Essays that got the world talking

2022

RECKONING WITH POWER AND PRIVILEGE

EDITED BY MICHAEL HOPKIN

Thames & Hudson | THE CONVERSATION

We wish to acknowledge the traditional owners of the land where the authors and editors of this book live and work. Particularly, we wish to acknowledge the traditional owners of the land on which Australia's universities stand, the land on which field work has been conducted, and the land on which much of the research cited in this book has taken place. We pay respects to all Aboriginal and Torres Strait Islander peoples as the First Peoples of Australia and Māori as tangata whenua in Aotearoa New Zealand.

First published in Australia in 2022
by Thames & Hudson Australia Pty Ltd
11 Central Boulevard, Portside Business Park
Port Melbourne, Victoria 3207
ABN: 72 004 751 964

thamesandhudson.com.au

These essays originally appeared on The Conversation (theconversation.com/au).

25 24 23 22 5 4 3 2 1

The essay 'If growing US–China rivalry leads to the "worst war ever", what should Australia do?' is an extract from *Lessons from History: Leading historians tackle Australia's greatest challenges* edited by Carolyn Holbrook, Lyndon Megarrity and David Lowe (NewSouth Books) published July 2022.

The essay 'Protests, "biznez" and a failed coup: a front-row view of the empire Gorbachev allowed to collapse' is an an edited extract of Monica Attard's essay in *Through Her Eyes: Australia's Women Correspondents from Hiroshima to Ukraine* by Trevor Watson and Melissa Roberts (Hardie Grant), published September 2022.

Thames & Hudson Australia wishes to acknowledge that Aboriginal and Torres Strait Islander people are the first storytellers of this nation and the traditional custodians of the land on which we live and work. We acknowledge their continuing culture and pay respect to Elders past, present and future.

978 1 760 76299 5 (paperback)
978 1 760 76306 0 (ebook)

A catalogue record for this book is available from the National Library of Australia

Cover design: Phillip Campbell
Typesetting: Cannon Typesetting
Editing: Paul Smitz
Printed and bound in Australia by McPherson's Printing Group

FSC® is dedicated to the promotion of responsible forest management worldwide. This book is made of material from FSC®-certified forests and other controlled sources.

Contents

PART II The power of hindsight

PART III The power to divide

PART VIII The power of hope

Editor's note

Michael Hopkin
Deputy Chief of Staff, The Conversation

Power and privilege: two words thrown into sharp relief by the biggest news events of 2022. In February, Russian President Vladimir Putin shocked the world by brutally invading Ukraine in a ruthlessly territorial power grab. In May, Australian voters handed Anthony Albanese the privilege of forming government – just the fifth time Labor has come to power from opposition since World War I. And in September, we bade farewell to Queen Elizabeth II after her unprecedented 70-year reign, and found ourselves wondering what kind of monarch King Charles III will be – and whether his reign may even be the one that ushers in an Australian republic.

Although this is in one sense simply a collection of the best essays published by The Conversation's Australia and New Zealand edition during 2022, there is also a unifying theme that runs through the book. All of the pieces published here confront, in some way, questions of power and privilege, and how they manifest themselves in our world.

In these pages, Michelle Arrow describes how the bravery of Brittany Higgins and Grace Tame in speaking up against entrenched power and privilege is helping to improve Canberra's culture, especially for women. Paul Strangio asks what kind of prime minister Albanese is likely to be, Joshua Black looks at how Scott Morrison is settling into post-prime-ministerial life, and Denis Muller casts a disparaging eye over the standard of campaign trail reporting.

Peter Abelson looks at which generation has the most financial power, Sally Larsen and Alexander Forbes ask whether the privilege of private school is really worth it, Tama Leaver and Rachel Berryman ask whether Mark Zuckerberg's Meta really deserves the privilege of setting the ground rules for what happens in the metaverse, and Hugh White ponders the prospect of perhaps the scariest power struggle of all: a war between the United States and China.

It was a privilege (although, speaking as an England fan, not always a pleasure) to watch Shane Warne rip through the opposition's batting order. Chris Wallace reflects on what turned him from a talented cricketer into a one-man cultural phenomenon who left us too soon, aged just fifty-two. And speaking of cultural phenomena, it was a daily ritual in my British student days to keep up with events in Ramsay Street. Now the curtain has come down on thirty-seven tumultuous years in Erinsborough. Sarah Casey and Juliet Watson weigh up the progressive credentials of the show that gave us Charlene the mechanic and Australian TV's first gay marriage.

We're yet to see how many of the issues covered in this book will ultimately play out. At the time of writing, the war in Ukraine rages on, the Albanese government is still setting out its agenda, the cost of rent, groceries and energy are climbing, the Omicron COVID wave continues to wash over us, and Australia is taking tentative steps towards deciding whether and how to enshrine a First Nations Voice to Parliament in the Constitution.

The world is an unpredictable place, with the power to shock, surprise, inspire or dismay. Thanks to the expertise in these pages, we have the privilege of understanding it a little better.

Michael Hopkin
September 2022

The year Australians turned the page

Michelle Grattan
Professional Fellow, University of Canberra

Prime ministers seldom turn out quite as expected. Bob Hawke's record as an economic reformer surpassed what anyone had anticipated. Kevin Rudd failed to live up to community hopes. Then there was Scott Morrison. After his 'miracle' election win of 2019, he was hailed as the great campaigner, acceptable to middle Australia, apparently set for political longevity. Inside the next term, he'd become deeply disliked and distrusted by Australian voters, who turfed him out in favour of a Labor government and a hefty – and unusual – crossbench.

Morrison lost, more than Anthony Albanese won, the 21 May election that was the turning point, in federal politics, of 2022. Australia's thirty-first prime minister, Albanese had been in parliament for a generation when he took office. Yet in the election campaign, voters were still getting to know him. He established himself as a neutral to slightly positive presence, someone who was 'not a bad bloke', a relatable figure with his much-repeated backstory of being brought up in council housing, the devoted son of a single mother. The important thing, it turned out, was that he was not Morrison, and Labor was not burdened, as in 2019, with over-heavy policy baggage and an unpopular leader.

Australians wanted change. They wanted the blowhard Morrison out. They wanted robust action on climate and integrity policy. With the spotlight having fallen on women's issues, they wanted more gender equity. And, with political trust dwindling again, after its rise in the pandemic, they wanted politics done differently. They were willing to elect Albanese because he and his party represented a decent, safe alternative. But Albanese had given only a line-sketch of what he would do and how he would operate in government. It will be some time before we see the full painting.

The road to a political fall

The final months of the Morrison government were ugly. The COVID crisis was difficult and divisive. And, on another front, the prime minister's character came under ferocious assault.

By late 2021, the public were exhausted from the COVID restrictions and disruptions. The health experts had lost some of their authority, as politicians claimed back their agency. People were desperate for life to return to something like normal, as it seemed about to do, and the prime minister played to that hope. Then Omicron hit, and summer was blighted. Once again the federal government, under fire for the initial slow vaccine rollout, was caught short – this time on rapid antigen tests. Morrison was further marked down on the competency test.

Meanwhile, on the character front, evidence mounted that Morrison lied. French President Emmanuel Macron had called this out publicly (over the ditching of the French submarines contract) in 2021. Leaked texts written by NSW premier Gladys Berejiklian (during the bushfires) and the Nationals' Barnaby Joyce (after former Liberal staffer Brittany Higgins alleged she had been raped by a colleague) later came to light. The message that Morrison was not to be trusted, amplified by Labor, resonated with the public. Morrison had no counter.

As the election approached, the objective evidence of the polls pointed to a Labor win. Yet many commentators were cautious. They'd been wrong in 2019. And there was the assumption, which turned out to be a myth, about Morrison's campaigning skills. Added to this, Albanese seemed lacklustre. The Liberals knew they were in deep trouble but hoped Morrison could tear down his opponent in the final race. They failed to understand that Morrison had already torn himself down. He had no political capital left. Albanese had a poor campaign, making mistakes, but Morrison – who had no forward agenda – was a busted flush.

Moreover, the government had another problem: the rise of the community candidates, dubbed 'teals' (from the campaign colour some adopted), who were fighting in previously safe Liberal seats on climate change, integrity and equity for women. All three issues had become red-hot, and Morrison was the worst possible leader to respond to this threat. He had persuaded the Coalition to embrace the 2050 net-zero target for the 2021 Glasgow Climate Change Conference, but it was too little, too late. He resisted a robust integrity commission, in the process breaking a 2019 election promise. And he was out of touch and ham-fisted in dealing with crises and issues affecting women.

While central features of Morrison's style – an obsession with control, a strong confidence in his own judgement, a penchant for secrecy – were always obvious, they were vividly highlighted by revelations after his defeat. It emerged that Morrison had had himself appointed to five ministries – health; finance; industry, science, energy and resources; treasury, and home affairs – in what was unprecedented and generally secret behaviour. Although his entry into health had some rationale, given the pandemic and the huge power vested in the health minister under the *Biosecurity Act*, and he moved into resources to override the minister on policy, Morrison's actions in relation to the other portfolios made no sense. But it was his breaches of convention in not informing the Cabinet (let alone the public) of his strange course, and even leaving most of the relevant ministers (including the treasurer) in the dark that caused the greatest shock. The Solicitor-General found while Morrison had not acted illegally, he had undermined 'the principle of responsible government' – because parliament could not hold a minister responsible if it did not know the person held the particular portfolio. Morrison's attempt to explain himself at a lengthy news conference was generally derided. Albanese, spotting a political advantage, called an inquiry by a former High Court judge, as Opposition members distanced themselves from their former leader.

Communities speak out: The teal phenomenon

Apart from the change of government, the 2022 election will be remembered for the success of the teals. They were supported by businessman Simon Holmes à Court's Climate 200 fund (established before the 2019 election to back community candidates committed to climate change action) and by groundswells of local volunteers. The teals showed the power that can be mobilised behind policies with strong community appeal. Their campaigns were highly organised and benefited from networking and the exchange of information on tactics. The fact they recruited so many volunteers reflected the potential for 'ground up' democratic movements at a time when the major parties have become hollowed out and faction-ridden, choosing candidates from narrow pools.

The teals were attractive to disillusioned Liberal voters in middle-class urban seats; they were also helped by 'strategic' voting on the part of some people who usually voted Labor. The Liberals tried to meet this threat entirely the wrong way. They denounced the teals as 'fake', pawns of Labor, and a party by any other name. With the most prominent teals being successful professional women, these attacks came across as disrespectful and patronising. It wasn't just the teals who benefited from the public's willingness to embrace more progressive causes and policies. The 2022 election also brought the Greens, with a set of progressive policies, to a high point, with four Lower House seats (previously one) and twelve senators (up from nine).

One question left hanging from 2022 is the long-term impact and future of the teals, who took six Lower House seats from the Liberals. The Albanese government has a majority in its own right in the House of Representatives, so the teals and other crossbenchers cannot determine votes. In the Senate the government needs the twelve Greens and an additional crossbencher to pass legislation the Coalition opposes. One obvious candidate for the extra vote is new ACT Senator David Pocock, a progressive who received Climate 200 funding and shares much of the teal agenda.

Whether the teals survive in the longer term, both individually and as a political force, will depend on their own performances, how issues play out, and whether the ground-up democratic movement they represent grows. Once crossbenchers win seats they are hard to move, which will work in teal MPs' favour. But will they have to find new issues to campaign on, if Labor has acted on their core agenda?

The teal seats present a major challenge for the Liberals under Opposition Leader Peter Dutton. Teal winners wiped out a substantial proportion of the moderates in the Liberal parliamentary party. Dutton, from the right, is much more attuned to appealing to outer-suburban, working-class areas than to voters in teal seats. Indeed, it is hard to see how, at the next election, the Liberals can put together a campaign that simultaneously pitches to outer suburbia and inner-urban areas. It is equally difficult to fathom how the Liberals can win back government if they continue to cede the teal seats.

'We don't want to waste a day'

Albanese might have made himself a small target for the election, but as soon as he was in office it was clear he wanted to move fast and his agenda would be substantial, if not all fully formed (or at least visible). Labor talks about two terms but, aware of the fickleness of politics, Albanese appears determined to pack as much as possible into this one.

A good deal of thought had obviously gone into the transition to power. Albanese projected an image of order as well as activity. Work was immediately started on the big policies, notably climate change and aged care. But also attended to were specifics that symbolised a new approach. Within days of the government being sworn in, the 'Biloela' Tamil asylum-seeker family, Priya Nadaraja, Nades Murugappan and their daughters, Kopika and Tharnicaa, in detention since 2018, were given approval to return to their Queensland town (in under three months they were granted permanent residency). Within several weeks, the highly contentious legal action against Canberra lawyer Bernard Collaery, for his part in exposing the Australian Government's spying on East Timor, was dropped.

More questionably, there was quick action that showed union influence on the new government. It defanged, by regulation, the Australian Building and Construction Commission, ahead of promised legislation to scrap it. The government also loosened disclosure requirements on superannuation funds, which smacked of being a sop to the industry funds.

The reaction of many Australians to the change of government had been one of relief at the end of a fractious era of hype and politicking, and the Albanese government's early days seemed to vindicate this. The government went about its business in an orderly way, the bombast as well as the punitive edge of the Morrison years disappeared, and senior ministers appeared on top of their portfolios. The public service was to be revitalised. Former University of Melbourne vice-chancellor Glyn Davis, a policy wonk, was brought in to head the prime minister's department. He replaced Phil Gaetjens, a former chief of staff to Morrison, who had been seen as a very 'political' head of the department.

Albanese had stressed he wanted to govern by 'consensus', and before the election had pointed to Bob Hawke's style as a model. Reprising Hawke's 1983 economic summit, Albanese called a summit on jobs and skills, as a prelude to Labor's October budget and a later employment white paper. Facing serious economic headwinds, Albanese was anxious to win and maintain the cooperation of business. He was well placed to do so. During Bill Shorten's leadership, Albanese had differentiated himself by arguing Labor needed to improve its relationship with business. He cultivated business, which greeted the Labor government positively, not least because it would bring certainty on the key climate issue, now critical to corporate sector planning.

Taking the new government to the world

Albanese's first days as PM were dominated by foreign travel. As it happened, a meeting of the Quadrilateral Security Dialogue (the Quad) had been scheduled for the week after the election. Albanese had himself (and several ministers) sworn in on the Monday after election day and immediately flew to Japan for the meeting. This provided him with the opportunity to meet US President Joe Biden, Japanese Prime Minister Fumio Kishida and Indian Prime Minister Narendra Modi.

Hard on the heels of the Quad trip, Albanese visited Indonesia. He then attended the NATO summit in Madrid (where Australia was among a small group of non-NATO invitees); he went on to France (repairing a relationship fractured over the broken submarine contract) and Ukraine. This was followed by his trip to the Pacific Islands Forum in Suva. With the Solomons having recently signed a security agreement with China, the new government was concerned to reassert Australia's presence in the Pacific region; Foreign Minister Penny Wong had already been dispatched to the region three times before the forum.

The government had a dual message in the foreign policy it presented to the world: continuity and change. Labor was firmly locked into the American alliance and had immediately embraced the former government's AUKUS agreement with the United States and Britain, which involved the supply of nuclear-powered submarines and other advanced technologies. But the element of change – the more ambitious climate policy – was crucial, and translated into a foreign policy entree with both Pacific countries and Europe. Albanese was able to use it to his advantage in establishing early relationships. But while the climate pivot was welcomed in the Pacific, as was the promise of more aid, it is unlikely that Australia's enhanced attention will curb China's determined extension of influence there over the longer term.

The arrival of the new government prompted signs of a possible defrosting of the China–Australia relationship. There were welcoming words from Beijing and some bilateral ministerial contact. But Albanese was cautious, not wanting to be entrapped, and making it clear Australia needed to see tangible action by China – notably, a winding back of the trade restrictions it had imposed on Australian exports. For its part, China's messages were conflicting and confusing, with vitriolic outbursts at times.

The Australia–China relationship is primarily a subset of the wider relationship between China and the West, and soon after the Albanese government's election, tensions at that broad level escalated dramatically over a visit to Taiwan by Nancy Pelosi, the Speaker of the US House of Representatives. When Labor announced a strategic review of Australia's defence force, one of those charged with undertaking it, former military chief Angus Houston, described current strategic circumstances as 'the worst I have ever seen in my career and lifetime'.

The emergence of the inflation beast

During the election, it was an easy, highly potent line from Labor: 'Everything is going up except your wages.' Cost of living emerged in the campaign as a damaging issue for the Coalition. But the new government faced a rapidly worsening reality, with inflation predicted to reach 7.75 per cent at year's end and economic growth figures downgraded.

Treasurer Jim Chalmers described the revised picture as 'confronting' and in his economic statement in the first week of the new parliament, he said real wages would only start to rise in 2023–24. The government had argued in the minimum-wage case that the lowest-paid should not be left behind, and the Fair Work Commission awarded a rise slightly above the then inflation figure. But this was quickly swallowed by the next rise in the CPI. Meanwhile, home owners were faced with increasing interest rates as monetary policy 'normalised' from the depth of the pandemic.

Australia's economic problems were mostly due to international forces, including the war in Ukraine and China's COVID lockdowns, although there were some local factors. Chalmers' strategy was threefold: to say he wanted to take the Australian people into his confidence, to lay as much blame on the former government as possible (including focusing on the debt it left), and to hold out the prospect of better times down the track. While support for Labor and Albanese held up well in the early polling, in Essential's late July poll, four in ten people said the government's handling of the cost of living was poor. The economic challenges, including the need for substantial budget savings, will test the government over its first year.

Climate policy turns a corner

Asked during the election campaign what his legacy would be, win or lose, Albanese replied, 'Acting on climate.' The government did not need parliamentary approval for its 43 per cent 2030 emissions reduction target. It had already registered the target under the Paris Agreement. But it was anxious to fix the target in legislation as an important signal to investors, and the business community was firmly behind the move.

This would be an early test of the Greens, emboldened by their election gains, and whose votes were needed in the Senate. The Greens had a dilemma. While their supporters wanted them to exert their muscle, they wore the legacy, from more than a decade before, of having stymied a Labor government's climate policy. Their big demand was for Labor to undertake to ban all new coal and gas projects. But the government held firm and the Greens, after some agonising, decided to support the legislation. In the spirit of inclusion, the government accepted some minor amendments from the teals, although it did not need their votes.

In the end, achieving the legislation was relatively easy, but the government could be under no illusion: the parliamentary stamp on the climate policy was only a beginning. Much detail was to be worked out. And the government was struggling with a gas crisis that had already brought the energy market to the brink. Australia's transition to a decarbonised economy was inevitable, but it would be bumpy and expensive. The promise of lower power prices was disappearing over the horizon.

In pursuit of a big target

In his victory speech, Albanese made specific reference to Labor's commitment to embracing the Uluru Statement from the Heart. That incorporates a treaty and truth-telling but most immediately, for this term, it means a referendum to put an Indigenous 'Voice to Parliament' into the Constitution.

The scale of this ambition is considerable. Since Federation, only eight of forty-four referendum questions to alter the Constitution have been carried. The hurdle is high, requiring a majority of states as well as an overall majority. If achieved, the Voice would likely be the most important social measure of the Albanese government's first term. A loss would be devastating, but for Albanese it is an opportunity that cannot be let pass. 'If not now, when?' he asks.

This would be another legacy. As he said during the Welcome to Country ceremony on the first day of the new parliament, 'You're not here for that long. None of us will be. When you're sitting on the porch, thinking about what you did, you can either have a source of pride or a source of regret.' While this issue will be formidable, its outcome will be a measure of modern Australia's attitude towards the continent's First Nations peoples.

Queen Elizabeth's death in September refocused attention on Labor's commitment to Australia becoming a republic, which had been underlined by Albanese appointing the first assistant minister for the republic. But this did not change his previously suggested timeline that this will be an issue for a second term. One big-ticket referendum is enough to handle at a time. If the Voice referendum is carried, that would give a second-term Labor government more confidence about the potential success of a referendum on the republic. Nevertheless, it would be challenging, with inevitable division among republicans between those favouring parliamentary appointment of the president and supporters of direct election. The latter model raises more complex questions and issues. If there is to be a republic, it is hard to see today's voters accepting anything less than being able to directly choose their head of state.

A leader facing hard times

A left firebrand in his young days, Albanese has moved a long way from many of his youthful political stands, while retaining his deep commitment to social justice. As prime minister, he wants to govern from the centre, and almost certainly will do so. He will aim to keep promises. Recent history has taught leaders the danger of breaking commitments, and Albanese often refers back to what he took to the people when he is warding off calls to change positions (for example, in relation to the legislated tax cuts that benefit higher-income earners). He says he wants to restore political trust and to foster a more civil political discourse. Those are testing aspirations in the modern polity, especially as a new government's capital erodes and another election approaches.

As a senior minister (and briefly deputy prime minister) in the former Labor government, Albanese understands the give-and-take of negotiation. He can be expected to bring that skill to his dealings inside and outside the parliament. While the early days saw him have his ministers take the limelight in their own areas, modern Australian governments are, to a significant degree, presidential, so coming years will see the burdens of office – the task of explaining, the receiving of blame – increasingly loaded onto Albanese's shoulders. In difficult circumstances, when politics and economics can be at odds, his most important ministerial relationship will be with his Treasurer, Jim Chalmers, the young bull who many would see as a future Labor leader.

Celebrating the government's first 100 days with an appearance at the National Press Club on 29 August, Albanese had much to be pleased about in his navigation of these early months. The Jobs and Skills Summit later in that week was hailed for its positive tone and the centring of women. The government skilfully used the summit to advance its agenda by trade-offs. The union movement had a major win with the government committing to extending multi-employer bargaining; the unions agreed to a boost in permanent migration, desperately needed by businesses to help with the acute labour shortages. Even with additional migrants and more TAFE places, however, there will be no early end to the dearth of workers in many sectors, especially aged care and child care. And regardless of the buzz about co-operation, substantial divisions flared over industrial relations reform. Nor was the government able to accommodate key items on summit participants' wish lists. Notably, the push to bring forward the implementation of the new, generous child care plan, from July 2023 to January, was rejected on the grounds of cost and operational difficulties. But the government did announce liberalised income limits for aged pensioners' earnings before their benefit is hit. Ironically, this had been a change recently advocated by Dutton.

Albanese has arrived in office with widespread goodwill but in very fraught times, at home and abroad. Events out of the government's control are likely to be major drivers in this parliamentary term, as they were in the last term. Albanese will be judged not just on all he can control, but on how he and his government respond to what will be outside their immediate control.

PART I

The power of leadership

We have Australia's most diverse parliament yet, but there's still a long way to go

Tim Soutphommasane
University of Sydney

The message from this year's federal election result was clear: Australians want a political reset. And not just on issues such as government integrity and climate change.

While much attention has been directed at the teal wave of independents, another change to the composition of parliament is taking place. This Australian Parliament is the most diverse yet in its ethnic and cultural background. Capital Hill has seen a substantial injection of colour.

A fitting result

Newly elected members Sally Sitou, Michelle Ananda-Rajah, Sam Lim, Zaneta Mascarenhas, Cassandra Fernando and Dai Le have bolstered non-European representation of the House of Representatives. The Indigenous ranks of parliament have also swelled, with the additions of Marion Scrymgour and Gordon Reid in the House, and Jacinta Price in the Senate.

In many ways, it is a fitting result to an election that had its share of controversies about representation. Labor caused consternation when it parachuted former senator (and ex-NSW premier) Kristina Keneally into its then safe south-western Sydney electorate of Fowler, cruelling the prospects of local Vietnamese-Australian lawyer Tu Le. A second captain's pick from Anthony Albanese, millionaire former political adviser Andrew Charlton, ran in the western Sydney seat of Parramatta, to the chagrin of local aspirants from multicultural backgrounds.

Such picks left many asking, with good reason: if worthy candidates from non-European backgrounds can't get preselected in multicultural electorates like Fowler and Parramatta, how can we get more diversity into parliament? It's a question that lingers, notwithstanding what this election has delivered.

Still a long way to go

If it feels like a surge of diversity has flowed through the parliament, it's only because there was so little to begin with. While those from a non-European background make up an estimated 21 per cent of the Australian population, they made up just a tiny fraction of the forty-sixth parliament.

The forty-seventh parliament features fifteen parliamentarians with an overseas non-European background, along with eleven Indigenous parliamentarians. That may sound like a strong result. It's certainly an improvement, and better than how many other major institutions in Australian society perform. However, we should put it in perspective.

It still means just a tiny fraction of the parliament (no more than 10 per cent) has a non-European or Indigenous background – far less than what you'd see if the parliament actually reflected our society accurately. Australia lags significantly behind the United States, United Kingdom, Canada and New Zealand.

It's not all about numbers, of course. We can't judge the calibre of our parliament solely on whether it's proportionately representative. Yet when sections of society can't see themselves within our public institutions, it is a problem. The very legitimacy, and quality, of those institutions can suffer.

A new phase?

For a long time, calls for greater multicultural diversity in politics have been typically greeted with indifference. It wasn't an urgent problem. Gender diversity was a higher priority. Political parties didn't feel the pressure from those supposedly excluded from the system.

That now has changed. Labor has been brutally punished for its Fowler move. A swing of more than 16 per cent saw the seat fall to independent (and former Liberal) Dai Le. Clearly, being from a non-European background isn't the electoral handicap political parties have sometimes feared.

Something generational is at play. Australia may once have comfortably accepted that newer arrivals were expected to play the role of the grateful supplicant in their 'host society'. But the children and grandchildren of yesterday's migrants don't see themselves as guests in their own country. They aren't happy refugees or cheerful migrants who are content to know their place. They're taking their lead less from the Anh Dos of the world and more from the AOCs (Democrat politician Alexandria Ocasio-Cortez) of US politics.

Demands about access and equity for people from non-English-speaking backgrounds have been replaced with calls for the equal treatment of 'people of colour' and for attention to 'intersectionality'.

We could be seeing a new phase in the evolution of Australia's multicultural project. While a triumph in many respects, Australian multiculturalism has to date fallen short on several counts. A celebration of cultural diversity has never been accompanied by a sharing of Anglo-Celtic institutional power. Or, for that matter, by a full reckoning with racial inequality and injustice.

That's why it will be interesting to observe this new parliament. The very presence of this new ethnic and cultural diversity will, in subtle and not so subtle ways, be felt in Canberra and beyond.

Critical mass matters. It is hard, for example, to imagine a more diverse parliament trying to wind back racial hatred laws (as parliament has done on more than one occasion with respect to the *Racial Discrimination Act*). Or to imagine a diverse parliament indulging other periodic bouts of race politics (think of the scaremongering over African gangs in Melbourne or the McCarthyist targeting of Chinese Australians).

All such excesses become much harder when the people debating such matters have skin in the game.

So don't mistake the wave of multicultural politicians for being a mere symbolic adornment in Canberra – the political equivalent of having exotic foods and festivals. It may feel like a subplot for now, but this could end up being just as significant as the teal revolution.

Making change, making history, making noise: Brittany Higgins and Grace Tame at the National Press Club

Michelle Arrow
Macquarie University

As a historian of the Australian women's movement, the past two years have been extraordinary to witness. Not only are we living through a once-in-a-century pandemic, which has had profoundly gendered effects, we have also experienced a feminist insurgency that has placed the issue of women's safety, and men's abuses of power, at the centre of our national conversation.

While many activists, journalists and advocates contributed to this insurgency, it exploded largely thanks to two young women: 2021 Australian of the Year Grace Tame and former parliamentary staffer Brittany Higgins. Both just twenty-seven, both say they were abused by men within institutions they ought to have been able to trust. Both rejected the expectation they should be shamed into silence about their experiences. In doing so, they have helped to rewrite enduring cultural scripts about sexual abuse and sexual assault.

Their joint address at the National Press Club on 9 February was a valedictory speech, a way to mark their extraordinary year in the public eye. But it was also a call to action, a warning against complacency in an election year.

Both made it very clear that, while hearing the voices of survivors of abuse and assault is important, it is not enough. As Higgins noted, the ways in which we discuss abuse are far too passive, 'as if sexual violence falls out of the sky. As if it is perpetrated by no-one.' Of the previous day's formal parliamentary apology to victims of alleged sexual harassment, assault and bullying, Higgins was grateful but sceptical: 'They are still only words. Actions are what matter.'

Tame and Higgins both made passionate pleas for structural change, for measurable action to prevent sexual abuse and assault. Tame called for government to take abuse seriously: to advance consistent national legislative change on sexual offences, and to spend more on preventive education to curb Australia's alarmingly high rates of abuse and assault. She calculated the Morrison Government spent 11 cents per student per year on prevention education, because it was 'primarily concerned with short-sighted, votes-based funding, not with long-term, needs-based funding'.

To those of us used to government by spin, obfuscation and photo-ops in hi-vis vests, Tame and Higgins' moral clarity and bluntness are exhilarating. Both vehemently ruled out the possibility of political careers – indeed, the journalists asking them about their political aspirations seem to misread their social and political roles.

They are advocates and activists, who use their public platform to articulate complex issues in clear, direct ways. Tame, in particular, clearly has no intention of playing by anyone else's rules, as her memorable side-eye to Scott Morrison at the Lodge demonstrated.

Their speeches also confirmed that their actions had rattled the Morrison government, whose response to them was ham-fisted at every turn. Tame revealed that in August 2021, a representative of a government-funded organisation (which she declined to name) had asked for her 'word' that she would not say anything about the prime minister on the evening before the 2022 Australian of the Year awards. 'You are an influential person. He will have a fear,' she was told. She speculated he had 'a fear he might lose his position, or, more to the point, his power'. The prime minister's office later said it had no knowledge of such a call to Tame and the person who made it should apologise.

Tame also reminded us the Department of Prime Minister and Cabinet conducted a review of the selection process for Australian of the Year not long after she won the award. This was an attempt at intimidation, as Tame noted, but it also spoke to the previous government's dislike of her fearless critique.

Higgins was consistently treated by many in the Morrison government as a political problem to be managed. In the wake of her allegations, Morrison commissioned not one, not two, but four reviews, all the while dragging his heels on a formal response to Sex Discrimination Commissioner Kate Jenkins' landmark *Respect@Work* report.

Higgins reminded us that implementing *Respect@Work*, especially the proposed 'positive duty' on employers to provide a safe workplace, would have 'impacted every single working woman in the country. And we just kind of let that moment slide by without thinking.'

Tame and Higgins dissected the previous government's performance on gender over the past year. Tame called out Christian Porter's reliance on a blind trust to fund his unsuccessful defamation case against the ABC. Higgins eviscerated the government's National Plan to End Violence against Women and Children for its 'vague and lofty' aims, its lack of targets and clear plans. She noted the shocking statistics on domestic violence that 'you've heard … rattled off at white-ribbon breakfasts … They should spur us to do whatever it takes. But instead they've become a sort of throat-clearing exercise that we all just kind of tolerate.'

Policy action on abuse and assault was a litmus test for the Morrison government's views on women. According to Higgins and Tame, it was a test the government failed at every turn.

In the 1970s, feminist activists told personal stories in public because of their belief that 'the personal is political'. Yet victims of sexual assault or abuse typically remained anonymous, because of the shame that was attached to these crimes.

More recently, advocates like domestic violence campaigner and 2015 Australian of the Year Rosie Batty, and now young women including Tame and Higgins, have personalised these difficult issues, making them harder for politicians to ignore. The #MeToo and #LetHerSpeak movements have centred on survivors and focused on hearing their stories. As Tame said in her NPC address: 'How beautiful is freedom of speech? I haven't always had it.'

One of the problems with a movement based on storytelling in public spaces is the brutal toll it exacts on survivors. Tame noted she had spent the past year being 'revictimised, commodified, objectified, sensationalised, legitimised [and] gaslit'. As US activist Tarana Burke (who is credited with starting the #MeToo movement) has pointed out, survivors 'shouldn't have to perform our pain over and over again for the sake of your awareness'.

There are other problems with placing too much emphasis on individuals like Tame and Higgins: two young white women can hardly represent all assault survivors, as Australian sociologist Shakira Hussein and others have pointed out. And we must be careful not to confuse justice for individuals with broader structural changes to protect all people from abuse and harassment.

But by speaking truth to power, Higgins and Tame have reinvigorated feminism for a new generation of young women. Back in the 1990s, older feminists were worried that young women were not taking up the feminist mantle. No-one is saying that now. Teenage girls know Grace Tame's name, and they admire her courage and her strength.

As investigative journalist Jess Hill and others have noted, the public face of Australian feminism in the 2010s was dominated by 'corporate feminism': seemingly preoccupied with getting more women on boards rather than raising the wages of low-paid female workers in aged care or child care, for example.

Sexual harassment is still, shockingly, endemic across Australia, and too many people have experienced sexual abuse and assault. By highlighting this problem – which at its core is about the gendered abuse of power – Tame and Higgins have mobilised a broad constituency of Australian women. They inspired thousands to march for justice and others to run for political office. Maybe they will play a decisive role in this year's federal election.

As Tame reminded us: '[Our leaders] may either be constructive or destructive. But every single one of them is arguably replaceable.'

A short history of the Aboriginal Tent Embassy: An indelible reminder of unceded sovereignty

Bronwyn Carlson
Macquarie University
Lynda-June Coe
Macquarie University

Aboriginal and Torres Strait Islander readers are advised this article contains the names of deceased people.

Often, people think about the Aboriginal Tent Embassy as something historical, dating back to the 1970s. But it should also be thought of as the site of the longest protest for Indigenous land rights, sovereignty and self-determination in the world.

In fact, this year, the Tent Embassy celebrates its fiftieth continuous year of occupation. Demonstrating its significance to Australian history, it was included on the Commonwealth Heritage List in 2015 as part of the Old Parliament House precinct.

In this momentous year, it's worth remembering how the Tent Embassy came to be, and acknowledging what it has stood for since its erection in 1972 – and the significance it still has today.

Aliens in our own land

The Tent Embassy began its public life on 26 January 1972. On that day, Michael Anderson, Billy Craigie, Bertie Williams and Tony Coorey left Redfern and drove to Ngunnawal Country (Canberra), where they planted a beach umbrella opposite Parliament House (now known as

Old Parliament House). They erected a sign that said 'Aboriginal Embassy'. With them on that day was their driver, *Tribune* photographer Noel Hazard, who captured the event in a series of photos.

The term 'embassy' was used to bring attention to the fact Aboriginal people had never ceded sovereignty nor engaged in any treaty process with the Crown. As a collective, Aboriginal people were the only cultural group not represented with an embassy. According to Aboriginal activist and scholar Gary Foley, the absence of an Aboriginal embassy in Canberra was a blatant indication Aboriginal people were treated like aliens in their own land.

Initially, the protesters were making a stand about land rights following then prime minister William McMahon's speech dismissing any hope for Aboriginal land rights and reasserting the government's position on the policy of assimilation. The Tent Embassy was therefore a public display of our disapproval of, and objection to, the policies and practices of the government.

It has since become an acclaimed site of our continued resistance to the continuity of colonial rule.

Demands of protesters

Police who were patrolling the area at the time of the Tent Embassy's erection asked the protesters what they were doing outside Parliament House. They said they were protesting and would do so until the government granted land rights to Aboriginal people. The police were said to have responded, 'That could be forever.'

As it turned out, it was not illegal to camp on the lawns of Parliament House, so the police could not remove the protesters.

Later, on 6 February 1972, the members of the Tent Embassy issued their list of demands to the government. The demands were clearly about our rights as Aboriginal people to our homelands, regardless of the fact cities were now built on the land or mining companies were interested in the bounties within. Compensation was called for in the instances where the land was not able to be returned. There were also demands for the protection of our sacred sites.

While the McMahon government cared little about negotiating with the protesters, the leader of the Opposition, Gough Whitlam, visited the Tent Embassy and publicly proclaimed a promise of

Aboriginal land rights under a future Labor government. There was widespread support for the Tent Embassy from Aboriginal and Torres Strait Islander people and allies across the continent, and indeed the world.

Media attention also grew as it became obvious the Tent Embassy and protesters were not going to move on. Other Aboriginal activists joined the embassy, including Foley, Isabel Coe, John Newfong, Chicka Dixon, Gordon Briscoe and many others.

Forced removal and revival

The government was not too keen on being reminded Aboriginal people were demanding rights, so it amended the Trespass on Commonwealth Lands Ordinance to make it illegal to camp on the lawn of Parliament House. This gave the police the authority to remove the protesters.

The ordinance was but a few hours old when police attempted to forcibly remove the embassy. They did so to the roar of the crowd chanting 'Land rights now'. A violent confrontation with police ensued.

On 12 September 1972, the ACT Supreme Court ruled against the use of the trespass laws, and the Tent Embassy was temporarily re-erected before being removed again the following morning. Then, at the end of 1972, the Coalition government led by McMahon lost the federal election to Labor. Whitlam was able to keep his promise in part – he did give the land title deeds to the Gurindji people. This was captured in the historical photo by Merv Bishop of Whitlam pouring a fistful of dirt into Vincent Lingiari's hand.

While this iconic image has become a demonstration of what might be possible, the work of the embassy is not yet done. Land rights across the continent have yet to be fully achieved.

The Tent Embassy was re-established in 1973 and remained until activist Charles Perkins negotiated its removal pending the enactment of the *Aboriginal Land Rights Act* in 1976. In the ensuing years, it occupied several other sites around Canberra, including the site of the current Parliament House. In 1992, it returned to its original site on the lawn of Old Parliament House to mark the twentieth anniversary of the original protest.

Eleven years later, much of the Tent Embassy was destroyed by fire in a suspected case of arson. The police once again attempted to remove protesters from the site under orders from the federal government's National Capital Authority.

An enduring symbol of protest

Today, the Tent Embassy remains on the lawns of Old Parliament House as a reminder of the successive failures of subsequent governments to address the demands for justice represented by the embassy and its people. As Foley reflects in his history of the embassy:

> That it has endured for [five] decades as a potent symbol rejecting the hypocrisy, deceit and duplicity by successive Australian governments is a testament to the refusal of large numbers of Aboriginal people to concede defeat in a 200-year struggle for justice.

Nowhere else in the world have we seen such longevity around a site of protest. The Aboriginal Tent Embassy is an impressive achievement that demonstrates the tenacity of Aboriginal and Torres Strait Islander people and our continued fight for the reclamation of our lands and sovereign rights as First Nations peoples.

Russia says peace in Ukraine will be 'on our terms', but what can the West accept and at what cost?

Alexander Gillespie
University of Waikato

July's assertion by Dmitry Medvedev, deputy head of Russia's security council (and former president), that the invasion of Ukraine will 'achieve all its goals' and that peace will be 'on our terms' raises an obvious question: what are those terms?

History suggests the answer may be a hard one. Modern Russian wars have followed a pattern: victory is either total (Chechnya or Syria) or it involves the dismemberment of the other country (Georgia or Ukraine after the first Russian intervention in 2014). Peace treaties are rare, and settlements – as Medvedev's comments implied – have been Russia's alone to approve. Opponents are expected to surrender, not negotiate.

And right now, Russian President Vladimir Putin may well believe he has the upper hand in Ukraine. Sanctions have hurt but not strangled the Russian economy. Western weapons and intelligence have slowed but not stopped the Russian advance, which grinds on with overwhelming and often indiscriminate use of force.

But with Russia now saying it will expand its war aims, and with the West continuing to pour arms into Ukraine, the risk of the invasion spilling into a larger conflict (by accident or design) slowly grows. Russian threats to European winter gas supplies suggest both sides are likely to escalate their actions rather than accept defeat.

The only safe way out will be through negotiation. But given what we know about Russian strategies and expectations, how will that be achieved?

What are the bottom lines?

Clearly, there is significant uncertainty about what terms Putin might agree to. Given he has denied the existence of Ukrainian statehood at all, he may believe Russia is entitled to it all. Or he may only demand international recognition of Russian claims to territory already conquered. Beyond that, he may really be looking for the disarmament of all parts of Eastern Europe that were once part of the Soviet Union.

While Putin's bottom lines remain unknown, the onus is now on Ukraine and its Western backers to set out their own terms for what is and isn't negotiable. Although it may be Ukrainian President Volodymyr Zelenskyy's country at war, ultimately peace will have to be settled by Putin and US President Joe Biden.

There appear to be four main questions that will determine what the bottom lines for peace will look like:

1. Should Russia be economically liable for repair of the damage caused by its invasion?
2. Should those accused of war crimes be brought to justice?
3. Should Ukraine's territorial integrity be retained, or should the country be divided and parts ceded to Russia (as former US secretary of state Henry Kissinger has recommended)?
4. What would ongoing security guarantees for the region look like?

What can the West live with?

The fourth question is particularly difficult, given the negligible respect currently shown for international law or treaty commitments. Rulings by the International Court of Justice that Russia should desist from its invasion of Ukraine have been ignored. Similarly, the treaties that had previously kept the peace in Europe by slowly building good faith and trust – governing the size of conventional military forces, the prohibition of missile defence shields, and the illegality of certain classes of nuclear weapons – are now largely void.

And so we may need to add a final question to that list, perhaps the most significant of all: even if an agreement can be hammered out over Ukraine, will the precedents and perverse incentives it creates be tolerable?

Avoiding something worse

None of this is easy. Compromise, cooperation and peace are, in the end, much harder than war. And there are certainly still many with hawkish views on why Putin must be stopped and his veiled nuclear threats ignored. But beyond Russia now being considered a significant and direct threat to the security, peace and stability of NATO countries, the wider global context cannot be ignored, either.

In 2021, world military expenditure surpassed US$2 trillion for the first time – 12 per cent more than in 2012. Nuclear arsenals are expanding and upgrading, as are emerging and largely unregulated military technologies in space, cyber capabilities, artificial intelligence and autonomous weapons systems. Ongoing tensions between China and the West, America, Israel and Iran, and webs of new military alliances (some visible, some opaque) on all sides, all contribute to a world that is becoming less peaceful according to the latest Global Peace Index.

Add to this the real threats to stability from climate change, a global food crisis, stretched supply chains and inflation, and the risk of Ukraine sparking or exacerbating something worse should be clear. Peace on the right terms must be the priority.

In the wake of the China–Solomon Islands pact, Australia needs to rethink its Pacific relationships

Patricia A O'Brien
Georgetown University

Like the Hunga Tonga–Hunga Ha'apai volcano that triggered a massive tsunami and sent shock waves around the world when it erupted on 15 January, the recently signed security deal between the Solomon Islands and China has also unleashed geopolitical convulsions of immense magnitude. The source of the spectacular volcanic eruption that was visible from space came from deep below the surface. Similarly, the controversial security deal, and Australia's alarmed response to it, also goes deep into history.

Solomon Islands Prime Minister Manasseh Sogavare has repeatedly described the China deal as an assertion of sovereignty. (Critics say it is the opposite.) China added to this discourse by accusing the Australian Government of 'disrespectful colonialism' in its unsuccessful attempts to dissuade Sogavare's government from formalising the deal. Yet then prime minister Scott Morrison defended Australia's response, claiming his government did not want to repeat the 'long history' of telling Pacific nations what to do. Morrison added: 'I'm not going to act like former administrations that treated the Pacific like some extension of Australia.'

Morrison was absolutely right about one thing – a long history shaped the recent deal. But were the Solomons treated like an extension of Australia? Did Australia exercise colonial power over the nation? Most crucially, how can Australia correct past mistakes and move forward given the new regional reality?

The 19th-century sugar plantations

Britain colonised the Solomon Islands from 1893. Unlike British New Guinea, where Britain transferred colonial control to Australia after Federation in 1901, the Solomons stayed under British control until 1978, when the islands gained independence.

That Britain was taking control of the Solomons at the end of the 19th century was a comfort to Australians in ways that echo the present. At the time, Australia was deeply 'concerned' about 'Great Powers … now established in the South Seas within a few days' steaming distance from

Eastern Australia, especially Queensland', wrote Brisbane's *Courier-Mail*. It continued:

> It is a great pity … that the colonial statesmen of former days had not foresight enough to grasp the importance of these South Seas territories and secure them, for their strategic as well as productive value.

And in words that sound remarkably like those being articulated now, the article predicted 'we will have to spend millions … because of the nearness of bases of possible hostile operations'.

The 'Great Powers' in question in 1898 were France, which was attempting to control all the islands south of the Solomons (present-day Vanuatu and New Caledonia), and Germany, which had claimed the arc of islands from the northern Solomons into New Guinea (excluding British New Guinea in the south-east).

Australian politicians had aspired to Britain controlling all South Pacific islands on their behalf from the 1870s. This was articulated by Australia's Monroe Doctrine, which held that Australia, backed by Britain, exclusively presided in its region. France and Germany challenged it in the 19th century, but the notion persisted along with Australian security concerns.

Although Australia did not officially colonise the Solomons, Australians exercised colonial powers there in other ways. The most egregious and devastating was through labour recruiting, which began in the islands around the 1870s. It is estimated some 19,000 Solomon Islanders worked on Queensland sugar plantations before most were repatriated in 1902. Recruiter mistreatment sparked cycles of violence in which white people were killed, and then these killings were avenged with official and unofficial punitive expeditions.

During – and after – World War II

Small numbers of traders and planters, many from Australia, established enterprises in the islands. Missionaries came too. But it was not until the Battle for the Solomons, which stretched from August 1942 to December 1943, that Solomon Islanders experienced colossal intrusions into their island homes.

Some Australians participated in this epic episode, but it was predominantly US forces fighting to halt the Japanese advance on

Australia. The importance of these islands to Australia's security was horrifically demonstrated.

After the war, and with decolonisation happening at a rapid pace, Australian politicians thought about how this wave of independence would affect the islands and how Australia might shape that change to preserve its security. The idea of a 'Melanesian Federation' was suggested. This would bind Dutch New Guinea (which became part of Indonesia in 1969), Papua New Guinea and 'The British Solomons'. But this idea relied on the new nations buying into it. They did not.

Another idea was incorporating New Guinea, and possibly the Solomons too, as a 'seventh state' of Australia. Future Australian governor-general John Kerr plainly articulated in 1958 the sticking point for this security guarantee: Australia would have to deal with 'racial problems' that 'we would have to solve on the basis of equality and genuine acceptance of New Guinea people in Australia'.

These ideas did not happen. Many Pacific nations have remained closed off from economic opportunities that would have drastically improved lives and permanently bound Australia to them through transnational communities.

Economics is key

The root causes of the Solomon Islands' problems since independence can be found in economics. Australia may have played a leading role in peacekeeping through the 2003–17 Regional Assistance Mission to Solomon Islands, but it did not take bold action on economic issues. Almost 13 per cent of Solomon Islanders live below the poverty line and just 70 per cent have access to electricity. China now seems to be offering an economic panacea that Australia did not.

Australia has to shed its longstanding aversion to Melanesian migration. Economic (rather than racial) exclusion is now the barrier keeping Pacific Islanders out of Australia. Communities have come via 'the New Zealand pathway', Samoa, Tonga and Fiji, and established themselves in Australia. They have created a vital remittance economy that has been even more important during COVID with the collapse of island economies.

Very few Australian residents originate from the strategic islands that arc around Australia's north. If people from these nations do come to Australia, it is through temporary means such as education programs or the Pacific Labour Scheme, which allows for employment in meatworks, agriculture, trades and cooking, hospitality and care. Recently, this scheme has suffered terrible publicity, with many workers claiming they were subjected to 'slave-like conditions', bringing to mind the Queensland plantation labour history.

Now that the geopolitical situation has become precarious, Australian politicians are again thinking about the islands and how major adjustments are needed to the ways things are done. A parliamentary committee reported in March 2022, suggesting ideas about compacts of free association, similar to those the Marshall Islands, Palau and the Federated States of Micronesia have with the United States. It also suggested more Pacific-friendly migration policies like those of New Zealand. The impacts of climate change are going to make all the pressures of life on Pacific islands more acute in the coming years.

Australia must take bold steps to reinforce its Pacific relationships and secure its strategic interests. Taking the humanitarian approach and integrating with Pacific islands is not only right, it is also the best way to support Australia's interests and shed its colonial legacies.

He's Australia's thirty-first prime minister. So who is Anthony Albanese?

Paul Strangio
Monash University

Karen Middleton's 2016 biography of Anthony Albanese concludes with a speech he made that year, on the twentieth anniversary of his election to parliament. 'I'm patient,' he told his clapping audience, 'I'm patient – I'm a Souths fan.' The South Sydney Rabbitohs are the rugby league club Albanese supports, which for the greater part of his adult life was notorious for its competitive underperformance.

The audience realised, of course, that in proclaiming his long-suffering dedication, Albanese was really alluding to his political vocation and his other underachieving 'tribe' – the Labor Party.

Albanese's journey in Labor politics has indeed been long and arduous. He was still a boy when he began accompanying his mother and grandparents to local branch meetings of the Labor Party; he remembers handing out leaflets for Gough Whitlam in 1972 when only nine. He formally joined the ALP as a teenager. Up to his ears in student Labor politics as an undergraduate, upon leaving Sydney University he went to work for the elder statesman of the NSW left faction, Tom Uren. By his mid-twenties he was assistant secretary of NSW Labor, and won the seat of Grayndler for the ALP in 1996 on his thirty-third birthday.

Even his path to leadership has been unusually slow. One has to go back to the middle of last century for an Opposition leader who was older (fifty-six) and who had served for longer in the parliament (twenty-three years) when first elected to that position. His wait for the chance to become prime minister has been far longer than most of Australia's recent national leaders. Kevin Rudd, Julia Gillard, Malcolm Turnbull and Scott Morrison averaged only around a decade between entering parliament and attaining office – for Albanese, it was a quarter of a century.

To continue the slow-burn theme, if Albanese is to be believed, his ambition for leadership formed late. Those who reach leadership positions are typically consumed with an aspiration for the top job from early in their parliamentary careers – if not before. They are fuelled by a sense of their own prime-ministerial destiny. Albanese is different. On his telling, it was only in 2013, on the defeat of Rudd's second government, that he first entertained thoughts of becoming leader. Until then he had contented himself with the role of 'counsellor and kingmaker'.

And still he had to wait. Despite winning a comfortable majority of the rank-and-file vote, he narrowly lost the leadership to Bill Shorten in 2013 because several of his left faction Caucus colleagues defected to support Shorten. Albanese then had to stay his hand in 2016 when Shorten's better-than-expected performance at that year's election insulated him from a leadership contest. When Shorten seemed poised for victory in 2019, Albanese must have figured his chance to be party leader had passed. But then came 'Morrison's miracle' and Albanese emerged as the only candidate to succeed Shorten within a demoralised Labor Caucus.

Playing the long game has also been the hallmark of Albanese's leadership over the past three years. Beginning with 'listening tours' of the regions where Labor badly faltered in 2019, most notably in Queensland, it has been painstaking and unglamorous graft.

As journalist Katharine Murphy has observed, to his detractors his approach has been akin to a campaign of 'attrition'. Those critics have harped on the theme of his leadership being a small target and his program prosaic. This is not how Labor wins office, they have insisted. Drawing on a sample size of three – the number of times Labor has claimed government from opposition since the end of World War II, under the leaderships of Whitlam, Bob Hawke and Rudd – the critics have argued the template for Labor success is a bold, transformative reform program and a charismatic, popular leader. Under Albanese, they complain, Labor has neither.

One can quibble at the edges of the critics' reading of history. Though Whitlam unquestionably heralded an expansive reform program in 1972, the Labor Party was sufficiently concerned about his image that it launched an unprecedented advertising blitz to humanise him in the eyes of the public.

When Hawke won in 1983, Labor's program for government was all but subsumed by the leader's messianic appeal, as encapsulated in the slogan 'Bob Hawke Bringing Australia Together'.

Rudd's victory in 2007 was on the back of a campaign in which Labor selectively staked out policy differences with the Coalition. The nerdy Rudd painted himself as more of a fiscal conservative than John Howard, and was reassuringly perceived as a kind of youthful version of the prime minister. In short, the idea of Labor relying on larger-than-life platforms and leaders to win government is exaggerated.

This is not to deny that under Albanese, Labor ran a considerably less daring election agenda than it did in 2019. Indeed, it is an irony – or confirmation that ideological tags count for nothing in the contemporary Labor Party – that the right faction's Shorten campaigned on an aggressively redistributive program spiced by 'class war' rhetoric about the 'big end of town'. In contrast, the left faction's Albanese has abandoned those redistributive measures and has been emollient in his language towards business.

The plan to curb franking credits was the first to go under Albanese, followed by the dumping of plans for changes to negative gearing, capital gains and, most recently, family trusts. As well, Labor has announced that in government it will not repeal the third tranche of the Coalition's tax cuts that benefit high-income earners. Simultaneously, Albanese has portrayed himself as a friend of aspiration. He believes, he says, in an Australia 'where nobody is held back and nobody is left behind'.

To be fair to Albanese, it makes sense Labor changed tack from 2019. The party's review of that defeat blamed it on 'a cluttered policy agenda that looked risky and an unpopular leader'. In a speech to the National Press Club on the release of that review, Albanese indicated he had got the message: 'too many people were confused or even frightened by our policies'. Elsewhere, he has pointedly noted none of Labor's past successful Opposition leaders campaigned on increases in taxes.

If there is a playbook to Albanese walking away from the Shorten program, then it is from the other side of politics. In 1996, heeding the lesson of John Hewson losing the unlosable election three years earlier on a radical neoliberal manifesto headlined by a new tax (the goods and services tax), John Howard renounced the GST as well as other contentious policies from Hewson's Fightback! program. Howard determinedly narrowed the points of difference with former prime minister Paul Keating, driving the latter to distraction.

Albanese has been unabashed about his strategy of not rejoining the battles of 2019, declaring he has no intention to 'relitigate the past'. To those who cavil that Labor has abandoned its ideals by dropping the redistributive policies, he has been equally blunt: 'One of my Labor principles is for Labor to win elections.' This might not be as caustic as Whitlam's famed put-down of the Labor hard left – 'Only the impotent are pure' – but the point is fundamentally the same. To change the nation, Labor first had to win at the ballot box.

The abandonment of the Shorten-era revenue measures has curtailed Labor's scope for campaign initiatives. According to the Coalition, Albanese was like a thief in the night, trying to steal his way into office on a meagre policy program. This is largely unfair. Beginning at a leisurely pace, Albanese gradually accelerated the rollout of policies.

Labor entered the campaign proposing, among other things, major investments in aged care, child care and social housing, manufacturing renewal, greater support for TAFE and universities, an upgrade of the electricity grid, a national anti-corruption commission and implementation of the Uluru Statement. During the campaign, this program was buttressed by further promises in areas like health, housing and pay equity for women workers.

Another conclusion of Labor's review of its 2019 election campaign was that there was an absence of a clear narrative binding together the party's policies. Albanese too has struggled in that space. In the second half of 2021, he seemed to be feeling his way there by talking about the reconstructive role of government following the crisis of the pandemic. This was potentially redolent of a great Labor reformist era (postwar reconstruction) and a sharp contrast to Morrison's 'can-do capitalism' mantra. Yet his prosecution of the case for the transformative power of government has remained inchoate.

Albanese's predilection, as exposed on the hustings, for wandering into verbal marshes has not helped either in providing coherence of theme. But the lack of a compelling storyline also goes back to the abiding caution of his approach.

The party's policy on a 2030 carbon emissions reduction target is an illustration. This is another area where Labor kept its powder dry, delaying the release of its target until after the Glasgow Climate Change Conference. When Albanese finally announced a reduction target of 43 per cent, it was almost as if the policy dare not speak its name. He declared it 'a modest policy. We do not pretend it is a radical policy.' Hardly the inspirational stuff of 'the great moral challenge of our time'.

Making amends for the disappointment of 2019 brings us squarely to the subject of leadership. If Shorten was a millstone on Labor's vote, a perusal of opinion poll leadership ratings indicates Albanese, though not popular, has not been subject to anything like the antipathy that dogged his predecessor. In the first half of this year, his leadership ratings edged into positive territory and, unusually for an Opposition leader, he was nipping at the heels of the incumbent on the question of preferred prime minister. This was a good place to be.

Probably the most consistent takeaway from the leadership polling over the past three years, however, is that Albanese has not made a major impression on the public. The relatively high number of respondents who have nominated 'Don't know' when asked to rate his performance has been an indicator of this. The pandemic is one reason Albanese remained indistinct in the electorate's mind. For stretches of the past parliamentary term, and particularly during 2020, he struggled for oxygen.

Yet undoubtedly the tepid response towards Albanese is also a function of the fact he has bent over backwards to be a non-threatening rather than arresting figure. For someone once styled as a warrior of the left, there has been nothing remotely incendiary from him.

That Albanese has journeyed a long way from his pugilistic younger days is a sign of maturity. But the charisma he displayed as a firebrand student politician has also leached away. He presents as a slightly rough-hewn, inoffensive type, workmanlike rather than exceptional. One senses he is more visceral than cerebral, with reserves of emotional intelligence. Colleagues testify that authenticity and decency are his defining attributes: a shorthand way of saying he is the antithesis of Morrison.

Altogether, Albanese's is an unusually modest persona for a prime minister, which goes with his insistence he never had a sense of entitlement to leadership. At the same time, there is a core of resilience and self-belief. His inner strength is rooted in the hard-scrabble backstory to which he routinely harks back. This is the story of being brought up as the only child of a single mother and invalid pensioner in council housing. His mother's struggles are the lodestar of his political vocation.

In another way, though, Albanese was blessed as a child. Like past Labor luminaries Whitlam, Hawke and Keating, he was the recipient of maternal special investment: what he remembers is his mother's 'absolute unconditional love' for him. While he might not have believed it was his destiny to be prime minister, his mother harboured that ambition for him. Middleton's biography records that she 'believed he could go far – as far as a person can go in the Australian political system'.

What sort of prime minister can we expect Albanese to be? He has referenced Hawke and, to the gall of Liberals, even invoked Howard as prime ministers he will take a leaf from. Hawke being the gold standard of modern Labor prime ministers, it is hardly surprising that Albanese looks to him as a role model. He says that, like Hawke, he will govern by consensus, bringing business, unions and civil society together.

The transactional business of forging networks of support is second nature to Albanese. It is a craft he mastered as a left faction operative in the hostile environment of the right-dominated NSW Labor Party.

There is evidence of his capacity for wrangling a middle ground. As leader of the House of Representatives during Gillard's prime ministership, he was integral to the functioning of Labor's minority government by closely liaising with the crossbenchers. Gillard later remarked: 'Albo is a very persuasive person. He's good at talking people into things.'

While Albanese's leadership style over the past three years has largely escaped analysis, it is notable he has mostly kept Labor united in common purpose. Walking away from the redistributive policies of the Shorten era required extensive consultation to work through the changes within the parliamentary party and beyond. In the end, the result was achieved with surprisingly little rancour. Albanese's collaborative abilities are also attested to by the strong leadership team he has assembled around him. In addition to his deputy, Richard Marles, and Labor's talented shadow treasurer, Jim Chalmers, that leadership group includes Katy Gallagher, Mark Butler, Kristina Keneally, Penny Wong and Tony Burke.

Like all Labor leaders since Rudd, Albanese insists he has learned the lessons of the dysfunction of that period of government. He will observe 'proper' processes allowing genuine debate in Cabinet. Albanese's team approach is a welcome contrast to the Coalition side, with Morrison giving the impression of running the show himself. Albanese's ability to orchestrate consensus will hold him in good stead for tackling thorny policy challenges, of which there will be many ahead.

Still, questions linger about whether Albanese has the stuff to be a substantial prime minister. Although a gifted transactional politician, does he boast the erudition and imagination to meaningfully shape the nation? He has demonstrated a flinty pragmatism over the past three years, but less certain is whether he has the driving sense of purpose required to achieve hard-fought-for reform.

And, like the best leaders, has he the ability to modulate his approach? Can he switch to a more dynamic, galvanising mode of leadership, or will the circumspection that has defined him in opposition shackle him in government? On the other hand, just maybe, his unassuming leadership will provide for a dogged but conscientious form of government that suits Australia's purposes.

By claiming victory in May, Albanese defied the critics and bent the template of how the ALP wins government from opposition. Non-heroic in leadership style, he has earned the right to be celebrated as a Labor hero who triumphed after an unusually protracted journey to the political summit.

Charles has been proclaimed king. But who is Charles the man?

Giselle Bastin
Flinders University

Charles Philip Arthur George, Queen Elizabeth II's eldest son, has finally ascended the throne as King Charles III.

As Prince of Wales, Charles has been there for as long as many of us can remember; every major moment in his life, from his birth through to his marriages and parenting of two sons, his public declarations about architecture, environmental sustainability and so on have been paraded before us in a regular drip feed of media coverage.

And yet, many Australians feel as if they know little about Charles the man.

A sensitive, solemn boy

Born in 1948 to the then Duke and Duchess of Edinburgh, Charles soon emerged as a solemn, sensitive young boy; he was loved but bullied by his father and loved but kept at arm's length by an emotionally distant mother whose first duty in life was to the Crown.

Prince Philip decided Charles would benefit from going to the same schools he had himself attended, and Charles was sent to the prep school Cheam in Hampshire, and later to Gordonstoun in Scotland – Charles hated them both.

After graduating with a 2:2 (lower second-class honours) from Cambridge – the first British royal ever to earn a university degree – and time spent in the Royal Air Force and Royal Navy between 1971 and 1976, Charles transitioned to civilian life and began to develop interests in the causes that would prove his enduring passion for the rest of his adult life: environmental sustainability, urban and rural conservation, architecture, spirituality, social reform and gardening.

He launched The Prince's Trust and the Business in the Community (BITC) scheme and oversaw the management of the Duchy of Cornwall.

The search for an heir

Throughout the 1970s the pressure grew for Charles to find a wife and cement the line of succession. His bachelor days whizzed by with a series of relationships with beautiful women (who were almost always blondes) who each seemed to be treated to endless afternoons gazing on admiringly while Charles played polo.

But there was a problem: in 1970 Charles had already met the love of his life, Camilla Shand, who would go on to marry military veteran Andrew Parker-Bowles in 1973. The woman Charles most wanted to marry was not in the running.

An heir, however, was required, and subsequently in 1981 Charles married the young Lady Diana Spencer in one of the most famous weddings of the 20th century.

For fifteen years the world looked on with fascination as the marriage produced two sons, William and Harry, before eventually ending in divorce in 1996.

One story that serves to sum up Charles and Diana's marriage concerns the interior decoration of their apartments in Kensington Palace and country estate, Highgrove.

Before his wedding, Charles lived in an apartment in Buckingham Palace described by royal biographer Sally Bedell-Smith as possessing a 'strong masculine flavour'. With Charles and Diana's subsequent move to Kensington Palace:

> … came Diana's pastels and chintzes to brighten the rooms made gloomy by limited sunlight […] Diana and Charles's divergent personalities defined their respective offices. Hers, the one room where sunlight flooded through tall windows, had two pink sofas and was brimming with embroidered pillows, porcelain figures, enamel boxes, and her childhood collection of stuffed animals. Charles's study was his man cave: small and dark, with stacks of books and papers, watercolour box, and sketch pads. From a portrait behind his desk, his mother gazed in silent judgment.

Upon his separation from Diana, Charles moved his own interior designer, Robert Kime, into Highgrove and charged him with the task of expunging 'all traces of Diana'.

The years after Diana's death saw a recalibration of Charles's public image. After a life spent in the shadows of the arc lamp of Diana's fame and popularity, Charles brought in a public relations team to reshape his reputation and to pave the way for the gradual acceptance of the now-divorced Camilla's as his future Queen Consort.

A man of contradictions

The Charles who is keen to stress that he is 'just an ordinary person in an extraordinary position' and someone to be 'treated like any other' person is one whose identity is nonetheless anchored in his royal heritage. This is the schism that besets his life.

For example, it has been reported he is someone who each day has a simple light breakfast, such as a boiled egg. Yet given his royal status, the egg must be cooked to perfection (four minutes exactly) and his cook boils several eggs in the event the one Charles is served does not meet his standards.

He has worn the same grey double-breasted suit for years as proof of his environmental credentials, yet he's a person for whom clothes are laid out each morning, and whose toothpaste (it has been noted, perhaps erroneously) is squeezed onto his toothbrush for him. A valet carries a special cushion Charles needs to have placed on nearly every chair he sits on.

His 'Farmer George' image (inherited from his ancestor George III, who earned the nickname because of his love for agriculture) rests alongside the reality that the gardens he tends belong to stately homes and palaces owned or managed by his own family.

As Bedell-Smith notes, Charles's:

> … cunning in extracting money from eager benefactors was perilously entwined with a weakness for the company and perks of the superrich […] he took full advantage of free yachts, flights on private jets, and estates for private vacations. From time to time his patrons turned out to be shifty, and Charles would find himself tarred by the tabloids.

Charles's many internal contradictions reflect both aspects of his character but have also been shaped by the royal system into which he has been born.

With the death of his mother, Charles is confronted with perhaps the most searing contradiction of his life: the moment he became king was one that he has waited for – often impatiently – for decades, and yet it was also the 'the moment he has most been dreading' for as long as he can remember.

PART II

The power of hindsight

Even in the political afterlife, Morrison departs from the norm

Joshua Black
Australian National University

Two months after his election defeat, Scott Morrison re-emerged as a subject of public discussion. First, there was a rumour about his interest in securing work with the Australian Rugby League Commission, which he promptly dismissed as 'pub talk'. Second, Morrison made his debut on the international lecture circuit with an address to the Asian Leadership Conference in Seoul. He seized that opportunity to criticise China and defend his own government's pandemic legacy, suggesting 'history would treat his government more kindly' than contemporaries have done.

Then the former prime minister went to Perth to deliver a sermon at the Victory Life Centre, the Pentecostal church led by conservative former tennis star Margaret Court. In his fifty-minute address, he stressed that Australians should put their trust in God rather than in governments or the United Nations. He also warned that prevailing feelings of anxiety – about the ongoing pandemic, the climate crisis or the cost of living – were part of 'Satan's plan'. With that performance, Morrison has signalled that he will likely depart from the established conventions of post-prime-ministerial life in Australia.

The leadership instability of recent years in both major parties has generated a relatively high number of ex-PMs. Their behaviour, and the reactions they receive, tell us much about our political culture.

Australia has never had more than eight former prime ministers alive at one time, and in the mid-twentieth century, three of them died in office. Today there are seven of them still with us, all of whom have seen their reputations rise and fall.

Australia's most successful former leaders have been those who deliberately try to embody generosity, magnanimity and a degree of bipartisanship. The first former prime minister, Edmund Barton, set that standard in 1903 when he resigned from the top job to continue his public service on the newly created High Court. His biographer Geoffrey Bolton suggested Barton enjoyed his transformation in public opinion from 'Tosspot Toby' to that of a 'well-regarded elder statesman'.

Several of Australia's postwar leaders have emulated that model. Gough Whitlam and Malcolm Fraser left the bitter politics of the

Dismissal behind them and dedicated themselves to humanitarian causes: Whitlam was Australia's ambassador to UNESCO in Brussels, while Fraser campaigned against apartheid in South Africa before joining humanitarian group CARE Australia. Both were highly critical of their successors.

Kevin Rudd has spent the past decade immersing himself in the challenge of US–China bilateral relations, and campaigning against the impact of News Corp on Australian politics. In 2016 he unsuccessfully sought Australia's nomination for the post of secretary-general of the United Nations.

In the recent past, Julia Gillard has similarly committed herself to causes such as the promotion of girls' education in Africa, chairing mental health support service Beyond Blue, and helming the Global Institute for Women's Leadership at King's College London. Her erstwhile critics at the *Australian* newspaper admitted that this was no 'miserable ghost'.

Conservatives have enjoyed their political afterlives too, albeit often in distinctly partisan ways. Earlier prime ministers such as George Reid and Stanley Melbourne Bruce were sent to London as Australia's high commissioner, working the British establishment. The aged Robert Menzies used his twelve years of retirement to write reminiscences, defend the British Empire from its inexorable decline, and enjoy the cricket. John Howard has studiously emulated Menzies (to the point of writing a book about him), although he remains a vigorous partisan campaigner during elections.

Even a highly unpopular leader can be rehabilitated in public opinion. Paul Keating's 'big picture' vision for Australia, which voters rejected heavily in 1996, looked more attractive after a decade of cultural division under the Howard government. By the same token, despite having lost his own seat in the landslide of 2007, Howard seemed a 'byword for stability' during the leadership turmoil of the 2010s, and there was much nostalgia about him.

Under Gillard, Labor sank to new lows in the polls, but in the years since her removal in June 2013 her reputation has recovered significantly – she is judged by some scholars to be the best prime minister post-Howard.

The public have had a little less tolerance for leaders who seem to be chasing money. John Gorton 'raised a few eyebrows' with his whisky advertisements, although Whitlam managed to get away with advertising spaghetti sauce because of his self-deprecating performance.

The popular Bob Hawke faced a fierce backlash in the 1990s following his explosive memoirs, his very public business investments, and his attempts to make money from short media appearances. It took time, some rewriting of history, and footage of beer consumption at the footy to rekindle his love affair with the public. Since Hawke, Australian politicians have followed their British and US counterparts by publishing memoirs in great volumes, but the lucrative international lecture circuit has been slightly less open to them.

It has been even more unseemly to be seen to act out of vengeance or bitterness. In the 1920s and 1930s, former prime minister Billy Hughes stayed in parliament and often caused significant headaches for his fellow non-Labor MPs, even voting to turf them out of office in 1929. Some felt him a 'great statesman and patriot', others a 'renegade'.

Billy McMahon remained in parliament for ten years after his defeat in 1972, apparently with no aspiration to leadership. In the more recent past, Rudd and Tony Abbott both stayed in parliament after initially losing the confidence of their parties, yearning to retake the highest office.

Malcolm Turnbull left parliament immediately on being removed in August 2018, and as Aaron Patrick has recently argued, he was outwardly bitter at his removal and passionately critical of his successor at every turn. Bitterness is a public emotion that alienates former leaders from their supporters.

The job of a former prime minister is awkward, defined by the past rather than the future, and by the absence of formal power. It is a role without a script. The awkwardness is embodied in Shaun Micallef's *The Ex-PM*, an ABC satire about a former prime minister who hires a writer to draft his memoirs, but finds he has no real story to tell.

But former leaders still have a meaningful role to play if they wish. They enjoy private offices, staff and travel privileges subsidised by the public. They retain their extensive high-level contacts and enjoy an enormous public platform from which to speak. Parting shots at colleagues and embittered book tours reflect a fractious political culture, but can be forgiven if the offender makes peace, finds a new calling, or develops a stately persona above the partisan din. In time, if they appear magnanimous, generous and 'above' daily politics, they can become a reassuring and encouraging presence within their partisan community.

By urging his audience not to trust in the institution of government itself, and by taking his Pentecostal rhetoric to such heights, Morrison is parting with former prime-ministerial convention. The congregation may have approved, but his fellow Liberal MPs appeared less enthused.

Such indulgences are unlikely to recultivate the respect of the electorate.

Morrison's multiple portfolios: Why the law has nothing to do with it

Frank Bongiorno
Australian National University

Emily Millane
University of Melbourne

The go-to defence of pretty much everyone entangled in the scandal of Scott Morrison's self-appointment to five ministerial portfolios other than his own, is that no laws were broken. But this alleged legality, which remains unclear, is barely relevant to any judgement that might be offered on the affair. Australia's system of government would cease to function without its actors being willing to observe conventions that do not have the status of law. It is no defence of one's behaviour to say that no law was broken as a result of it.

Australia has a written Constitution, but any casual reader of its text would gain little idea of how the political system actually works. Ministers hold office 'during the pleasure of the Governor-General'. The document does not mention the office of the prime minister. It does not speak of a Cabinet. The lifeblood of the system is convention and practice, and they are not to be found in the ink of the Constitution. Many of these conventions and practices were inherited from Britain and then adapted. In Australia, following developments in Canada in the late 1830s and 1840s, this agreed practice was sometimes called 'responsible government'.

'Responsible government' was a colonial adaptation of a model that was also evolving in Britain. That is why we use the term 'Westminster system' as a catch-all for Australia's system of parliamentary government. The most famous and influential account of the Westminster system appears in Walter Bagehot's *The English Constitution* (1867). Its central feature, wrote Bagehot, distinguishing it from the more drastic separation of powers and antagonism between branches of government characteristic of the presidential system of the United States, was 'the close union, the nearly complete fusion, of the executive and legislative powers'.

The lower house of a parliament, ostensibly elected to make laws, would in practice find 'its principal business in making and in keeping an executive' that 'should be chosen by the legislature out of persons agreeable to and trusted by the legislature'. Under Westminster convention, a Cabinet requires the confidence of the popularly elected chamber, which, in turn, is the mechanism for the government's accountability to the nation.

Morrison did not apparently see that in secretly having himself sworn into a range of portfolios, he was misleading parliament and preventing the accountability that Bagehot saw as the essence of the system. Instead, in seeking to justify his behaviour, he used a phrase that US president Harry S Truman had as a sign on his desk: 'The buck stops here.' In this vein, during his subsequent press conference to explain himself, Morrison referred multiple times to popular expectations of him, such as that he was responsible for 'every drop of rain'. Morrison seems to imagine the public believed government started and ended with him.

Morrison has since apologised to Cabinet colleagues for not having told them he signed up to their portfolios in secret. But it is telling that he has not apologised to the parliament for misleading it, nor to the Australian people for misleading them.

There was a time, not all that long ago, when phrases such as 'individual ministerial responsibility' and 'collective ministerial responsibility' were meaningful. The first was the principle that ministers were responsible to parliament and therefore to the people for what went on in their portfolios – they could not pass the buck to advisers or public servants, even if an error or misdeed had occurred in those quarters. Collective ministerial responsibility referred to Cabinet's responsibility as a body for its own decisions. If a minister felt so strongly opposed to a decision agreed by Cabinet that they could not publicly support it, the solution was clear: they would need to resign.

These were textbook concepts in high school Australian politics classes. It was widely understood that they were ideals and theories, that they would be applied differently according to context. But they were understood as Westminster conventions with genuine force and importance, even if an abrogation of convention did not carry the same consequences as a breach of law.

In contrast, we now seem to have a system in which it is considered a legitimate defence of one's highly unconventional behaviour to say that no law was broken. But this is not a legitimate defence in a system of parliamentary government that rests substantially on convention. It is rather a serious menace to democracy.

The electorate's concerns with institutional integrity manifested in this year's federal election result. But Morrison's highly secretive, underhanded accumulation of power would likely not be the fodder of a federal anti-corruption commission. This is all the more reason to be concerned at his 'Nothing to see here' attitude.

In an interview with Sky News's Paul Murray – his first one-to-one since the revelations came to light – Morrison made a blink-and-you'll-miss-it observation. He said that during the pandemic, the premiers had to make decisions they were responsible for, 'like I had to be responsible for the decisions I was accountable for'. Morrison still didn't get it. Transparency and accountability go hand-in-hand, and he had avoided both through his actions.

When the agreed way in which our politics is conducted is eroded, what happens then? Conventions are enforced by their usage. As the parliamentary practice guide notes, 'conventions are subject to change by way of (political) interpretation or (political) circumstances and may in some instances be broken'. But they cannot simply be set aside without serious and detrimental effects on the way in which we are governed. When they are broken, the system on which they rest eventually becomes broken too.

When prime ministers leave office, their reputation often enters a phase of decline, only later to revive as circumstances change, memoirs appear, and historical evaluation and scholarly biography replace instant analysis and the hot-take. We have seen this trajectory in relation to a progression of national leaders, including acknowledged giants such as Robert Menzies, Bob Hawke, Paul Keating and John Howard, and in more recent years, for Julia Gillard.

The revelation of Morrison's secret ministries has damaged a reputation that was already in sharp decline before the election of May 2022. Time will tell whether future historians will find brightness in what at present seems an irreparably tarnished prime ministerial legacy.

The election shows the conservative culture war on climate change could be nearing its end

Matthew Hornsey
University of Queensland
Cassandra Chapman
University of Queensland
Jacquelyn Humphrey
University of Queensland

Former treasurer Josh Frydenberg's shock loss to an independent running on a climate action platform wasn't a fluke event. 'Teal' independents have ousted five of Frydenberg's colleagues, all harvesting votes from the conservative heartland and all calling for more action on climate change. Amid the wreckage, Frydenberg was asked whether the Liberals needed to rethink their policies on climate change. His response – that he didn't believe Australia had been 'well served by the culture wars on climate change' – deserves analysis.

Who started the culture war on climate change? And are we nearing its demise? Our research, published in the same month as the election, provides some clues.

We found that approximately a third of Australians – predominantly conservatives – maintain that climate change is not caused by human activity, but rather by natural environmental fluctuations. Crucially, however, we also found signs the conservative position against climate science has weakened over time. The election results reinforce this message, with a projection of six teal independents nationwide and two new Greens seats in Queensland.

As such, this election may well be remembered as the first crack in the dam wall of conservative-led climate scepticism.

How climate science became political

Historically, science has been excluded from left and right political culture wars. Science, it was agreed, was best left to the scientists. For example, shortly after definitive evidence emerged that chlorofluorocarbons were eroding the ozone layer, an international treaty committed to phasing them out. The response was swift and apolitical: in the 1980s you couldn't tell how someone voted from knowing their stance on CFCs.

Unfortunately, this can't be said for climate science. In 1965 there was enough scientific buzz about the dangers of carbon emissions that US president Lyndon B Johnson delivered a message to Congress sounding the alarm. But the seeds of the climate culture wars were sown soon after. With the ear of senior politicians – and supported by think tanks and private corporations – a campaign of misinformation was started that came straight from the Big Tobacco playbook: to convince people to do nothing in the face of impending danger, you need to convince them the science is not yet in.

The campaign to scramble the science on climate change was remarkably effective: in the 2000s, 97 per cent of climate scientists agreed about anthropogenic climate change, but people incorrectly believed scientists were divided on the issue. A scientific conclusion had been effectively positioned as a 'debate'.

Originally, this had little to do with conservatism. In the early 1990s in the United States, educated Republicans saw more scientific consensus around climate change than Democrats. But this pattern has since dramatically reversed. Climate mitigation became perceived by conservative elites as ideologically toxic – a Big Government response designed to regulate industry and the freedoms of individuals. Among the right, politicians, think tanks and media all started to coach other conservatives on how to think about climate change.

The consequence was that a scientific issue became a political issue. Researchers investigating the predictors of climate scepticism found political allegiance blew everything else out of the water: it was more important than people's personal experience of extreme weather events, their levels of education, or even their science literacy.

Australia and the climate divide

In the early 2010s, the culture wars on climate science in Australia escalated dramatically. It became routine for conservative politicians to question climate science (former prime minister Tony Abbott famously proclaimed climate science as 'absolute crap' in 2009) and one-third of mainstream newspaper articles were climate-sceptical.

A short history of Australia's climate response

- **1980s**
  Australian climate warnings begin.
- **Early 1990s**
  Leadership changes stall action.
- **December 1997**
  Howard demands special treatment in Kyoto.
- **2007**
  Rudd ratifies Kyoto, promises climate action.
- **November 2011**
  Gillard government passes carbon price.
- **July 2014**
  Abbott ditches the emissions trading scheme.
- **September 2015**
  The Turnbull era begins.
- **2016**
  Turnbull rules out emissions intensity scheme.
- **October 2017**
  Finkel proposal rejected in favour of National Energy Guarantee (NEG).
- **August 2018**
  Scott Morrison becomes PM, dumps the NEG.
- **2019**
  International condemnation.
- **May 2020**
  Emissions reduction technology plan released.
- **October 2021**
  No new targets at Glasgow (COP26).
- **May 2022**
  Australia's 'climate election'.

We recently analysed twenty-five polls conducted by Essential Research over ten years, collecting representative data on Australians' beliefs about climate change. We found scepticism levels were staggeringly high by international standards. Over the last decade, about four in ten Australians either said climate change isn't driven by human activities or they 'don't know' what's causing it. Most of these people were conservatives.

But scepticism has tailed down from the high-water mark in 2013, particularly among conservatives. Our data suggest the trigger for this change has been the string of record-breaking annual global temperatures since 2015.

Climate scepticism isn't inherently conservative

As the Liberal Party and conservative voters ponder what happens next, it's worth remembering that rejection of climate science is not an inherently conservative position. International data suggest the link between conservatism and climate scepticism is largely an issue for the United States and Australia. In most countries there is no such reliable relationship. Indeed, in the United Kingdom it was the conservatives who led the local phasing out of coal.

Pro-climate conservative leaders around the world – such as Australia's Malcolm Turnbull, and Arnold Schwarzenegger and John Kasich from the United States – remind us that mitigating climate change is something that dovetails with conservative values: protecting traditional ways of life, maintaining national security and independence, and catalysing green jobs and innovation. Similarly, the success of the teal independents highlights that many conservative Australians want climate action. The election result could pressure the Liberal Party into deleting climate science from the culture wars.

This will not be easy. Australia is the world's leading exporter of coal, and in the past, inaction on climate change has been an effective wedge issue for harvesting traditionally left-leaning, blue-collar votes. But extracting climate policy from the culture wars would be game-changing in terms of our ability to unite in the face of the climate crisis, and conservatives are the ones most equipped to do so.

As the Liberals reflect on the loss of a generation of future leaders in blue-ribbon seats, they may just decide that now is the time.

How the 'reality-distorting machinery' of the federal election campaign delivered sub-par journalism

Denis Muller
University of Melbourne

The nightly television news coverage of the 2022 federal election was among the most juvenile and uninformative in fifty years. Given that about 61 per cent of Australians get their news from television in an average week, this matters.

The pattern was set early on: unimaginative, slavish, PR-stunt footage of the leaders, combined with young go-getters in the travelling media packs trying to make a name for themselves with gotcha questions. It is a pattern that has been developing for a long time, and for which editorial leadership in Australia's main newsrooms is responsible – leadership of my own generation included.

More than thirty years ago, it became obvious to editorial executives that having their senior political correspondents travel with the leaders was a waste of time and resources. Instead, the senior correspondents were encouraged to base themselves in Canberra and to be selective about where and when they went on the road. They attended campaign launches and major set pieces such as leaders' debates or National Press Club appearances, but otherwise they focused on analysing issues and trends as they emerged. Relatively junior staff took their places 'on the bus'.

The reason it became a waste of time and precious resources to keep the senior people on the bus was that the party apparatchiks and campaign managers imposed increasingly limited access to the leaders and increasingly absurd secrecy about the travel schedule. It got to the point where the itinerary for the day would be slipped under journalists' hotel doors in the early hours of the morning.

In these ways, the parties became able to exert a high degree of control over the media coverage. It is very difficult to prepare questions to put to the leaders if you have no idea where you will be the next day, what the leaders will be doing, or what opportunity you will get to ask a question. As a result, journalists and camera crews have become hostage to the party machines – news takers rather than news makers.

They find themselves trailing around factories, building sites, hospitals and playgrounds, shooting footage of the most banal but politically self-serving kind: helmets and hi-vis vests; Scott Morrison as a welder, pastry cook, hairdresser or whatever else he is dressed up as; Anthony Albanese having an earnest cup of tea with an elderly voter or bent over some unsuspecting child at a daycare centre.

Then comes the fleeting stand-up media conference, often outdoors against random background noise. Ten metres away and robbed of any meaningful preparation, the reporters shout questions that may or may not have anything to do with what they have just seen or with any issue of the remotest relevance to voter concerns. Was there a question about climate change, corruption or gender equality at any of those stand-ups? Fitting such questions into the scenario controlled by the party machines is next to impossible.

So the stage is set for the gotcha question. They have their place, as the one to Albanese in the first week about the unemployment level showed. It revealed him as astonishingly ill-prepared, but as John Howard said that night: 'So what?'

After that, Albanese was peppered with them, and seemed quite unable to muster anything like Adam Bandt's classic response when confronted with something similar: 'Google it, mate.' But as Howard implied, it told us nothing about Albanese's capabilities as a potential prime minister. His confidence strong once he had won the prime ministership, Albanese asserted himself in the face of the media pack: 'You will not get the call earlier if you yell. Day one. Let's get that clear.'

This unedifying routine affects all news coverage, but television journalists suffer from it the most. The exigencies of television news bulletin production leave them little scope for persistent questioning and little time to prepare their scripts. It is all about grabs and pictures. Newspaper journalists at least have the luxury of a little more time to prepare their print-edition stories, even if they have to file quickly for their online editions.

What can editorial executives do in the face of this? For one thing, they do not have to run the tiresome, cliched footage of politicians doing stunts. Shoot it by all means, but there is no need to use it unless something newsworthy happens.

For another, they need to do a lot more to brief their junior staff on the bus about questions that might constructively inform the audience. Take the unemployment figures. The outgoing prime minister and treasurer were understandably proud of the 3.9 per cent unemployment figure that came out in the last week of the campaign. But this statistic is in part an artefact of the participation rate. When people are so discouraged they stop looking for work, the unemployment rate looks better. So why not a question to the prime minister or treasurer about the participation rate? Or about underemployment?

Relatively inexperienced reporters being herded and hustled on the ground need not only guidance but also support in the form of necessary background information.

More strategically, it is time to call a halt to arrangements that coopt the media into acting as a publicity arm of the two main parties. The new reality is that there are three main forces in Australian politics: Labor, the

Liberal–National Coalition and the Greens/Independents. Each attracted roughly one-third of the primary vote at the 2022 election. This means the media will be paying more attention to the third force than they traditionally have, and so gives the media more leverage in dealing with the two main parties, which no longer have the power of a duopoly.

The media should insist on receiving travel schedules in reasonable time, on having media conferences held in settings where the exchange can be conducted civilly and, where there is time, for the leaders to be subjected to questions of substance, including follow-up questions.

As the COVID-19 media conferences showed, these can elicit useful information because journalists are, on the whole, not piranhas but intelligent people keen to do right by the public. It is not they, as individuals, who are to blame for the appalling television coverage we have seen over the past six weeks, but the whole reality-distorting machinery in which they are caught up.

Boris Johnson says his time as UK PM was 'mission largely accomplished'. How does that actually stack up?

Ben Wellings
Monash University

Boris Johnson has declared his time as United Kingdom prime minister was 'mission largely accomplished'. How does that self-diagnosed legacy stack up?

Nothing is inevitable in politics, but Johnson's political demise in July 2022, and his yielding of the top job to Liz Truss after the ensuing two-month leadership contest, might be as close as we get to such inevitability. This was not so much because of the growing pressure to oust him once revelations of his wrongdoing occurred. Rather, it was because of the well-known character flaws of chaotic self-management and flagrant disregard for responsibility that he brought to the job of prime minister.

Nevertheless, he has left a significant legacy, both politically and for the United Kingdom as a whole – albeit this is not to say his legacy was part of a coherent ideology or governing strategy. Contrast Johnson with Margaret Thatcher who, although reviled on the left of politics, was recognised as having a well-formed plan and effectively implementing it. Conversely, Tony Blair had an electoral strategy and was feared on the right for over a decade for winning the middle ground of politics from the Conservatives (although many Labour voters never really forgave Blair for hollowing out the party).

So what is Johnson's legacy?

It is hard to see any order in Johnson's chaos. He was seen as a fixer, a prime minister who governed through and by crises. The list of his main legacies will run as follows.

Mission largely accomplished 1: Brexit and UK unity

Johnson will be best remembered for getting Brexit done. However, this is not quite right. Brexit is not done yet, certainly not in Northern Ireland. The statecraft required to get the UK out of the European Union was focused on political concerns in England and paid little regard to those parts of the UK that voted to remain.

The push for Scottish independence has entered a new phase, with the Scottish Government sending its plans for a referendum on separation from the UK in 2023 to the UK's High Court.

Mission largely accomplished 2: Levelling up

The flipside of Brexit was 'levelling up'. This was a plan to reinvest in those relatively deprived areas in the north and midlands of England that had voted to leave the European Union.

There have been many plans to overcome the north–south divide in England; none have really achieved their stated aims. The cancellation of the Leeds branch of a high-speed rail project doesn't look like a promising departure from the norm.

Mission largely accomplished 3: Pandemic response and the economy

Of course, it might be too early to tell just how successful Brexit has truly been. Its medium- and long-term effects are yet to become apparent.

This is most obvious in regard to the economy, which was hit by the pandemic only weeks after the UK formally left the EU in January 2020. The anticipated 'Brexit opportunities' have certainly not arrived for the fisherpeople who were a key source of support for the 'leave' campaign back in 2016.

Although Johnson is often seen as having got the big decisions on the pandemic response right, his record is chequered here even before Partygate. His initial avoidance of emergency meetings spoke to his disregard for process and avoidance of responsibility.

Mission (actually) accomplished: Lack of trust in politics

What Johnson may have fully accomplished is destroying trust in politics. His greatest legacy will take some time to become apparent.

At the electoral level, Brexit was built on the support of those who had lost faith in the ability of politics and politicians to change their lives for the better (see above about Tony Blair). Johnson squandered the trust that those people put in him through his disregard for the responsibilities that go with the role of PM, and his lack of empathy for the situation of others he so obviously wished to rule.

Who were the candidates to replace him?

Two candidates faced the party's 160,000 grassroots members, vying to become Johnson's successor: former chancellor of the exchequer (Treasurer) Rishi Sunak, and Foreign Secretary Liz Truss. With his high-taxation policies, Sunak is what passes for a liberal among conservatives. This arguably weakened his chances against the eventual victor Truss, who presented herself as the continuity candidate.

About 160,000 members of the Conservative Party were involved in the vote that delivered victory to Truss in early September. This is where former prime minister David Cameron's legacy, rather than Boris Johnson's, has come to fruition. Back in 2010 the Conservatives were often described as stale, pale and male. Cameron selected female and ethnic minority candidates for safe seats (contrast this with the Australian Coalition's difficulties over quotas). Those decisions are now bearing fruit: the choice came down to selecting Britain's third female prime minister or its first non-white one.

Conservative fortunes

As Enoch Powell famously wrote: 'All political lives, unless they are cut off in midstream at a happy juncture, end in failure.' Johnson's political demise can hardly be described as coming at a happy juncture.

Yet, for all his flaws, Johnson bequeaths his successor a healthy parliamentary majority – down from eighty in 2019, but still a very strong seventy-three. Even with a huge swing away from the Conservatives, the Labour Opposition – which has ruled out a coalition with the Scottish National Party – still has a proverbial mountain to climb. The Conservatives may be dining out on Brexit and Johnson's single election win for some years to come.

Johnson signed off on his last prime minister's questions in the House of Commons by quoting the Terminator: 'Hasta la vista, baby.' His time as prime minister has come to an end; but for a natural-born grandstander like Johnson, we can be sure he'll be back.

Protests, 'biznez' and a failed coup: a front-row view of the empire Gorbachev allowed to collapse

Monica Attard
University of Technology Sydney

It's unlikely that in 1970, when I was twelve, I could have imagined myself covering the collapse of an empire. Nor could I have dreamed that fifty-one years later, my passion for Russia would still be alive, if battered by its barbaric invasion of its neighbour, Ukraine, in February 2022.

But back then, when I was a young girl, I did dream of being a foreign correspondent; in particular, a foreign correspondent in what was then the Soviet Union. From that romantic notion to doom-scrolling social media for news on the latest atrocity in Ukraine is quite the narrative arc.

As far back into my childhood as I can recall, there were dinnertime conversations about how brutal capitalism could be, how Joseph Stalin had saved Europe from fascism – and my favourite story of all, how the brave Soviet experiment with socialism would reap the benefits of communism at some point, sometime, in the future.

A new world, in the nirvana of time and place, where all human beings would live as equals! My father was from war-torn Malta, and he was a 'believer', at least in a better world. He remained that way to the end.

And when he encouraged me to go the Soviet Union for the first time in 1983, I was wearing his rose-coloured glasses. Everything seemed to be on the way to nirvana – even the empty shops, the long queues for offcuts of substandard meat, and the clothes shops that sold thousands of copies of just one item of clothing in the same size and the same colour. This, I reasoned, was a place sacrificing something – life – for something better.

From nothing to something, to uncertainty again

In 2022, after thirty years of Russia's integration into the global economic and financial system, that long-lost world of deficits – the word Russians used for everything not available – was ancient history.

But by March 2022, the nirvana of nascent capitalism born in the 1990s had abruptly and eerily been shut down, thanks to the deep and wide sanctions imposed by the West on an invading belligerent Russia.

It's been a long road from nothing to something to uncertainty again. The world is yet to see whether Russians will again rise against a ruler whose voracious appetite for land and blood has returned them to an Orwellian nightmare.

In 1983, when I first travelled to Russia with a friend in the dead of winter, Orwell was hovering in my mind. Although nothing I saw could have been further from my own reality, I reasoned there was purpose. The driver sent to ferry us from the then only international airport in the capital was such a welcoming touch, I thought. The driver was of course associated with the UPDK, the Directorate for Service to the Diplomatic Corps, an agency of the Foreign Affairs Ministry charged with looking over the shoulder of any and all foreigners who dared then visit for leisure or work.

UPDK still does much the same job, if now under commercial auspices – although as Russia's President Vladimir Putin tightens the noose around the freedoms won by his own people, the agency may well return to its darker days. But back in 1983 there was still, for me, romance to the Russian capital. The streets from Sheremetyevo Airport to the city centre were virtually empty, because cars were in deficit, and the trip took a brisk 15 minutes. Magic, I thought – no traffic.

Arriving at the decrepit and now demolished Intourist hotel on what was then Gorky Street, it was like being in the twilight zone. These two young female foreigners couldn't figure out what all the men and women hovering at the front of the hotel were up to. Maybe they were there to greet us? How friendly, I thought. It turns out they were awaiting tourists of the male variety and businessmen to proffer the wares of what we discovered was a highly lucrative trade in sex work.

Inside, surly desk workers looked over our documents and briskly marched off with our passports, which was a momentarily discombobulating feeling. But when they returned minutes later with our passports in hand, I thought – how efficient! All foreigners, still to this day, need to have their passports registered with UPDK, as though our arrival at the airport and delivery to Intourist hadn't already been clocked.

A rickety lift took us to our floor, where a babushka sat on a chair in the hallway, arms comfortably perched over her bosom, scowling at us for reasons unclear. Still, I thought kindly of her; it was icy cold outside and this poor woman had to come to work.

Looking out our hotel window overlooking Gorky Street, we spied huge red banners with Lenin's image fluttering in the wind. 'That must be the Lenin Museum', we decided. This place is going to be easy to navigate, I thought. The next day, we decided to put our lives on the line and make our way across Gorky Street through foot-high snow underpinned by ice.

Gorky Street was what in Australia we'd call a highway – six lanes wide and connecting the heart of the city centre, across from the Kremlin, to the outer reaches of the city. We hadn't seen the underpass to allow foot traffic to avoid the car traffic, which led to our first brush with the law. In the end, taking pity on us, the militsiya, or local police, accompanied us to the underpass and across the road, from where we emerged – like magic – just below the fluttering Lenin banners.

Sadly, a near hour-long effort to cross the road didn't get us to the Lenin Museum. As we looked up Gorky Street, there were Lenin banners fluttering everywhere. Most were worse for wear – much like the rest of the city as it turned out – but flutter they did, as if to say, 'Welcome to the land where we all sing from the same song sheet.'

Only briefly in the scheme of time has this turned out to be untrue. The more than thirty years between 1991, when the Old Order collapsed, and 2022, when it threatens to rise again, was perhaps the nirvana.

Foreign correspondent

When I was a child, being a foreign correspondent seemed like the best job in the world, particularly for a kid from the inner western Sydney suburbs at a time when travel was expensive and rare. I didn't see the inside of an aeroplane until I was seventeen.

But as a child, I imagined the vest-wearing, bespectacled, notepad-carrying reporter in fields of war, penning stories for faraway Australia, hungry for news from the world out there, far, far away from our marooned island nation. And so it came to pass for this dreaming migrant child, carrying the burden common to my socio-economic and racial class of low expectation. Just minus the vest. But it didn't come easily.

I had spent years in newsrooms, commercial and the ABC, spiriting myself over to the then Soviet Republic of Russia each year on my annual break to poke around and observe. I'd been travelling in and out of the USSR, the Union of Soviet Socialist Republics, since that first trip in 1983. Friends in Paris who, as young university students on exchange to Moscow State University, had met some like-minded Russians, led me to a woman who would become my lifelong friend.

Natasha Yakovleva was a film archivist with the state archives. She died recently, so trips to Moscow now feel empty. Back in 1985 when I met Natasha, she was as curious about me as I was about her, and surreptitiously she showed me the weird and wonderful underbelly of this intriguing city, about which, oddly, I felt I understood less and less with each visit.

By 1989, the ABC was ready to open a Moscow bureau and post its first correspondent. I was devastated when the job didn't come my way, although when the second position did later that year, I was happy not to have been the first correspondent in. Establishing a physical bureau, navigating the vagaries of UPDK and hiring support staff while filing on a big story would have been a herculean effort for a then young, single female.

Soviet society was thought by its members to be matriarchal. And in the sense that women carried the major burdens of life, including family life, in a country of constant deficits, perhaps it was. But men, like everywhere else, in every significant aspect of life outside the home, held all the power.

Operating as a foreign correspondent in this environment was often confusing. My questions were always entertained, but I was invariably considered exotic for having asked. My desire to understand the place was always welcomed but my curiosity was considered, by some, a little unbecoming for a woman.

The one saving grace for me was that socialism had given the Soviet people a strong sense that everyone was in the same sinking boat – men, women and children. There was an affordance of empathy for hardships suffered and help when help was needed. That made a difference in reporting the place.

The demise of the Soviet Union was slow, burning with disappointment and rage and, of course, with anticipation. By the time I arrived as a correspondent, it was well and truly underway, though the end couldn't have been imagined.

Politically and geo-strategically isolated, the Kremlin plastered over the long and obvious economic disasters while holding out the promise of better days to come. And coercion was the tool of choice to ensure people maintained the faith, much as now in 2022, even if the faith is no longer communism but nationalism.

Mikhail Gorbachev came along in the mid-1980s. Perestroika (political and economic reinvention) and glasnost (openness) gave people the right to think for themselves about how they wanted to live and work.

But it enraged the bureaucrats and the hard left of the Soviet Communist Party. As a result, it wasn't a smooth, seamless transition from diktat to free thinking, and it brought societal schisms – some of which were entirely predictable, some of which were not.

There were those who feared freer thinking would let loose the hounds of capitalism, which would kill off the achievements of their forebears whose blood and hard work had built the Soviet industrial base and, of course, rip away the sureties on which their lives were built. There were those who thought just a little freedom would do the job of making people feel valued and hopeful of a better life, and give them the chance to do something for themselves, outside the regime's boundaries, to make their lives better. And there were those who wanted the chains to be thrown off completely.

Add to that potent mix fourteen largely resentful republics outside of Russia (the most politically and economically important republic of them all), and the result was years of social upheaval, from the Kremlin to the most far-flung corners of the Soviet empire.

The reverberation from that upheaval, the breaking apart of a 70-year-old federation of states built on dogma and held together by coercion and fate, is what the world now sees playing out in Ukraine.

By 1989, when I arrived in Moscow as a correspondent, even the most fearful regularly took to the streets in protests for and against Gorbachev's rule. There would be tens of thousands, sometimes even a million or more people, crushing into each other, carrying each other along with sheer body weight, overseen by scores of KGB and militsiya.

We saw this again on the streets of Russia's big cities in 2022 as people protested Russia's invasion of its neighbour, only this time the protests were smaller in number, people were instantly arrested, and they were entirely unified in what they wanted – no war.

Back in the late 1980s and early 1990s, the protests were almost confused; some wanted a break put on reform, others wanted more and faster reform. There were uprisings against rulers and parliaments across the fifteen Soviet republics, the most frightening of them being when local Soviet officials defended their political fortresses with force, though relatively few were killed. As punishment, the food-producing republics and their subjects who wanted freedom from Moscow imposed food blockades on the capital. Deficits of cars, furniture and clothes produced by decades of a malfunctioning economy suddenly seemed quaint, even preferable.

Throughout it all, I had a group of Russian friends holding my hand, taking me to the edges of Soviet society, where I could see how people were experiencing the teetering of an empire. Some of them are still holding my hand to help me understand what rage and fury brought their country to invade its neighbour.

When the USSR finally collapsed in December 1991, I again felt as I had when I first travelled there in 1983: I was in the land of the brave. Their new world was something neither they nor their forebears could ever have imagined. Now, in 2022, it all seems threatened.

Russia and women

The odd thing about Russia's relationship with women was the strange contradiction at its heart. While women had and have no real power, they simultaneously had and have all the power.

They cleared those underground crossings of ice and snow in labour for which they were physically unsuited. They were prevalent among university graduates in medicine and engineering, even if that led to a downgrading in the salary and status of both professions. They rarely appeared on politician roll calls, yet their influence was evident in politics. And, most certainly, the influence of women's thinking, needs and demands was evident in the manoeuvrings of local communities. There was a respect, and it was not secret.

When it came to journalism, some of the toughest were women. Anna Politkovskaya is a name still recognised in the West. Her fearless reporting of the war Russia waged against the semi-autonomous republic of Chechnya as it tried to break away from Moscow remains a high point of independent journalism in a country where that has never been easy, and where it now appears to have been snuffed out completely by a new law penalising journalists for telling the truth about the war with Ukraine.

When Politkovskaya was gunned down returning to her apartment in Moscow in 2006, the Russians I knew were sad but not shocked. They expected something to happen to her. Who writes about atrocities perpetrated by the Kremlin without consequence?

Politkovskaya's murder – and the murder and harassment of dozens of journalists, activists and politicians since 2006 – put paid to any notion that media in Putin's Russia was free in the sense we understand media freedom in the West.

But like all those killed or harassed, Politkovskaya was respected, heard. The Kremlin might wish to forget her and her reporting, but many haven't. To this day, no one sits at her desk at *Novaya Gazeta*. (In March 2022, following two warnings from the censor, the paper suspended its operations until, it said, the end of Moscow's so-called 'special military operation' in Ukraine.)

Still, the retort I hear most often about this assassination is – why didn't she just stick to issues that were safe to cover, issues that women should cover? There's that odd relationship with women, again.

'Biznez' and the mafia era

Into this I waded, in my early thirties, single, very excited to be on my first posting and covering what appeared to me then to be the most consequential story in the world. The USSR was in its death throes.

Gorbachev was tussling for authority with Boris Yeltsin, and on the streets, Russians were rooting for both men. The hard left of the Communist Party was keeping a watchful, anxious eye on the new liberties granted: the ability to trade; the new television programs which questioned; the protests which, while overseen by a still operative KGB, gave the newest freedom of all – the right to protest.

Even though many in my circle thought that if communism was going to survive, it would need more than a little miracle, no one thought it would collapse. The system was corrupt and few showed any real loyalty to it. But the system did provide free health care, education and accommodation. Cradle-to-grave security was a big deal.

Russians also knew that the nirvana Lenin had promised, Stalin had corrupted and Brezhnev, Andropov and Chernenko had failed to revive was gone – as an idea as much as an achievable destination. But life without the Communist Party was still unthinkable.

The new buzzword was 'biznez'. Making do in a nation of deficits was no longer cutting it. Even the class of people who proudly maintained 'they pretend to pay us, we pretend to work' were looking to find ways to do their own thing. My local state cafe, which rarely had anything but diluted coffee to offer its customers, and from which its manager, Galia, made a paltry amount of money each month, suddenly changed.

Galia was an imposing figure: tall, graceful and gracious, and most of all, determined. She decided to offer the locals something new – real coffee, food and service. With her blonde beehive perched atop her strikingly Slavic face, Galia tapped into her contacts in the caviar industry, sourcing bucketloads of the stuff, red and black. When word spread, the customers came, queuing around the block to buy a slice or two of bread with caviar, and Turkish coffee that tasted real. She was in business for a good six months before the cafe was firebombed.

The era of mafia had taken hold, with thugs whose only way of doing 'biznez' was to extort. Galia refused to pay for protection and her business was annihilated. This was life as the Communist Party lost control.

While danger was everywhere for those Russians trying to make a go of the new trade freedoms, fear of it was abating among others. By 1990, just six months before Russians experienced their first dance with democracy with the election of President Yeltsin, young people were making their voices heard. They would gather on street corners to deride the "party mafia" that guarded its own turf and operated protection rackets to ensure only a new class of post-communist entrepreneurs could live well. People weren't afraid to talk about the issues anymore.

On television, Vzglyad, or Outlook, was a talk show hosted by the immensely popular Alexander Lyubimov, the son of a well-known spy. Looking back now from Putin's Russia, this was a high point of media freedom. Lyubimov openly discussed with guests the ills of Soviet communism, what people wanted from government, how they would get it, what Gorbachev was doing right and wrong, how the feud between Yeltsin, president of the Russian republic, and Gorbachev, the last leader of the Soviet Union, might hinder progress towards a capitalism-based nirvana.

In 1990, my friends could barely believe what they were watching. Now, in 2022, even using the word "war" to describe the Russian invasion of Ukraine is penalised. As I spend nights doom-scrolling for information on the war with Ukraine, I wonder how Lyubimov feels about the gains he forged being squashed so comprehensively?

As a correspondent, I would often hit the streets back then to test the limits of the newfound intolerance of the regime, and the reactions, while mixed, had one idea in common. Living as they had was no longer possible; personal freedom couldn't be the price for cradle-to-grave security.

Of course, few ordinary folk followed their desire for more freedom and a better life in a functioning economy to its logical conclusion. They thought the old structures could be reformed, renewed, revitalised. Certainly, no one I knew thought the old structures might actually collapse under the weight of the reforms. Not even Gorbachev.

And so, as 1990 ushered in a newly empowered Yeltsin, who held court at the Russian parliament, oddly named the White House, the demands for more grew louder and louder – led by the non-Russian republics. The Communist Party was becoming very tetchy indeed.

Putin is different

On 19 August 1991, Russia – and the world – woke to startling news. Gorbachev had been put under house arrest while holidaying with his family in Crimea. In the dead of night, a group of eleven men (of course) had hastily put together a State Committee on the State of Emergency (GKChP) to return the USSR to its 'natural' pre-Gorbachev state.

Led by the KGB chief, Vladimir Kryuchkov, the committee declared that the Soviet Union was falling apart. It said Gorbachev had refused to return order to the country and the protesters had eroded the authority of the state; extremism had taken hold. The GKChP encircled Moscow with tanks, and by morning, the capital had erupted in fury, fear and concern for Gorbachev, who was by then incommunicado.

On 24 February 2022, when Putin sent Russian tanks across the border into the Donbas region of Ukraine, proclaiming his intent to rid Russia's neighbour of its extremists and Nazis, I thought of what Gorbachev had said about the Emergency Committee many years after the failed 1991 coup: 'I said to them they must be mad if they think the country would simply follow another dictatorship. People are not that tired.'

Russian shelling may yet break the Ukrainian resolve to fight. But it won't be soon. Putin is now assessing how much fight the Ukrainians have in them and how many urban Russians still have memories of 1991 coursing through their veins. The difference: Gorbachev was largely unwilling to turn his military against his people. Putin is different.

When, in August 1991, the centre of Moscow was occupied by its own military, with columns of tanks rumbling through its main streets and soldiers armed with assault rifles fending off angry citizens, Muscovites screamed for sanity to prevail. 'Go home to your mother', was the most frequent refrain. 'Do you know what you are doing?' was another. While there was animosity towards Gorbachev for failing to deliver on his reforms, he was preferable to the putschists.

I felt safe, mostly. But never safer than when I scrambled onto a tank to speak with a group of soldiers in their early twenties. They looked terrified, like they wanted to jump off the vehicle and go home. Today in Ukraine, some young Russian conscripts have been doing just that – refusing to use force to overcome the Ukrainians who've stood in their path. Not enough of them have yet decided to defy their leaders to turn the tide, but the war is still young.

Through three days of heartache, confusion, mayhem, destruction, defiance, resilience and hope, Russians and the world were united – the GKChP must fail. Little did anyone know that its resolve to turn back the tide would be eroded by internal disorder. Defence minister Dmitry Yazov and KGB chief Kryuchkov were at odds while the other committee members, overwhelmed by their own anxieties, drank themselves into a stupor. They had all failed to understand how perestroika and glasnost had changed their own people.

By day three, their efforts to end the Gorbachev era looked shambolic. Their so-called 'constitutional transfer of power' was over before it had begun. The grave errors the putschists had committed were evident – Yeltsin, the leader of the defiant, had not been arrested, the TV tower had not been captured, allowing media to broadcast the truth, mass arrests had not taken place.

Putin, a student of history, has no doubt studied the dying moments of the August 1991 putsch. He has not committed the same mistakes in Ukraine.

This is an edited extract of Monica Attard's essay in Through Her Eyes: Australia's Women Correspondents from Hiroshima to Ukraine *by Trevor Watson and Melissa Roberts (Hardie Grant), published September 2022.*

American exceptionalism: The poison that cannot protect its children from violent death

Emma Shortis
RMIT University

I had always been afraid of America. Once, in Alaska, we had dinner with a man my father was working with, and he actually uttered the line – that iconic American saying, so ridiculous as to be almost unbelievable – *Guns don't kill people. People kill people.* I thought he was joking, attempting some kind of irony. He wasn't.

When I got a fellowship at Yale a decade later, a big part of me did not want to go, and especially did not want to take my husband and our almost-two-year-old daughter with me. Going on to a school or college campus in the United States is demonstrably risky. At the beginning of May the Wikipedia category page listing school shootings in the United States already had twenty-six entries for 2022 alone.

Still, I wasn't afraid enough not to go. Or perhaps I was just more afraid of what people would say if I said I wasn't going to Yale because of guns. The pull of America is strong, even to those who know.

By the end of May, it happened again. An eighteen-year-old gunman entered an elementary school in Uvalde, Texas and shot and killed nineteen children and two teachers. The children were all nine or ten years old. The police didn't help them.

Over the weekend, an eleven-year-old girl explained to the media that she had survived by smearing the blood of her dead friend over herself and pretending that she was dead, too.

The conversation is the same. The National Rifle Association held its convention a few days after the shooting, in Houston. Texas Senator Ted Cruz said, 'We must not react to evil and tragedy by abandoning the Constitution or infringing on the rights of our law-abiding citizens.'

The beacon of democracy and freedom, the shining light on the hill, the force for good in the world, cannot, will not, protect its own children.

Child's play in gun country

On one of our last days in New Haven, in the northern summer of 2018, I took my daughter to the Yale Peabody Museum of Natural History. Like everything at Yale, the museum is extraordinarily well funded. It's free for Yale students and is always hosting community events, mostly for local schoolchildren.

On that particular day, one of the first real days of New England summer, when the green had exploded and the air was thick with humidity, the museum was quiet. We spent what felt like hours in the children's discovery room, listening to the elderly volunteers worry about the black mould in the leafeater ant colony and marvelling at the poison dart frogs. I held my daughter's hand as we walked down the grand stone staircase, under the watchful glass eyes of the pink giant squid, to see the fossils. I chuckled, again, at the glorious 1940s mural that spanned the length of the Great Hall and its red-eyed, cartoonishly angry *Tyrannosaurus rex*. Clara ran around and around the main display, insisting on touching the fake rocks even though she knew she shouldn't, yelling at the top of her lungs, 'Rrrrraaaa Mummy, I'm a dinosaur, rrrraaaa!'

For some reason, as Clara did her little dino routine, I looked up and noticed two boys watching from the discovery room above. They were both white: nine, maybe ten. As I watched, one of the boys, standing right in the middle of the window, pretended to cock a shotgun. He lowered it slowly, while his little friend laughed, and proceeded to shoot everyone in the hall below. Shoot, reload, shoot, reload. He shot my daughter as she ran laps around the brontosaurus.

It was pretend. I knew it was pretend. But I could barely stand. I was frightened, of course. But it was the vicious rage that nearly knocked me down. Rage at the kid standing in the window, at his friend, at their parents, their grandparents. All of them.

This fucking country.

Parkland and a student revolution

On campus, there were regular reminders of the danger: bag searches before lectures, or complete bag bans in the case of particularly important speakers like Henry Kissinger or Al Gore. Yale was relatively safe, of course, insulated by privilege. But everyone operated under the assumption that it was only a matter of time until the next one, even if it was more likely to be somewhere else.

We arrived in New Haven in August 2017. The next mass school shooting happened on 14 February 2018. If anything, we waited longer than we had anticipated.

On that winter day, a nineteen-year-old man walked into Marjory Stoneman Douglas High School in Parkland, Florida and shot and killed seventeen people with a semiautomatic weapon; fourteen of those victims were aged between fourteen and seventeen years old. Seventeen others were seriously injured. The gunman had purchased the AR-15 he used legally. It was the worst school shooting in American history.

In the United States, Parkland, and the extraordinary young survivors who became the face of a movement, dominated the news for weeks. Through their activism, those students, along with organisations like Moms Demand Action, have seized the narrative and are doing everything they can to create change. In the month after the Parkland murders there were huge protests all over the country. In the 'March for Our Lives', half a million kids descended on Washington, DC, with Parkland survivors at the forefront. Children all over the country walked out of school, supported by organised events in basically every city in the land.

Parkland has largely fallen off the mainstream radar now. It reappears periodically, more often than not because one of the young survivors, traumatised by this hideous act of cruelty, has decided they cannot take it anymore. Other survivors are forced to publicly relive their trauma, again, whenever there is another one. Because despite the appalling public suffering of those children and their extraordinary organising, the shootings have not stopped.

Since Parkland, there have been many more mass shootings in the United States, in schools and elsewhere. By one count, there were 417 mass shootings (defined as an incident in which four or more people are killed) in 2019 alone. In the following year – in fact, before 2020 was even over – Americans had purchased more guns than in any of the years before: seventeen million. Seventeen dead teenagers. Seventeen injured. Seventeen million more guns.

Toxic American gun culture is a hideous outgrowth of American exceptionalism, and just like that exceptionalism, there is nothing else like it in the world. In any other Western country, when white kids die, something happens. But at Parkland, at Sandy Hook, at Virginia Tech, at Columbine, the kids who died were mostly white. They were seemingly middle class. The fact that white, privileged children are being killed and nothing is being done about it is extraordinary, in the truest sense of the word. The American political system – built on, and sustained by, white supremacy – is willing to sacrifice its children to keep its guns.

Those guns have become symbols of that white supremacy, as conservative forces in the American media encourage and spread the same hateful, violent ideologies that meet their logical endpoints in supermarkets in Buffalo, as they have since even before the nation was founded. The suffering Americans willingly inflict on each other, on their own children, is as horrifying as it is mundane.

But it wasn't always this way.

The Second Amendment, Reagan and racist politics

The Second Amendment to the US Constitution forms the centrepiece of American gun culture and conversations about how to dismantle it. It is one of the ten amendments to the Constitution that form the Bill of Rights, ratified in 1791. Its words are no doubt familiar, but they are worth repeating: 'A well-regulated Militia, being necessary to the security of a free State, the right of the people to keep and bear Arms, shall not be infringed.'

The amount of ink spilt in legal, philosophical, historical and political debates about the true meaning of those twenty-six words defies assimilation. What is inarguable is that those words were composed by white men worried not so much about an individual's right to buy and use the kind of weaponry their 18th-century minds could scarcely imagine, but about protecting the political revolution they had led and institutionalised.

The Second Amendment reflected contemporary fears that a standing army, in service to the state, would present an unacceptable threat to true freedom. (A freedom that, it must always be pointed out, was reserved only for white people.) It did not anticipate that the standing army of the new nation would go on to become, two centuries later, the biggest and most dangerous in the world, or that it would feed into the vicious circle of American militarism. The men who wrote it did not anticipate that it would be used to excuse the murder of American children. Their indifference to the murder of children they would not have considered American – Black Americans, Native Americans – must sit at the heart of any attempt to historicise the Second Amendment and its consequences.

But that amendment's morphing into a unique political monster was not inevitable, and is in fact fairly recent. Until the 1980s, interpretations of the Second Amendment tended not towards permissiveness but to control. In the 1930s – a century and a half after the ratification of the Bill of Rights – both the federal government under President Franklin Roosevelt and the Supreme Court actually curtailed gun rights. In the late 1960s, in the aftermath of the successive assassinations of President John F Kennedy, Dr Martin Luther King, Jr and Senator Robert F Kennedy – and, critically, the rise of the Black Panther movement – the Lyndon B Johnson administration oversaw the passage of the 1968 *Gun Control Act*.

For decades, gun-control measures were successful at least in part because they were aimed at curtailing the ability of Black people to own guns. Not uncoincidentally, from its founding in 1871 until the mid-1970s, the NRA offered mostly bipartisan support to gun-control measures. It was not until the mid-1970s that gun culture and the role firearms play in American politics began to resemble what we are familiar with today. As the NRA radicalised, it built enormous political force. In 1980 the association endorsed a presidential candidate for the very first time. Ronald Reagan had largely been in favour of gun-control measures precisely because they were aimed at disarming African Americans. But by the 1980s, that had changed.

During Reagan's second term, Congress passed the 1986 *Firearm Owners Protection Act*, which did exactly as its name suggests. Even an assassination attempt on that most beloved of NRA presidents five years earlier did not shake what was quickly becoming an entrenched politics of gun rights, particularly on the right. Four decades ago, the Republican Party became the party of the NRA, and it remains so today.

Clinton's assault weapons ban

At the end of the Reagan era, as a triumphant United States emerged victorious from the Cold War and the 1990s promised a new era of American ascendancy, things looked like they might change. A new president sought to emulate his Democratic forebears in successfully enacting significant gun-control measures.

In 1993, President Bill Clinton signed the *Brady Handgun Violence Prevention Act,* which created a national register of background checks. The following year, the *Public Safety and Recreational Firearms Use Protection Act* – more commonly known as the assault weapons ban – was passed as part of the infamous omnibus Crime Bill of 1994. The Act specifically banned military-style semiautomatic weapons.

The NRA, which had spent an eye-watering (at the time, anyway) US$1.7 million trying to get gun-friendly congresspeople elected, vowed electoral revenge. But in this new era, coverage mused that maybe the NRA's electoral influence was, at long last, waning, and in the new political culture of the 1990s, technocratic bipartisanship seemed to be winning out. Jimmy Carter and Ronald Reagan had written to Congress in support of the ban. It passed the House and the Senate easily.

But the promise of the 1990s was always an illusion. Clinton's assault weapons ban did not signal a systemic change in American gun culture so much as a brief interregnum. The ban was full of loopholes and included what would turn out to be a catastrophic sunset clause. The Act came into force in September 1994 and lasted for a decade. It was not renewed.

Attempts to revive the Act have repeatedly failed. And even before it had expired, it was clear that it had not worked to prevent mass shootings.

Columbine: The first televised mass shooting

On 22 April 1999, over four years before the assault weapons ban expired, two teenage gunmen shot and killed twelve students and two teachers at Columbine High School in Colorado. Inspired by Timothy McVeigh and the Oklahoma bombing, they had planned the attack for a year.

McVeigh and his apprentice were both white supremacists, motivated by extreme right-wing views – including a hatred for federal government – that took on a new virulence during the Clinton presidency. That connection is largely forgotten, now.

Columbine, which in fact is deeply connected to the racist history of both the gun rights movement and the US political system, was far from the first mass shooting, and far from the last. But it was the first to be televised. Columbine became the first in a long line of what has become an all-too-familiar international spectacle of unfathomable grief and astounding political failure.

Columbine did not shake American gun culture. The reluctance to really reckon with Columbine – to recognise and address the systemic failures that allowed it to happen – has meant that the pattern continues. Though at the time it seemed such a cataclysmic event that the idea it would *not* lead to some kind of reform was unfathomable to those of us watching from afar, Columbine was very quickly attributed not to structural failures but to errant individuals, high-school bullying and video games – just as Ted Cruz scrambled to blame Uvalde not on gun laws but on insecure schools, calling for them to 'harden up' and have just one door (with armed guards) accessible to the outside.

Nothing much has changed since Columbine, aside from documentarian and campaigner Michael Moore's successful effort to get Walmart to stop selling ammunition – and even that small victory didn't last. Since Columbine, the failures have piled up like the dead bodies at Virginia Tech (2007), Fort Hood (2009), Aurora (2012), Charleston and San Bernardino (2015), Orlando (2016), Las Vegas (2017), Parkland (2018) and now Uvalde (2022).

Defying logic and compassion

There is no clearer example of the failure of American democracy than this incomplete list of massacres. Over 60 per cent of Americans are in favour of some kind of gun-control measures, such as background checks or a ban on military-grade assault weapons. The failure of Congress, the presidency and the courts to prevent these ongoing tragedies – and at times their efforts to make it easier for them to occur – defies all logic and compassion.

In recurring debates over gun control, Americans and international observers alike turn their eyes beyond American shores – more often than not, across the Pacific to Australia and, more recently, New Zealand.

Not long after President Clinton oversaw the passage of the temporary assault weapons ban in the United States, a lone gunman massacred thirty-five people in Port Arthur, Australia. As the American version of the story goes, the public outpouring of grief and anger after that already rare event created what the *New York Times* has described as a 'national consensus' that gun control was the answer. The subsequent reforms, enacted by a conservative government, are described in alternatively incredulous and envious terms – although even the *Times* can't resist importing American arguments into its coverage of Australia, mischaracterising a national 'debate' about gun reform around the nature of the controls and their legacy.

Still, the implied logic, the rationality, of the Australian reforms, and later Jacinda Ardern's in New Zealand, is unmistakable. So too is the deep sense of resignation that such reform is not possible in a country so burdened by the unique nature of its foundation and politics. Ardern got a standing ovation at Harvard University in May after giving a speech about gun control. It won't change a thing.

What Australians and New Zealanders fail to understand when we ask ourselves why Americans can't just do what we did is the nature of American exceptionalism, its depth, and how it defies rationality.

We can recite our own national statistics all we like. Scots, New Zealanders and Australians, with their hearts in the right places, do it after every massacre, and we will do it after the next one, and the one after that. And American parents will be forced, again and again, to share their grief with millions of viewers on television. Even before Uvalde, it was easy to imagine the new president, so accomplished at mourning, shedding his own entirely genuine tears at the first school shooting that occurred under his administration. It is also easy to imagine that, just like his predecessors, he won't change a thing.

Australians should never pretend that we have the answers to the failures of American gun control. It isn't helpful, or kind, when smug Australians look condescendingly at the United States and its failures to rationally address its own deeply embedded and violent culture. We tend to underestimate the power of the NRA, which has the entire Republican Party and too many Democrats on its payroll. A lot of us underestimate the power of American white supremacy. We also underestimate American reverence for the Bill of Rights and the Constitution, from those opposed to gun control and those in favour.

Americans, meanwhile, tend to overestimate the power of the NRA, and have allowed that power to become self-perpetuating. The NRA is powerful because it has created a narrative that sees that power as permanent and unshakable. Combined with the force of American exceptionalism, that power – real and imagined – leads not to action but to resignation and acceptance among the very people who are in a position to change things.

American institutions are seemingly powerless to enact gun reform because so many Americans believe – consciously or not – that any cost or sacrifice is worth it to live in the best country in the world. Even the potential massacre of their own children.

An elite inured to violent death

Yale University is full of immensely powerful and influential people, and people who will go on to hold positions of immense power and influence. Four out of the nine Supreme Court justices, including Trump appointee Brett Kavanaugh, are graduates of Yale Law School (the other four went to Harvard; Trump's final appointment, Amy Coney Barrett, went to Notre Dame). Five Yale alumni have gone on to become president (Bill Clinton, George HW Bush, George W Bush, Gerald Ford and William Taft). Yale graduates are everywhere that matters in American politics. They are journalists, foreign policy types, Wall Street brokers and congresspeople. They've served at every level of almost every presidential administration, in every agency, every department, every lobby group and every think tank.

They also went to school about 40 kilometres from Newtown, Connecticut – the home of Sandy Hook Elementary School. I didn't know that, when I arrived. It wasn't until Parkland prompted discussions about school shootings with my colleagues that I realised just how close it was.

On 14 December 2012 – exactly five years and two months before Parkland – a gunman entered Sandy Hook Elementary and murdered twenty children aged between six and seven years old, along with six adult staff members. He shot himself when police arrived.

Many Yale faculty, especially those with families, don't live in the college town of New Haven. They live instead in the leafy outer suburbs, in big New England weatherboard houses with rolling lawns and trees that turn red and gold in autumn, and where everything sparkles under a blanket of pristine white snow in winter. On that day, 14 December 2012, their children's schools went into lockdown. Before it became clear what was happening, those parents didn't even know which school was under attack. They thought their children might be dead.

I'm not sure if the existential horror of this was just new to me, an outsider, but by the time I was there, five years after Sandy Hook, what struck me most was the sad resignation of every single person I spoke to at Yale about Sandy Hook and Parkland.

By that time – more than halfway through my fellowship – I had grown accustomed to the ritual of the very powerful and influential people I met asking me what I might do next, after Yale. When everyone is connected to someone, your answer to that question might make or break the rest of your life. In the five months prior to February 2018, I had answered it very carefully, probably with visible desperation. But after Parkland, I got braver. I changed my answer.

We were going home, I started to say – we were going home because we could not send our child to school here. We could not live with the unadulterated existential horror of our three-year-old doing lockdown drills 40 kilometres from the site of the mass shooting of twenty other babies. We couldn't do it.

The response I got never, ever varied. Sure, they would reply – that's a reasonable position. But a ripple across the forehead, a tiny frown, almost always gave them away. I could see a switch flicking. I was either written off as lacking ambition or encouraged to reconsider – to look at this or that program, or university.

In all honesty, it was only then – despite over a decade of study, despite multiple visits – that I really understood the poison of American exceptionalism. These powerful, rich people were utterly convinced that the United States, and perhaps especially the small corner of it that they occupied, was the best possible place in which to be, and *it was worth it to be there*. It was worth the risk of Sandy Hook.

They were, of course, partly insulated from that risk. Their kids went to schools with better security than most; they had money and health insurance. But it was still a risk. They had been exposed to that risk directly. The pervasiveness of the threat means that gun massacres can and do happen to people who are otherwise protected from the most excessive cruelties of American society. To take just one example: in 2017, a gunman opened fire on a mostly white crowd at a country music festival in Las Vegas. It was the deadliest mass shooting in American history.

They were all horrified by gun violence, of course. They were sad, and frightened. But they weren't angry. They were resigned to the continuing occurrence of mass shootings of children: just another thing that happens in America.

Powerful Americans would see this as unfair, of course. But after nearly four years of reflection, I do not know what else to take from it. These enormously powerful and influential people had decided that not only was the risk worth it, but that they could do nothing about it. The result of that failure – of Yale, of the other Ivy Leagues, of the institutions of American political power – is a country awash with fear and violence. In the United States, there are more guns than people. Americans purchased seventeen million guns in 2020, after Parkland; they already had 400 million. Put another way, 5 per cent of the world's population owns 45 per cent of the world's guns.

That population suffers from the highest rate of gun-related deaths in the developed world. Gun violence kills roughly 40,000 people every year. It is now the leading cause of death for American children. The guns that kill those children are manufactured by American companies deeply ingrained in the American military industrial complex. American capitalism is geared towards war.

The result of all this is also a powerful elite, riding the conduit from the Ivy Leagues to government and Wall Street, inured to violent death and absolved of personal responsibility.

'The Blob' and institutionalised violence

That group of powerful people make up the courts, the government and 'the Blob' – the foreign policy establishment made up of academics, think tanks and government. The Blob is what takes Americans to war, where they use weapons similar to, and worse than, the AR-15 that killed children at Marjory Stoneman Douglas High and at Sandy Hook Elementary. The Blob sends Americans to fight unwinnable wars, where they shoot people with guns, and then some of them come back and threaten the very fabric of the democracy powerful Americans so revere and that they had promised to protect. One investigation found that nearly one in five of the assailants who stormed the Capitol on 6 January 2021 had a military history. Some of them were former or current law enforcement officers. Many of them were wearing military-grade body armour, just like the man in Uvalde.

Joe Biden's Blob might look and sound different to Donald Trump's, but it won't do anything to really address this violence. Biden's Blob is made up of the same kind of people who have failed to act before. The 2020 Democratic Party Platform said all the right things about ending gun violence, including conducting universal background checks and banning the manufacture of assault weapons. They invited X González, a Parkland survivor, to narrate a stirring video about gun violence at that year's Democratic National Convention. But even in that video, you could almost hear the resignation in González's voice.

The President and First Lady visited Uvalde on Sunday. President Biden said all the right things; his grief was visceral, and genuine. But it all came, as CNN reported, 'without promise of major legislative action to prevent further carnage'. And Biden's promise that he 'will', as one mourner begged him, 'do something' doesn't factor in the prospect of the Democrats losing their tiny congressional majority in November. Lawmakers are in talks now, but even if they do keep their majority, holding a coalition of Democrats together to pass even the most basic of gun-control measures would be incredibly difficult.

More broadly, none of this addresses the institutional failures that have let the gun lobby torpedo gun-control efforts for decades. And it doesn't reflect on the nature of American exceptionalism – on why twenty-six words written over 200 years ago hold American society hostage, and why powerful Americans allow that to continue.

It doesn't address why those words are held up as uniquely good in the world, despite the way they are weaponised against Americans themselves. It doesn't ask why it is that so many powerful Americans who know better, who know that most of the rest of the world doesn't have to live with the very real threat of their children dying at school at the hands of their peers, have decided that that risk is worth it, for them and their fellow citizens.

That exceptionalism has allowed every generation of American children since Columbine in 1999 to face an existential threat in their own schools, in the full knowledge that the people who hold power and influence in their exceptional country are unable and unwilling to protect them.

This is Joe Biden's 'beacon', Ronald Reagan's 'force for good in the world'. This is what American exceptionalism does, at home and abroad: it puts Americans on a permanent war footing, against each other – against their own children – and against outsiders. This is the true face of the country that rules our world.

In mid-2018, we drove out of New Haven for a weekend away in upstate New York. Summer had finally arrived, and everything was green and full of life. The drive was beautiful, not at all like the ten-lane American highways we had grown accustomed to, but tree-lined and skirting around rivers and lakes. Clara was asleep in the back seat as it dawned on the both of us where we were. As we followed the curves of Berkshire Road, we saw the signs for Newtown, and, a little later, Sandy Hook.

Nothing is worth that. Nothing.

We lost the plot on COVID messaging. Now governments will have to be bold to get us back on track

Stephen Duckett
University of Melbourne
Sarah Duckett
King's College London

Overall, Australian governments managed the first two years of the COVID pandemic well. Border closures and state actions such as lockdowns averted 18,000 deaths in 2020 and 2021. This came at a cost in terms of the separation of families and friends because of border closures, disruption to schooling and economic activity, and individual stress. Still, the public supported these measures and thought state governments had managed the pandemic appropriately. Support for the Australian Government was also high, at least until mid-2021, when the bungled vaccine rollout caused that support to plummet.

Then, in mid-2022, we were seized in the grip of a fresh COVID wave. Hospital systems and ambulance services came under severe strain, not just because of an increase in patients but because the virus had decimated their own workforces. Governments now appear to be much more reluctant to introduce measures to curb its spread, a big difference from the start of the pandemic in 2020.

So how did it come to this?

Contest of values and rhetoric

Despite the much-vaunted National Cabinet, for most of 2020 and 2021 there was no coherent national leadership of the COVID-19 response. Then prime minister Scott Morrison and other federal ministers downplayed COVID risks and undermined state public health measures. They attacked lockdowns, state border closures and school shutdowns, while dog-whistling to anti-vaxxers. This weakened the states' social licence to pursue effective public health measures.

The differences between the Australian and state governments were in part due to different weighings of the risks of COVID. In 2020 and for the first half of 2021, there was either no vaccine or not enough vaccines, and the prevalent virus strain was quite virulent. As a result, other public health measures were key to controlling the pandemic and minimising hospitalisations and deaths. But from the middle of 2021, the rhetoric and messaging changed. Led by the Australian Government, there was increasing talk of 'living with COVID', reducing restrictions and reopening borders, with the underlying assumption being that, with vaccines, the pandemic was under control. Even the advent of the Omicron wave in late 2021 didn't lead to a reset, as it was dismissed as 'mild'.

There have also been ideological differences throughout the pandemic. Morrison preferred 'personal responsibility' to mandates, the latter of which was viewed pejoratively. Individual responsibility is a comfortable position for conservative politicians who tend to minimise the role for government. In contrast, the very essence of public health is that it is an organised response by society, to quote a standard definition of the field.

The federal electoral context

By early 2022, the effect of undermining the social licence was increasingly prevalent. The public, especially those who had borne the brunt of the more extensive public health measures, were tired of lockdowns.

The evidence about vaccine waning had not yet become apparent, so reliance on vaccines was seen as the appropriate principal public health response. 'Living with COVID' was becoming the dominant narrative.

Around the same time, anti-vaxxers had begun to get organised and protested against any public health measures. States sniffed the wind and began to roll back their restrictions.

A Melbourne joke from 2021 went like this:

Question: What is the hardest part of a one-week snap lockdown?

Answer: Week five.

The federal Coalition attempted to paint Labor as the party that would reintroduce lockdowns and border closures. The Labor Opposition did not want to talk about the pandemic to dodge that bullet.

Post-election politics

This long history is necessary context for the confusion we see today. Despite its defeat at the election, the Morrison government's pandemic legacy is hindering Australia's ability to manage the COVID response because of the weakening of the social licence to regulate.

Labelling the more transmissible Omicron variant as mild hasn't helped, as low average severity coupled with high incidence still leads to overburdened hospitals. The Morrison government's rhetoric of personal responsibility has proved hard to shift as well. It is certainly seductive: 'It is your job to protect yourself and if you don't, tough luck, you will wear the consequences.'

Of course, that position assumes we are all perfectly rational decision-makers and we bear the full cost of our decisions. Neither is true. We tend to discount the future consequences of our decisions, and we are unrealistically optimistic about the chances of getting COVID and its consequences. Just one person's infection can have a big impact on others – for example, if they are hospitalised, that impedes access to hospital beds for others – so the cost of poor choices by one person potentially falls on others too.

The public health messaging is also confusing. If I have had only two doses, am I 'fully vaccinated'? Does 'individual responsibility' involve my lugging a very heavy HEPA filter to ensure clean air in any room I go into? Is the Omicron variant genuinely mild? If so, why do we see all those stories about hospital problems?

And what is the right thing to do about masks? Are cloth masks any good? Or should we all have N95s? And should they then be subsidised? And if masks are 'strongly recommended', why are they not mandated?

It all comes back to the COVID social licence. What proportion of the public will accept a mask mandate? If the public is not convinced of the threat or benefit to themselves and others, compliance will be low. This means public health leaders need to talk up collective responsibility and collective benefit, the antithesis of the individual responsibility mantra. This has been missing from the national response.

Talking up individual responsibility means leaders don't have to lead or shape collective behaviour. Media hype about regulatory fatigue, a fraught catch-all concept where the evidence is still developing, hasn't helped either. Both New South Wales and Victoria face elections in the coming months. Neither government wants to be attacked as the government of lockdowns and mandates when the risks of not acting have been downplayed for so long.

So where to from here? Public health messaging over the first half of 2022 has been woeful. Political leaders are sometimes seen in masks, but mostly not. There has been little messaging about third and fourth doses, and so we have poor third-dose rates, despite what we now know about vaccine waning. The 'Omicron is mild' message has led to a 'No worries, mate' insouciance among the public.

Political and public health leaders must now exercise leadership. Public health requires collective action, not simply a reliance on the easy cop-out of individual responsibility. This will require a carefully planned transition from the discredited positions that have made a public response so much harder now than it was a year ago, and consistent positions across party lines that put the public's health ahead of cheap political shots. Leaders need to adopt a more nuanced approach to responding to COVID, jettisoning the simplistic all-or-none dichotomy. Finally, the mainstream media also need to resile from their knee jerk rejection of any public health action as akin to lockdowns and economic catastrophe.

PART III

The power to divide

Are Vladimir Putin's nuclear threats a bluff? In a word – probably

Matthew Sussex
Australian National University

Russian President Vladimir Putin habitually rattles his nuclear sabres when things start looking grim for Moscow, doing so long before his ill-advised invasion of Ukraine.

In February 2008, Putin promised to target Ukraine with nuclear weapons if the United States stationed missile defences there. In August that year, he threatened nuclear war if Poland hosted the same system. In 2014, Foreign Minister Sergei Lavrov warned that Russia would consider nuclear strikes if Ukraine tried to retake Crimea. A year later, the Kremlin said it would target Danish warships with nuclear missiles if they participated in NATO defence systems. And within the space of a few months – in December 2018 and February 2019 – Putin warned the United States that nuclear war was possible, then promised to target the American mainland if it deployed nuclear weapons in Europe.

Since the invasion of Ukraine, the Kremlin has waggled its nuclear arsenal so many times it's starting to become tedious. Even the most peripheral slight is apparently fair game, like former president Dmitry Medvedev's invocation of nuclear retaliation if the International Criminal Court pursued war crimes investigations against Russian soldiers.

Deterrence

One explanation for Russia's behaviour is that it's attempting to deter NATO from attacking it. For nuclear deterrence to be effective, states possessing such weapons require three things, commonly referred to as the 'Three Cs': capability, communication and credibility.

Russia certainly has the first of these. With nearly 6000 nuclear warheads, it's the world's most heavily armed nuclear state. It also communicates – loudly and with regularity – those capabilities.

But the question of credibility remains an open one, reliant on the perceptions of others. Put simply, America and other nuclear states must believe Russia will use nuclear weapons under a certain set of conditions, typically in retaliation for a similar attack or when it faces a threat to its survival.

But will it really use them?

Russia's declared nuclear doctrine identifies the circumstances under which it would employ nuclear weapons in a fairly rational and sensible manner. Its 2020 Basic Principles on Nuclear Deterrence stress that Russia reserves the right to use nuclear weapons 'in response to the use of nuclear and other types of weapons of mass destruction against it and/or its allies'. Or, if Russia comes under such severe conventional attack that 'the very existence of the state is in jeopardy'.

Putin spokesman Dmitry Peskov addressed this directly on 28 March, stating 'any outcome of the operation [in Ukraine] of course isn't a reason for usage of a nuclear weapon'.

Yet this has not prevented widespread acceptance of the view that Russia would use nuclear weapons in order to seize the advantage in escalation control. This idea, commonly referred to as 'escalate to de-escalate', is even embedded in the US 2018 Nuclear Posture Review's assessment of Russian intentions.

But the Kremlin's perpetual nuclear signalling has much more to do with its attempts to intimidate and attain reflexive control over the West. In other words, it's seeking to get the United States and other NATO members to so fear the prospect of nuclear war that they will accede to Russian demands. That makes it a coercive strategy, but crucially one that relies on never actually being tested.

There are plenty of signs this is working. In April 2022, German Chancellor Olaf Scholz based his decision not to supply heavy weapons to Ukraine on the justification that 'there must not be a nuclear war'. A number of Western commentators have also begun reconsidering the 'nuclear taboo', worrying Putin might resort to nuclear weapons in Ukraine if he feels backed into a corner, or to turn the tide of the war. One particularly agitated opinion piece in the *New York Times* called for immediate talks before major-power war became inevitable.

Little sense in Russia going nuclear in Ukraine

But what if the Kremlin's recent nuclear threats are aimed less at NATO and more at Kyiv? Under those conditions, the logic of nuclear deterrence (threatening a non-nuclear country) do not apply.

There are several reasons Putin might seek to use nuclear weapons against Ukraine: a decapitating strike, to destroy a large portion of

Ukraine's armed forces, to cripple Ukrainian infrastructure and communications, or as a warning. This also generally means using different types of nuclear weapons. Rather than large city-busting bombs, Russia would employ smaller non-strategic nuclear warheads. It certainly has plenty of them: about 2000 warheads in Russia's stockpile are tactical nuclear weapons.

But none of these scenarios make sense for Russia. While Moscow has returned to regime change in Ukraine as a war aim, using a nuclear weapon to take out Volodymyr Zelenskyy would be difficult and risky. It presupposes ironclad intelligence about his location, entails significant loss of civilian life, and requires Moscow to accept substantial destruction wherever Zelenskyy might be. It would hardly look good for victorious Russian forces to be unable to enter an irradiated Kyiv, for instance.

Punching nuclear holes in Ukrainian lines is equally risky. Ukraine's army has deliberately decentralised so it can operate with maximum mobility (often referred to as 'shoot and scoot'). Putin would have to order numerous nuclear attacks for such a tactic to be effective. And he would be unable to prevent radioactive fallout from potentially blowing over 'liberated' portions of Donbas under Russian control, not to mention western Russia itself.

Another possibility is a high-altitude detonation over a city, doing no damage but causing a massive electromagnetic pulse. An EMP attack would fry electrical systems and electronics, bringing critical infrastructure to a standstill. But again, it would be difficult to limit EMP burst effects to Ukraine alone, and it would leave Moscow with very little remaining usable industry.

Finally, the Kremlin might seek a demonstration effect by detonating a nuclear device away from populated areas, or even over the Black Sea. This would certainly attract attention, but it would ultimately only be of psychological value, without any practical battlefield utility. And Russia would join the United States as the only countries to have used such weapons in anger.

Is Russia rational?

In all this, there's naturally a big caveat: the assumption Russia's regime is rational.

Having accrued vast personal fortunes and a taste for luxury, Russia's rulers are likely in no hurry to commit suicide in a major nuclear cascade. However, since there's no way of being certain, the West must continue to take Russian nuclear posturing seriously – but also with healthy scepticism. Indeed, if the West capitulates to Russian demands due to fears of nuclear war, it will further embolden Putin and show other nations nuclear brinkmanship is appealing.

But Russia arguably faces the bigger risk here. If Putin uses nuclear weapons against Ukraine or a NATO member, it would also make it very difficult for states that have quietly supported it (such as China) or sought to benefit from its pariah status through trade (like India) to continue to do so. It would also likely engender a broader war that Putin has tried hard to avoid.

Let's continue to hope Moscow, although often misguided, remains rational.

If growing US–China rivalry leads to the 'worst war ever', what should Australia do?

Hugh White
Australian National University

Should Australia join the United States in a war against China to prevent China from taking America's place as the dominant power in East Asia? Until a few years ago the question would have seemed merely hypothetical, but not anymore.

Senior figures in the Morrison government quite explicitly acknowledged that the escalating strategic rivalry between the US and China could lead to war, and their Labor successors do not seem to disagree. That is surely correct. Neither Washington nor Beijing wants war, but both seem willing to accept it rather than abandon their primary objectives.

There can be no doubt that if war comes, Washington would expect Australia to fight alongside it. Many in Canberra take it for granted that we would do so, and defence policy has shifted accordingly. Our armed forces are now being designed primarily to contribute to US-led operations in a major maritime war with China in the Western Pacific, with the aim of helping the United States to deter China from challenging America, or helping to defeat China if deterrence fails.

In fact, the risk of war is probably higher than the government realises, because China is harder to deter than they understand.

The biggest war since World War II

If war comes, Australians would face a truly momentous choice. Any choice to go to war carries special weight, because the costs and risks that must be weighed against the potential benefits are qualitatively different from those involved in other policy choices. A nation's leaders must decide whether those exceptional costs and risks are justified by the objectives for which the war is fought.

That is a big responsibility even for the relatively small wars that Australia has joined in recent decades in Iraq and Afghanistan. But a war with China would be nothing like those. Once fighting began, there would be little chance of avoiding a major war, because the stakes for both sides are very high, and both have large forces ready for battle.

This would be the first serious war between two 'great powers' since 1945, and the first ever between nuclear-armed states. It would probably become the biggest and worst war since World War II. If it goes nuclear, which is quite probable, it could be the worst war ever. A decision to fight in that war would be as serious as the decisions to fight in 1914 and 1939, which were arguably the most important decisions Australian governments have ever made.

It is important to be clear what the decision would be about. If war comes, it will be sparked by a dispute between the United States and China over something like Taiwan or the South China Sea. But the specific dispute would not be the reason we would go to war with China, any more than we went to war in 1914 over the fate of Belgium or in 1939 over the fate of Poland. On both occasions, the decision for war was driven by our concern to help prevent a defeat in Europe that would destroy British power in Asia, which we then relied on for our security.

We would go to war with China to preserve the US strategic position in Asia on which we depend for our security. That is not quite the same as saying that we would fight to preserve our alliance with the US. Many people assume that that would be our primary objective, because the US might abandon its commitments to us if we failed to support it.

But Washington's disappointment with us does not threaten our US alliance nearly as gravely as Washington's defeat by China. As long as it has strategic ambitions in Asia, Washington will have good reasons to help defend Australia. What would destroy the alliance would be American defeat and withdrawal from Asia.

Australia would be profoundly affected by a US–China war whether we joined the fighting or not. That might tempt some to think that our decision wouldn't matter much one way or the other. That obviously overlooks the consequences for those who actually serve, and the possibility that Australia itself could be targeted. But more importantly, it overlooks the possibility that Australia's decisions would influence decisions elsewhere – including in Washington.

Recent scholarship has highlighted the remarkable weight given to Australia's attitudes by British policymakers in the crises of 1914 and 1938–39. Douglas Newton has shown how, at a critical moment, Britain's choice for war in 1914 was nudged by Australia's eager support, while David Lee and David Bird have shown the influence of Stanley Bruce and Joseph Lyons on Britain's innermost councils in 1938 and 1939. The possibility that Australia's choices might help to shape the ultimate decisions for war or peace in Asia over the years ahead makes it all the more important that we weigh those decisions carefully.

Choices for war are profoundly shaped by historical analogy. Often this is the primary driver of a decision, in part because there is so little else to go on – nothing like the kind of data that can guide decisions on, say, tax policy or health policy. We decide whether to go to war or not largely by looking at what our predecessors did in previous crises. Much depends, then, on which earlier crises we choose to consider, on how well we understand them, and on how closely yesterday's crisis resembles today's.

As Australia considers whether to join a US–China war, it is natural and prudent to look for guidance to the two previous occasions when we have faced comparably serious choices: 1914 and 1939. When we do this, we find an acute contrast between the way in which these two choices are now understood.

Two world wars, two lessons

Today, no-one seriously doubts that we – Australia and its allies in the British Empire – were right to go to war in 1939 against Nazi Germany, nor that we were wrong not to go to war over the Czech crisis of 1938. This was also the seemingly universal view of those who lived and fought through the war. In 1961 the historian AJP Taylor noted how little interest there was in contesting the accepted view of these momentous decisions. The same is true today. World War II is seen as a war that had to be fought.

The contrast with 1914 could hardly be starker. No-one today seems seriously to doubt that World War I should not have been fought. Again, today's judgement matches the verdict of those who lived and fought through the war itself. Throughout the troubled decades from 1919 to 1939, there was an almost universal belief that the war had been a ghastly mistake and should never have been fought. Ever since, and despite lively debates about details of the debacle that led to war, especially how much of the blame lay with Berlin, the clear consensus has endured that war came that long-ago summer through the collective folly, weakness and ineptitude of the statesmen involved.

The British wartime prime minister, Lloyd George, writing soon after the war ended, said the nations of Europe 'slithered over the brink' into a war that none of them intended. *Sleepwalkers*, the title of Christopher Clark's notable recent account of how it all happened, suggests how little those essential judgements have changed.

The intriguing thing about these very different verdicts is that the underlying reason for Britain and the Empire going to war was much the same on both occasions. It was to prevent the domination of Europe by a single power that would then be strong enough to threaten Britain itself, and hence Britain's capacity to defend its empire, including Australia.

Both times Germany threatened to upset the balance of power between the European great powers, on which Britain had relied for centuries to safeguard its security across the English Channel and thus allow it to project power around the globe to build and defend its empire. After 1918 this seemed a wholly insufficient reason to go to war. And yet when the same strategic logic drove Britain and its empire to war again in 1939, it seemed entirely justified.

Why the difference? One important reason concerns who did most of the fighting. In World War I the hardest fighting was done by Britain and France on the Western Front. In World War II it was done by the Soviet Union against Germany in Europe, and (as we all too easily forget) by the

Chinese against Japan in Asia. That is why, for all its horrors, the second world war was less horrific for Britain and Australia than the first.

But the main reason is of course the nature of the Nazi regime. During World War I, many lurid things were believed about the evils of Prussian militarism, and some of them no doubt were true. But no-one would compare them with the truly astonishing evil of Nazi Germany, which turned out after the war to be far worse even than most people had imagined. As the liberation of Europe in 1944 and 1945 revealed the reality of life under Nazi rule, it was hard to doubt that this was a challenge that had to be defeated.

Not surprisingly, the lessons that have been drawn from 1914 and 1939 are very different – indeed, they are diametrically opposed. After World War I it was universally accepted by national governments that war on that scale must be avoided at almost any cost. It was therefore always better to compromise and accommodate the ambitions of a country that wanted to change the international system in its favour, rather than fight to defend the status quo. The word used was 'appeasement'.

The lesson drawn from 1939, and especially from the failure of the last gesture of appeasement at Munich in 1938, was never to make concessions to any power that seeks to expand its influence in the international system. Accommodation only encourages further demands. An unshakable refusal to compromise, backed by a clear determination to fight if necessary, will probably force the challenger to back off, thus avoiding war. And if they do not back off, then better to fight sooner before the challenger gets any stronger. They will have to be fought sooner or later, before they become too strong to be stopped.

It is not surprising that this stark and simple rejection of the lessons of 1914 should have appealed to people during the six hard years of World War II. It is a bit more surprising that it has retained such a strong influence ever since. Today these simple, powerful precepts remain perhaps the most potent element of that vague set of ideas, preconceptions and prejudices that provide the intellectual framework for foreign and strategic policymaking in the Western, and especially the Anglo-American, world.

The ideas that we should always be willing to fight rather than compromise, and that the more willing we are to fight, the less likely we are to have to fight, took on the aura of timeless precepts of universal application. As such, they had, and have, obvious appeal. They make difficult policy decisions look easy, and allow leaders and their advisers to look and sound tough.

But the results have not always been happy. The 'lessons of Munich' inspired Britain's debacle in Suez, the United States' defeat in Vietnam, its invasion of Iraq in 2003 and many other mistakes. These failures are easy to explain.

Lessons of history are inevitably tied to the original circumstances of time and place from which they are drawn, and how well they apply to new situations depends on how much and in what ways the new circumstances resemble the original ones. The lessons drawn from the failure of appeasement in 1939 are specific to the circumstances of that failure, and some of those circumstances were very unusual.

Above all, the shadow of Nazi Germany was unusual and perhaps unique in several critical ways. One was the sheer evil of the Nazi regime, to which we have already referred. Another was its unusually stark and clearly stated strategic ambitions. From *Mein Kampf* onwards, Hitler made clear that he planned to do more than build Germany's position as the leading power in Europe by expanding its influence over other countries. He wanted to destroy other countries by seizing and occupying large tracts of territory to provide *Lebensraum* for the German people.

A third was Nazi Germany's potential to realise its ambitions on the basis of its formidable national power – economic, demographic, technical and organisational – compared to its neighbours. Against this kind of challenge, the only possible response may well be, as the lessons of Munich suggest, unwavering and uncompromising opposition; if necessary, by fighting a major war.

But neither Gamal Abdel Nasser's Egypt, nor Ho Chi Minh's North Vietnam, nor Saddam Hussein's Iraq were anything like Hitler's Germany. The dangers they posed were nowhere near as serious as was assumed, and the costs and risks of resisting them by force turned out to be much higher than expected, certainly higher than could be justified to avert those dangers. Even more strikingly, however, the lessons of Munich had relatively little influence on a number of much bigger questions.

The postwar architecture hammered out between US president Franklin Roosevelt and Soviet leader Joseph Stalin at Yalta, based on the United Nations, was premised on a spirit of accommodation and compromise. Even more strikingly, so was the West's approach to the one adversary it faced in the postwar decades that was in some ways comparable with Nazi Germany: the Soviet Union. Western leaders sometimes invoked the follies of Munich to advertise and justify hardline Cold War postures, but their policies were most often guided by a prudent recognition of the need to negotiate understandings with Moscow in order to avert the danger of war.

This was of course all the more imperative as the Soviet capacity for nuclear warfare grew. In the 1950s even the archetypal opponent of appeasement, Winston Churchill, became a fervent advocate of negotiation with Moscow to settle differences in order to avoid nuclear war. In the darkest moment of the Cold War, the Cuban Missile Crisis, President JF Kennedy was influenced much more by the lessons of 1914 than by those of 1938–39, which prompted him to offer the concessions that defused the crisis. In any case, the policy of détente that evolved in the aftermath of that crisis owed a lot more to the lessons of 1914 than those of 1938–39.

It seems clear that, as a new Cold War looms between the United States and China, the lessons of 1939 loom much larger than the lessons of 1914, both in Washington and Canberra. Washington has made it clear that it has no interest in seeking an accommodation with China that would meet any of China's aims to expand its influence in Asia and beyond. Washington's talk of preserving the 'rules-based liberal order' plainly embodies its intention to perpetuate the old status quo of US primacy, and its emphasis on meeting China's military challenge reflects its willingness to go to war with China rather than to compromise that objective. In Canberra, Scott Morrison made clear the influence of Munich on his policy when, launching his government's Defence Strategic Update in 2020, he explicitly compared today's strategic circumstances to those of the 1930s and early 1940s.

Is this the right way to think about the problem of China? To be clear, the question is not whether we should try to resist China's ambitions but how far we should resist them, and at what cost. Should Australia be willing to go to war, whatever the cost may be, to preserve the US-led regional and global order, and block any expansion of Chinese power and influence? Or should we be willing, reluctantly, to accommodate some of China's ambitions by accepting an expansion of its influence, in order to reduce the risks of war? It is not a simple question.

The lessons of Munich do not seem to offer a very helpful guide to answering this question. The Chinese Communist Party has many faults and is responsible for much brutality and oppression, but it is not by any stretch comparable to the evil of the Nazi Party. China today is certainly strategically ambitious, but there is no serious reason to fear that – the special case of Taiwan apart, its claim to which the rest of the world acknowledges – it seeks to conquer and absorb others' territory. And although China is set to become the most powerful country on Earth, it cannot dominate and subjugate such strong neighbours as India and Russia. Overall, then, the risks that China poses to the regional and global order, though significant, are not like those posed by Nazi Germany, or indeed the Soviet Union.

On the other hand, a war with China may well be as costly as the world wars of the twentieth century, or even more costly, especially if it becomes a nuclear war. That would be an almost unimaginable disaster even if our side won – a victory, as Churchill wrote of World War I, 'bought so dear as to be almost indistinguishable from defeat'.

Moreover, there is no reason to assume that we and our allies would win. Indeed, it is hard to see how a major war with China could be 'won' without the kind of full-scale invasion or subjugation of the enemy's country that brought victory in the two world wars. It is somewhat easier to imagine how China could defeat the United States – by imposing such heavy costs that Washington decides to abandon the war, and withdraw from Asia to the Western Hemisphere.

That raises the very real possibility that a war with China launched to preserve the US's position in Asia might well end up destroying it, just as World War I destroyed the empires that went to war to preserve themselves in 1914.

The limits to accommodation

What, then, do the lessons of 1914 offer as a guide to our policy choices today? In the 1920s and 1930s, the majority of those who survived World War I would have been quite clear about the answer. They would have said we should avoid war at almost any price, by being willing to go a long way to accommodate China's ambitions by according it a much larger share of influence and authority in the international system. They would have been confident, however, that China's ambitions could be constrained by limits imposed, not by armed force, but by a powerful international institution – the League of Nations – and by what they called 'international public opinion'.

They repudiated war as an instrument of policy, but they placed great faith in these alternatives to achieve what war, or the threat of war, had long been relied upon to do. Of course, this did not work. As the historian EH Carr wrote just before war broke out in 1939, their misplaced confidence in these constraints, and what he later called 'the almost total neglect of the factor of power', did much to create the crisis that then confronted Britain with no alternative but to go to war again.

We would be wise, then, not to follow their example. Where then to turn? We might begin by noting that the lessons of 1914 and of Munich are both aberrations. They depart from much older traditions of statecraft that developed over many centuries as the modern European state system emerged and evolved.

Those traditions do not by any means forswear war. Indeed, as former US secretary of state Henry Kissinger, one of their foremost contemporary exponents, wrote in the first page of his first book: 'those who forswear war will never have peace'. But the aim is always to achieve the maximum advantages without war, and that entails a willingness to negotiate and accommodate; to appease, in other words. War is not an alternative to accommodation; it is used to set the limits to accommodation and to enforce those limits.

This approach prevented any single power dominating Europe for centuries, and after the 1815 Congress of Vienna, it prevented any Europe-wide wars for almost a century until 1914. Seen in the light of this tradition, the appeasers' mistake at Munich was not that they accommodated Hitler over Sudetenland, but that they failed to make it absolutely clear that they would go to war to deny him the rest of Czechoslovakia, or any of Poland.

As that example makes clear, the key to this kind of statecraft lies in deciding where to set the limits to accommodation. These are hard decisions to make. As we have seen, one of the attractions of the lessons of Munich as a template for strategic decision-making is its simplicity. But it achieves simplicity by lazily assuming that all ambitious powers are essentially the same and must be treated the same by refusing any accommodation.

Taking a more responsible approach requires careful judgements about the current and probable future extent of an adversary's ambitions and power, and nuanced assessments of the implications for our future security. Then we can judge how far we can afford to accommodate them before the costs and risks of doing so exceed the costs and risks of the war we would need to fight to stop them.

Looking back, for example, it is interesting and instructive to think about the alternatives to war in August 1914. Had Britain stood aloof, France and Russia may well have been defeated, leaving Germany the unquestioned leading power in Europe. That appeared an unacceptable outcome to the majority of the Cabinet in Whitehall, but a minority argued that Britain could live with it more easily than it could bear the burdens of war, and in the light of events since then they were probably right.

After all, the Germany of 1914 was not Nazi Germany. And Australia might well have been better off had the arguments for peace prevailed in Whitehall. Not only would we have been spared the losses we suffered, but Britain would have remained a stronger global power better able to defend its Pacific dominions than it proved to be in 1941.

Rhyming history

History does not repeat itself, but it does rhyme. As we face the challenge of a rising China, we can hear the clear echoes of the choices faced by our predecessors in the last century and the centuries before that. Those echoes tell us that to meet that challenge, we need to do a lot more than mouth slogans about Munich.

We have to think carefully and realistically about the nature of China's challenge to the old order in Asia, the kind of new order that might be created to accommodate it, the safeguards that would be required to protect our most vital interests in that order, and how that might be achieved at minimum cost and risk. We must also think about how best we can influence our major ally as it addresses the same questions, because its answers will have immense significance for us.

All this is a formidable task. Indeed, it is probably the most demanding foreign policy task that Australia has ever faced. But we should not be surprised by that when we remember that China's rise is the biggest shift in Australia's international setting since Europeans first settled here in 1788.

In meeting that task, it falls to the present generation of political leaders, policymakers, commentators and, ultimately, citizens around the world to navigate one of the biggest, swiftest, most disruptive and most dangerous power transitions in modern history. One might say, too, that it falls to the current generation of historians to contribute to that work by offering a deeper understanding of the choices that were made by earlier generations navigating similar transitions.

That is not easy, because the accepted versions of earlier episodes like 1914 and 1938–39 are encrusted with tradition, sentiment and ideology, and few historians have sought to challenge or overturn these accepted versions. Perhaps more will step forward as the nature and seriousness of today's choices, and the need to illuminate them with lessons from the past, become clearer.

One key element of such work will be the methodologically vexed but undoubtedly stimulating exploration of counterfactual histories. To assess and learn from the decisions of 1914, we need more nuanced and sophisticated views of how Europe and the British Empire would have fared had Imperial Germany dominated the Continent. To assess and learn from the decisions of 1938 and 1939, we need to better understand what might have happened had different decisions been made.

We also need to recognise and meditate on what might have happened had 'our side' not won the last two major-power wars. Because we might not win the next one.

This is an edited extract from Lessons from History: Leading Historians Tackle Australia's Greatest Challenges, *edited by Carolyn Holbrook, Lyndon Megarrity and David Lowe (NewSouth Publishing, July 2022).*

US Supreme Court overturns *Roe v. Wade*, but for abortion opponents, this is just the beginning

Prudence Flowers
Flinders University

On 24 June, the US Supreme Court handed down a ruling overturning *Roe v. Wade*, the landmark 1973 decision that found there was a constitutional right to abortion. In *Dobbs v. Jackson Women's Health Organization*, the court ruled 6–3 that: 'The Constitution makes no reference to abortion, and no such right is implicitly protected by any constitutional provision.'

Abortion regulation has now been returned to the individual states. Yet rather than resolving the debate over abortion in the United States, we will likely see a dramatic escalation of abortion lawsuits and legislation. That is because the goal of abortion opponents has always been to stop abortion nationwide. Overturning *Roe v. Wade* is just the beginning.

Roe v. Wade has been under constant attack

For forty-nine years, *Roe v. Wade* has been under constant attack from opponents of reproductive rights, surviving repeated legal challenges and reaffirmed on multiple occasions by the Supreme Court. Despite the political controversy and polarising rhetoric from Republican politicians, 2021 polling indicated 80 per cent of Americans support abortion in all or most cases, and at least 60 per cent support *Roe v. Wade*. However, after former president Donald Trump was able to fill three Supreme Court vacancies, conservatives had a 6–3 majority on the bench.

The end of *Roe v. Wade* seemed inevitable, and the question became whether the judgement would be gradually gutted or overturned in one fell swoop.

What can Biden and the Democrats do?

In early May, a draft of Justice Samuel Alito's majority decision was leaked, indicating *Roe v. Wade* would be overturned. Protests from abortion rights supporters erupted, including outside the Supreme Court and the homes of conservative justices. President Joe Biden swiftly issued a statement insisting a 'woman's right to choose is fundamental', and his administration has spent the intervening months meeting with abortion rights advocates. However, there is little of substance the President or congressional Democrats can do to reverse the decision.

In mid May, the *Women's Health Protection Act*, which sought to codify abortion rights, was defeated in the Senate. And although Democrats have a majority in both houses of Congress, without filibuster reform they do not have the numbers to pass legislation, which has stymied much of the Democratic agenda during Biden's presidency. While Biden responded in July by issuing an executive order to protect access to medical abortion and contraception, this will offset only some of the likely consequences of the new abortion landscape.

Meanwhile, in the days after the May leak, congressional Republicans met with prominent anti-abortion leaders to discuss a nationwide ban on abortion after six weeks. Such a move would shift the contours of the abortion fight back to the national stage and would ensure abortion is front and centre in the 2024 presidential elections.

State laws on abortion access and provision

With the overturning of *Roe v. Wade*, abortion access and provision will be shaped by a patchwork of state laws. At the time of the decision, thirteen states already had 'trigger' laws on the books to criminalise abortion on the overturning of *Roe*. As of August, ten states had banned abortion outright, and a further five had outlawed abortions after six weeks of pregnancy.

States hostile to abortion have also begun debating how to close legislative 'loopholes', considering laws that are more extreme than any previously proposed. In addition to pursuing abortion bans, including from the moment of conception, many of the new laws no longer allow for abortion in cases of rape or incest. Provisions that would allow abortion to protect maternal health are being so narrowly defined as to render them almost meaningless: in Oklahoma, one Republican complained the proposed law did not ban abortion in instances of ectopic pregnancy, a condition fatal to the pregnant person if left untreated. And Louisiana Republicans debated language that would have charged abortion patients with homicide.

Opponents of abortion are also strategising about how to prevent patients from accessing abortion from out-of-state providers, including discussing banning interstate travel and making abortion providers and support networks subject to legal sanction. Nineteen states already ban the virtual provision of abortion care, and opponents of abortion are particularly keen to criminalise and limit patient access to medication abortion provided via telehealth.

The National Right to Life Committee has drafted model state legislation that would make it illegal to provide information on self-managed abortion via phone, internet or website, effectively targeting the First Amendment right to free speech.

Some states have laws enshrining the right to abortion

Supporters of reproductive rights have also been galvanised by the looming end of *Roe v. Wade*. Sixteen states, primarily on the east and west coasts, as well as the District of Columbia, have laws enshrining the right to abortion.

California has passed laws protecting abortion providers and patients accessing care from out-of-state civil lawsuits, while New York has passed a package of laws that would make it an abortion 'safe haven'. Advocates are pushing the White House to challenge any law criminalising out-of-state travel to receive an abortion. A Jewish synagogue is suing the state of Florida, claiming the state's abortion ban violates religious freedoms protected by the First Amendment.

Impact on abortion patients

Politically and legally, the struggle over abortion rights is primed to explode nationwide, with no foreseeable end in sight. Yet the impact of the Supreme Court decision will be most acutely felt by abortion patients.

Most of the toughest abortion bans and regulations are in the South and Midwest, rendering abortion inaccessible in a vast geographic stretch of the country. Approximately half of US women and girls of reproductive age live in states where abortion is or will become illegal. Overturning *Roe v. Wade* will result in the closure of more than a quarter of the nation's abortion clinics, placing huge pressure on the remaining providers to offer time-sensitive care to patients likely travelling hundreds of kilometres from home.

Banning abortion does not stop abortion

Banning abortion does not stop abortion, nor does it reduce the number of abortions. Regardless of their home state, pregnant people will still seek abortions, although they may need significant resources to do so and could face criminal sanctions.

The majority of abortion patients in the United States are already from vulnerable and marginalised populations. The devastating consequences of this decision will fall primarily on the shoulders of those least able to bear it.

How the US Supreme Court has become right-wing

Adrian Beaumont
The Conversation

The US Supreme Court's annual term usually finishes at the end of June, so late June is when the most important decisions are likely to be announced. On 23 June, the court struck down a New York state law that restricted the carrying of guns outside the home. On 24 June, it denied a constitutional right to an abortion, overturning its own 1973 *Roe v. Wade* ruling. On 30 June, it ruled against the Environmental Protection Agency's regulations on fossil fuels.

From an international viewpoint, the EPA ruling is the most significant. Other countries can set their own gun and abortion laws, but climate change mitigation efforts require international cooperation. According to a May 2021 report, China was responsible for 27 per cent of global greenhouse gas emissions in 2019, with the United States second with 11 per cent of emissions.

How did the Supreme Court become right-wing? Unlike Australia, judicial appointments in the US are politicised. Democratic presidents will try to appoint left-wing judges and Republican presidents will try to appoint right-wing judges. Supreme Court judges are lifetime appointments. Presidents nominate judges who are subject to confirmation by only the US Senate, not the House of Representatives.

Up until late 2020, the court had a 5–4 right majority, but Chief Justice John Roberts sometimes sided with the left, most famously in the June 2012 decision that upheld Barack Obama's *Affordable Care Act* (Obamacare).

In February 2016, right-wing justice Antonin Scalia died. Obama was still president at the time, and replacing Scalia would have given the left a 5–4 majority. But Republicans controlled the Senate, and majority leader Mitch McConnell denied a vote for Obama's nominee, Merrick Garland. McConnell's ruthlessness was rewarded when Donald Trump unexpectedly defeated Hillary Clinton at the November 2016 presidential election. Trump nominated Neil Gorsuch to replace Scalia, and his nomination was confirmed by the Republican-controlled Senate in April 2017.

In July 2018, right-wing justice Anthony Kennedy retired. After a vicious confirmation fight that involved allegations of rape, Kennedy was succeeded by Trump's nominee Brett Kavanaugh in October 2018. At the November 2018 midterm elections, Democrats gained control of the House, where all 435 seats are up for election every two years. But senators have six-year terms, with one-third up every two years. The seats up in the Senate last had elections in 2012, a great year for Democrats. Republicans gained two net Senate seats in 2018 to extend their control.

In September 2020, left-wing justice Ruth Bader Ginsburg died. McConnell ruthlessly rammed Trump's nominee, Amy Coney Barrett, through the Senate in late October, shortly before the November 2020 election that Trump lost. This is why we now have a 6–3 right Supreme Court: Obama did not get a chance to replace the right-wing Scalia, while Trump had three nominees approved, including Ginsburg's replacement.

Left-wing justice Stephen Breyer announced he would retire at the end of the term, and President Joe Biden's nominee, Ketanji Brown Jackson, was confirmed by the now Democratic-controlled Senate in April. Jackson has now replaced Breyer, but she replaced a left-wing judge, so the 6–3 right majority remains.

The Supreme Court is historically unpopular, but so is Biden

A Gallup poll conducted in June, before the major decisions were announced, had 25 per cent of respondents expressing a great deal or quite a lot of confidence in the Supreme Court, down from 36 per cent in June 2021. That's the lowest confidence in the court in Gallup's polling, which goes back to 1973; the previous low was 30 per cent in 2014.

A recent FiveThirtyEight article cited seven polls that asked whether voters approved or disapproved of the 24 June abortion ruling. Disapproval led in all seven polls by 7–23 points, with an average lead of 15.6.

The bad news for Democrats is Biden's ratings are at a near-record low compared to past presidents. In the FiveThirtyEight aggregate, 55.9 per cent disapprove of Biden's performance and 39.2 per cent approve (net −16.7). That's worse than Trump, who had a −10.2 net approval at this stage of his presidency. Since presidential approval polling began with Harry Truman (president from 1945 to 1953), Biden only beats Truman at this stage of previous presidencies: Truman fell to −19 net before rebounding into positive net approval.

Inflation and the resulting drop in real wages explain a large amount of Biden's unpopularity. US inflation increased 1 per cent in May alone for a twelve-month rate of 8.6 per cent, the highest since 1981. Real weekly earnings dropped 0.7 per cent in May; they are down 3.9 per cent in the twelve months to May. As well as economic factors, I believe a perception that Biden has been weak in both the Afghanistan withdrawal in August 2021 and the current Russian invasion of Ukraine has damaged his ratings.

Midterm elections were set for early November, with all 435 House seats and one-third of the Senate up. FiveThirtyEight had Republicans leading the Democrats by 2 per cent in the race for Congress, little changed from before the abortion ruling. While the close polls gave Democrats hope, they did not account for Republican efforts to tie Democratic candidates to the unpopular Biden, or for a greater Republican likelihood to vote. The FiveThirtyEight House model gave Republicans an 87 per cent chance of winning control of the House, and a 55 per cent chance of claiming control of the Senate.

In my opinion, the economy is likely to be far more important to most voters than abortion.

Long-term electoral trends look bleak for Democrats

In April, I calculated the percentage of people living in cities with populations of over 100,000 in four countries: the US, Australia, the UK and Canada. A total of 68 per cent of Australians lived in cities of over 100,000 people, but only 29 per cent of Americans. In the US, high-income white people have moved to 'suburbs' outside cities, and these swung to Democrats in 2020, helping Biden win.

Like the Australian Senate, the US Senate has the same number of senators for each state (twelve in Australia, two in the US), and this makes it highly malapportioned, with high-population states like California, Texas, Florida and New York getting the same number of senators as the lowest-population states. Analyst Nate Silver said in May that this means the US Senate has a large skew towards groups that are trending towards Republicans (rural and small town voters).

In the US overall, suburban and urban voters make up 52 per cent of the population, compared with 48 per cent for rural and small town voters. But in the average state, rural and small towns make up 61 per cent of the population, while suburban and urban voters comprise just 39 per cent.

In 2024, Democrats will be defending twenty-three Senate seats and Republicans just ten; these will include Democratic defences in Montana, Ohio and West Virginia, which Trump won easily in both 2016 and 2020.

If Republicans gain a permanent lock on the Senate, they will be able to deny future Democratic presidents legislative or judicial wins. The US could be heading for a future where only Republican presidents are able to govern effectively.

Australia is failing marginalised people, and it shows in COVID death rates

Gemma Carey
UNSW Sydney
Ben O'Mara
UNSW Sydney

Australian Bureau of Statistics data show that people living in poverty or disadvantage are three times more likely to die from COVID than the wealthy. This statistic is alarming, but it gets worse when we begin to look more closely at particular communities.

ABS data show the rate of death from COVID for people living in Australia who were born overseas was almost three times more than those born in Australia when standardised for age (6.8 deaths per 100,000 vs 2.3 deaths). The rate of death from COVID for people living in Australia from the Middle East was over twelve times that of people born in Australia (29.3 people per 100,000).

These statistics are damning. They tell us you're more likely to survive COVID if you were born here, grew up speaking and reading English, are educated, and earn a good income. They undermine the idea that Australia has good-quality, universal health care that has been accessible during the pandemic.

Poverty makes you sick

Most health problems, and the care needed to address them, follow what we call 'the social gradient'. This term is shorthand for the idea that those with the most resources – be it money or education – have better health and get better treatment than those with fewer resources.

In short, poverty makes you sick. It does this by limiting your access to services and supports, through money or other factors such as the type of job you work. People at the 'lower end' of the social gradient also tend to receive poorer-quality health care.

Unfortunately, this social gradient is now clear in the data on Australian COVID deaths. For example, some people from Middle Eastern countries and other migrant or refugee communities have poorer employment conditions, such as janitorial jobs in hospitals. These jobs expose people to COVID, who then bring the virus home. They have also needed to keep working in these high-risk jobs throughout the pandemic so they can afford basic living costs like food and rent.

There are also major barriers to medical care for, and information about, COVID for particular communities. During the Delta variant wave in Victoria and New South Wales, we saw this result in people from refugee and migrant backgrounds dying at home before receiving any medical care for COVID.

Authorities attributed this to a reluctance to seek health care. This reluctance can stem from a lack of culturally and linguistically appropriate healthcare communication and services. Many people also distrust authorities, including the police and army, due to experiences in their home countries. Being scared of authorities is a legitimate fear when you have come from a country where authorities may kill you. This has been exacerbated by governments in Australia choosing to 'police' the pandemic. Large fines were threatened to people who broke COVID public health orders.

This fear of fines and authorities likely contributed to a reluctance to seek medical care, and in turn more deaths. And messaging around authoritarian approaches to those who break COVID health orders is likely to have exacerbated this. Many have also been excluded from government support.

Australian governments and health services have been failing parts of our community, from those with low incomes to people from non-English-speaking backgrounds.

What can we do right now?

There is a range of actions we can take to rectify the high rates of death among refugee and migrant communities.

Policy-wise, the federal government could extend access to Medicare and social safety net support for people experiencing issues with temporary visas, such as asylum seekers living in the community who are appealing a decision on a visa application and are not eligible for Medicare. Adding specific Medicare items for refugees and migrants may also encourage more culturally and linguistically inclusive medical care in the health system. These changes would help provide more affordable, accessible and inclusive health care, particularly for asylum seekers and refugees dealing with visa issues, and help prevent loss of life.

Governments should also involve refugee and migrant communities in the development and implementation of actions to reduce COVID deaths. Communities know what they need in a crisis – we need to find new ways of listening. A top-down, middle-class response to a pandemic will create services and supports that only work for the middle class. It's vital we look to the evidence of what may best help refugee and migrant communities reduce the risk of infection, involve them meaningfully in this process, and sharpen our focus on making life in Australia fairer, more inclusive and, hopefully, safer for all.

What has to happen next?

Currently there are major gaps in understanding what may best support refugee and migrant communities to reduce the risk of infection and harm from COVID. More research is needed. However, that research needs to be led by peers in communities and be easy to access and participate in. In other words, we cannot repeat the mistake of creating approaches that work for just the middle class.

Best practice tells us multiple forms of research are required, and in culturally and linguistically inclusive ways. Survey-based research must be conducted in hospitals, health centres and other clinical environments to understand how barriers to medical care and information for COVID can be addressed to better meet the needs of people from refugee and migrant communities. The research could identify more culturally inclusive ways of managing vaccinations, testing and recovery from virus symptoms.

This must be backed up by in-depth research to explore the experiences of a diverse range of communities. Just as disadvantaged groups are not all alike, neither are refugee and migrant communities – despite commonly being lumped under the term 'culturally and linguistically diverse'. Communities who are recently arrived or longer settled – all from different countries – have different needs.

We need more listening, and less-punitive approaches.

Long COVID should make us rethink disability and the way we offer support to those with 'invisible illness'

Marie-Claire Seeley
University of Adelaide

Australia has only a handful of specialists familiar with managing what happens when the nervous system can't properly regulate the body, as sometimes occurs with long COVID. While long-COVID clinics are being set up, there are no government-funded clinics for this type of nervous system dysfunction, and private waiting lists are now long.

From the outset, long-COVID sufferers faced the same prejudice experienced by patients before them who sought assistance through Centrelink and the National Disability Insurance Scheme for the effects of post-infection conditions. Disability insurance schemes worldwide are driven by definitions and checklists that allow non-medical workforces to assess and approve candidates for support services, but those with 'invisible illness' rarely meet these criteria.

If we are to manage the tidal wave of impairment and disability bearing down on us, policymakers must heed the warnings that have been sounding for the past two years. We'll need to rethink disability and support.

First warnings

In November 2020, data later published in *The Lancet* were presented to the Chinese Academy of Medical Sciences. The researchers warned of persistent symptoms after COVID, including fatigue, cognitive dysfunction, palpitations, chest pain, depression, insomnia and headache. The colloquial term 'long COVID' was soon coined. Varying iterations of the name followed (including 'COVID long haulers' in the United States). Many clinicians use the more scientific descriptor 'post-acute sequelae of COVID-19'.

Long COVID is not a new phenomenon. Various post-infection illnesses have been documented in the medical literature for decades. And such conditions bear a striking resemblance to each other. First, an individual is knowingly (or unknowingly) exposed to a pathogen (a virus, bacterium or other microorganism). An acute illness of varying degrees of severity ensues before a partial or complete recovery. But following 'recovery', a broad range of symptoms emerge. And these lead to functional decline – in other words, they stop the sufferer from doing the daily activities they would normally be able to do.

Two of these conditions, postural orthostatic tachycardia syndrome and myalgic encephalomyelitis or chronic fatigue syndrome, appear closely related. And their symptoms look a lot like long COVID, too. Both seem to affect more women than men, and additional immune problems are often present.

These similarities support the theory these illnesses result from a hypervigilant immune system. This creates an immune response that inadvertently causes damage to the fragile autonomic nervous system (which regulates the body's normal functions, like heart rate and blood pressure) while attempting to rid the body of the invading pathogen. However, there are a plethora of other theories and more investigation is needed.

An old stigma

Lack of understanding about these syndromes is reflective of the broad stigmas attached to them – the idea they are psychosomatic and involve the mind and body. The origin of these stigmas can be traced to a series of publications in the latter half of the twentieth century that addressed outbreaks of illnesses after exposure to unknown pathogens.

In 1970, the *British Medical Journal* published an article by two psychiatrists who had reviewed the case notes of 198 patients from the Royal Free Hospital in North London, where an outbreak of an unknown pathogen had occurred fifteen years prior. The authors determined the disease had no identifiable organic origin and was therefore likely to be caused by 'epidemic hysteria'. This conclusion was partly justified by the high proportion of women among those infected with the illness.

Publication of this theory in a pre-eminent scientific medical journal gave credence to what became an enduring narrative. The result has been a chronic lack of interest and investment in these debilitating invisible illnesses, which can render people unable to work or participate in society.

A question of definition

The burden of these systemic failings now weighs heavily on a society faced with a worldwide tsunami of post-COVID conditions. And it goes some way to explaining the collective shrugging of shoulders by health authorities when it comes to providing answers for sufferers.

Estimates of how many people infected with COVID go on to develop long COVID vary from 5 per cent to 40 per cent. The large variance is a result of the initial absence of a consistent or unifying set of diagnostic criteria.

Recently the World Health Organization provided a definition of post-COVID conditions. It includes those with a history of likely or confirmed infection with SARS-CoV-2 (the virus that causes COVID) who experience lingering symptoms for longer than two months, which are unexplained by an alternative diagnosis. Defining the illness allows clearer characterisation of who is affected. Long COVID is now known to affect any age group and may be unrelated to initial infection severity. This evidence prompted the US Centers for Disease Control and Prevention to detail an ominous warning about post-COVID health problems that 'can last weeks, months, or years'.

Multiple case series and observational studies have now identified a high burden of nervous system dysfunction in long-COVID patients. Several studies, including one published in the *Journal of the American College of Cardiology*, demonstrated that up to 95 per cent of long-COVID patients also meet the international criteria for postural orthostatic tachycardia syndrome. This syndrome can cause lightheadedness, brain fog, fatigue, headache, blurred vision, palpitations, tremor and nausea. These symptoms are often incompatible with carrying out normal daily tasks, which explains why unemployment and disability are high among postural orthostatic tachycardia syndrome patients, despite their young age.

The next wave

Back in March 2021, the American Autonomic Society released a statement warning of the rising presentations of patients to autonomic specialist referral centres with symptoms of post-COVID postural orthostatic tachycardia syndrome. Of particular concern was the insufficient number of physicians familiar with this type of dysfunction to treat the condition. This situation is mirrored in Australia, where only a handful of specialists are familiar with managing such complex cases.

Contrary to popular medical opinion and widely held beliefs, effective therapies exist for underlying conditions like postural orthostatic tachycardia syndrome, which is prevalent in long COVID. Early intervention is key. Treatment needs to be fully explored and implemented before disability support services can be sought.

Time to listen

Our health systems need to absolve themselves of past sins and pay attention to the overwhelming voice of the current sufferers of long COVID and those with other post-infection syndromes or invisible illnesses who have endured decades of medical neglect. Treatment options need to be made available and multidisciplinary teams need to upskill to manage these conditions.

A redefining of what it is to be disabled needs to be explored. Most importantly, these definitions should not be tied to a single cause but to the manifestation of symptoms that culminate in the disability.

By naming Pennhurst, *Stranger Things* uses disability trauma for entertainment. Dark tourism and asylum tours do too

Joanne Watson
Deakin University

The Netflix sci-fi horror series *Stranger Things* is vividly soaked in 1980s nostalgia, famously catapulting Kate Bush's 1985 song 'Running Up That Hill' to the top of the music charts in 2022. In season four, series creators the Duffer brothers introduce viewers to Pennhurst Mental Hospital for the criminally insane (which was also mentioned in season one). Viewers follow teenage sleuths Robin and Nancy into Pennhurst, where they are granted permission to speak with Victor Creel, imprisoned because he is thought to have brutally murdered his family.

Although the Pennhurst Mental Hospital portrayed in *Stranger Things* is fictitious, the location was inspired by the Eastern Pennsylvania State Institution for the Feeble-Minded and Epileptic. Later named the Pennhurst State School and Hospital and located in the woods of

Chester County, Pennsylvania, it was founded in 1908 and shut down in 1987. More than 10,000 people with intellectual disability and mental illness lived at Pennhurst, many spending their entire lives within its walls.

The real Pennhurst has become a tourist attraction, like dozens of empty asylums around the world, including some in Australia. But as we seek out thrills, we shouldn't forget these institutions held real people, or their stories.

Pennhurst, then freedom

Pennhurst was a place of segregation, power, abuse, neglect and torture, fuelled by society's perception that people with intellectual disability were a dangerous threat to social order. At the dawn of the 19th century's eugenics movement, people with intellectual disability existed on the lowest rung of the human hierarchy. Ultimately, they were removed from the human gene pool through institutionalisation and sterilisation.

In 1987, in response to the disability rights movement's loud call for deinstitutionalisation, and after groundbreaking litigation brought by a resident and her family, the state of Pennsylvania closed Pennhurst's doors. The courts agreed those in state care had a constitutional right to appropriate treatment and education. More than 1000 Pennhurst residents began lives of worth and value in the community.

In 2010, Pennsylvania sold the site. Today, Pennhurst exists as a 'dark tourism' destination. Pennhurst Asylum entertains visitors with 'jump scares' around a narrative of depraved criminality that simultaneously erases and evokes the inhumane treatment of the people who called Pennhurst home.

Real people, real stories

To those who lived there and their supporters, Pennhurst is more than the horrors of its past and the commercialisation of its future. For Dennis Downey and James Conroy, editors of *Pennhurst and the Struggle for Disability Rights*, Pennhurst represents 'one of the great, if unrecognised, freedom struggles of the twentieth century', fanning the flames of the global deinstitutionalisation and independent living movements.

Following Pennhurst's closure, most Western nations began closing institutions. This independent living movement was a precursor to the 2006 United Nations Convention on the Rights of Persons with

Disabilities. Article 19 of the convention obliges signatory nations to ensure 'the equal right of all persons with disabilities to live in the community, with choices equal to others'. And Article 12 asks signatory nations to recognise that all citizens, regardless of disability, have 'legal personhood' and therefore should enjoy autonomy and respect.

The convention charges signatory nations with an unequivocal obligation to firmly make the traumatic experiences of institutionalisation a thing of the past, while acknowledging and preserving the stories of trauma as narratives of dignity and respect.

A global ghost tour

Pennhurst is one of many 'haunted' tourist attractions worldwide inspired by the traumatised lives of people with disability.

A hemisphere away, high on a hill, overlooking the rural town of Ararat in western Victoria, Australia, stands Aradale Lunatic Asylum, location of the notorious J-Ward. During its years of operation from 1867 to 1993, it was home to more than 10,000 people with disability. Like Pennhurst, the past two decades have seen a transformation of Aradale into a tourist attraction, exploiting the very real and horrific life experiences of the people who called it home. Thrill-seekers can join the Aradale ghost tour and be haunted by ghostly 'tickling, strange smells, banging sounds, shadows, and other spooky sensations'.

Tours and 'paranormal investigations' also operate at the former Mayday Hills Lunatic Asylum in Beechworth, Victoria. Tours of Sydney's Gladesville Mental Hospital, formerly Tarban Creek Lunatic Asylum, are currently on hold due to COVID.

Shuttered institutions that were once home to people with disabilities in the United States, Norway, Austria and South Korea are regularly grouped into terrifying online itineraries.

Acknowledge and preserve their stories

Dark tourism operators sell thrilling customer experiences, but the stories of people with disability who lived behind the walls of institutions like Pennhurst and Aradale are much darker. By relying on offensive and misguided portrayals of people with disability as horrifying, dangerous and criminal, operators exploit the ways in which residents were treated for commercialised entertainment.

Ironically, London's Bethlem Hospital (from which the word 'bedlam' originated) reportedly ran tours for curious visitors to gawk at residents until 1770. But today, the Bethlem Museum of the Mind houses archives and art 'to support the history of mental healthcare and treatment'. An upcoming exhibition explores how 'experiences of trauma, mental distress, contact with mental health services and everyday life can shape and disrupt a person's sense of home'.

Netflix and filmmakers like the Duffer brothers have an opportunity to acknowledge and preserve the stories of institutionalised communal trauma. A simple dedication to Pennhurst residents could even be added to a *Stranger Things* episode or opening credits. It could educate a generation of world citizens about the crimes of the past and the intrinsic personhood of all of humanity.

Will NASA rename the James Webb Space Telescope in light of the Lavender Scare controversy?

Alice Gorman
Flinders University

The first images from the James Webb Space Telescope are astounding. With its deep infrared eyes, the telescope is illuminating regions of the universe with never-before-possible clarity.

The telescope is a collaboration between NASA, the European Space Agency and the Canadian Space Agency. More than 300 universities, companies, space agencies and organisations are involved. But in all the excitement, it's easy to forget the Webb telescope has been the subject of controversy. It's named after a NASA administrator who has been associated with the persecution of queer people in the 'Lavender Scare' of the 1950s and 1960s.

Who was James E Webb?

James Edwin Webb was born in 1906 in North Carolina. He gained degrees in education and law, and spent time in the US Marine Corps. He held a senior position in the State Department from 1949 until the early 1950s.

In 1961, US president John F Kennedy appointed Webb to the position of NASA administrator, the second since the agency had been established in 1958. In this role, he was responsible for the Apollo program to land humans on the Moon. He was very successful in lobbying for support from Congress, and also navigated NASA through the difficult aftermath of an incident in which three Apollo 1 astronauts lost their lives in a capsule fire on the ground. Webb pushed for science to be prioritised in the Cold War environment, where every space mission was a political tool. He also promoted 'psychological warfare' (or propaganda).

Webb left NASA in 1968, before Apollo 11 flew to the Moon. In later life, he served on various advisory boards and was involved with the Smithsonian Institution, the US flagship cluster of museums, education and research centres in Washington, DC. He died in 1992.

What was the Lavender Scare?

During the Cold War, Western capitalist democracies feared communist infiltration. This became known as the 'Red Scare'. The 'Lavender Scare' was entwined with this paranoia. Its proponents argued that, because of the social stigma attached to their sexuality, LGBTQ+ people were at risk of being blackmailed into becoming Soviet spies. From the late 1940s, under the influence of Republican politician Joseph McCarthy, LGBTQ+ people were purged from US Government employment.

Webb's exact role in the Lavender Scare is hotly debated. Several astronomers petitioning to have the telescope renamed have noted Webb (while at the State Department) was involved in high-level meetings about Lavender Scare policies. In a *Scientific American* article published last year, authors led by cosmologist Chanda Prescod-Weinstein wrote:

> The records clearly show that Webb planned and participated in meetings during which he handed over homophobic material. There is no record of him choosing to stand up for the humanity of those being persecuted.

But according to a 2021 *Nature* article:

> David Johnson, a historian at the University of South Florida in Tampa who wrote the 2004 book *The Lavender Scare*, says he knows of no evidence that Webb led or instigated persecution. Webb did

attend a White House meeting on the threat allegedly posed by gay people, but the context of the meeting was to contain the hysteria that members of Congress were stirring up. 'I don't see him as having any sort of leadership role in the Lavender Scare,' says Johnson.

Is it any better if Webb was passively enacting the policies rather than leading the persecution? Other government departments did actively oppose the investigation and sacking of LGBTQ+ employees.

Echoes of controversy

Space instruments are usually named via a consultation process, often with the public invited to contribute their ideas. It's also not unusual for spacecraft names to be changed. For example, the 1991 Gamma Ray Observatory was renamed for physicist Arthur Holly Compton after its launch. The Webb telescope's name was reportedly chosen by NASA administrator Sean O'Keefe in 2002.

NASA's official response to the controversy is that there is 'no evidence at this point that warrants changing the name of the telescope'. Whatever Webb's role in the Lavender Scare, the question for some observers seems to come down to whether he was personally homophobic.

Framing the issue like this has echoes of another controversy: the complicity of German rocket scientist Wernher von Braun in the Third Reich. Von Braun, who was a member of the Nazi Party and an SS officer, played a pivotal role in the US space program. Today, NASA mentions von Braun's Nazi past on its website. But space historian Michael J Neufeld says 'his Nazi record was not widely known until after his death'.

Many excuse von Braun's political allegiance by arguing he just wanted to launch rockets into space.

Where to from here?

The James Webb Space Telescope is a touchstone for issues that have come to the fore in recent times. For example, there has been a backlash against the memorialisation of colonial 'heroes' who perpetrated violence against Indigenous and enslaved people, leading to statues all over the world being toppled. Some decry the idea of inclusivity as the ultimate in 'wokeness'; others argue that maintaining historical barriers to participation in science – based on race, class, gender and disability – means we lose potential talent.

In a world where we are facing increasing environmental challenges and declining numbers of researchers in scientific fields, we need all the talent we can get.

Science is meant to be objective and have no prejudice. In reality, scientists and science administrators are people like any others, with their own ideologies and flaws. The question is whether we judge them by the standards of their time or by those we hold today.

In the end, perhaps we should remember that the Outer Space Treaty of 1967 proclaims that space belongs to *all* humanity.

PART IV

The power to unite

How the James Webb deep-field images reminded me that the divide between art and science is artificial

Cherine Fahd
University of Technology Sydney

The first task I give photography students is to create a starscape. To do this, I ask them to sweep the floor beneath them, collect the dust and dirt in a paper bag, and then sprinkle it onto a sheet of 8 × 10-inch photo paper. Then, using a photographic enlarger, they expose the detritus-covered paper to light. After removing the dust and dirt, the paper is submerged in a bath of chemical developer.

In less than two minutes, an image slowly emerges of a universe teeming with galaxies. I love it when the darkroom fills with the sound of their astonishment the moment they realise the dust beneath their feet has been transformed into a scene of scientific wonder.

I was reminded of this analogue exercise when NASA's James Webb Space Telescope shared the first deep-field images. The public expression of wonder is not unlike that of my students in the darkroom. But unlike our makeshift starscapes, the deep-field images capture an actual galaxy cluster, 'the deepest, the sharpest infrared view of the universe to date'.

This imaging precision will help scientists to solve the mysteries of our solar system and how we fit into it. But they will also inspire continued experiments by artists who address the subject of space, the universe and our fragile place in it.

Creating art of space

Images of the cosmos afford considerable visual pleasure. I often listen to scientists passionately describing the information stored in their saturated colours and amorphous shapes, what the luminosity and shadows are, and what lurks in the deep blacks that are spotted and speckled. The mysteries of the universe are the stuff of science and of the imagination.

Throughout history, artists have imagined and created proxy universes: constructions that are lyrical and speculative, alternate worlds that are stand-ins for what we imagine, hope and fear is 'out there'. There are the photo-real drawings and paintings of Vija Celmins, the night sky painstakingly drawn or painted by hand with extraordinary detail and precision. There are David Stephenson's time-lapse photographs that read as lyrical celestial drawings reminding us that we are on a moving planet, Yosuke Takeda's ambiguous starbursts of colour and light, Thomas Ruff's sensuous star photos made through the close cropping of the details of existing science images he bought after failing to capture the cosmos with his own camera.

There's also the incredible work of the Blue Mountains–based duo Haines & Hinterding, where polka dots become stars, black pigment is the night sky, and bleeding coloured ink is a gas formation. They make rocks hum and harness the Sun's rays so we can hear and smell its energy.

These artworks highlight the creative drive to draw on science for the purposes of art. The divide between science and art is an artificial one.

Pictures of our imaginations

The Webb telescope shows science's capacity to bring us images that are aesthetically imaginative, expressive and technically accomplished. But – strangely – they don't make me feel anything. Science tells me these shapes are galaxies and stars billions of years away, but it isn't sinking in. Instead, I see a fabulously constructed landscape like James Nasmyth's famous Moon images from 1874. In my imagination, I picture the Webb images as made of fairy lights, coloured gels, mirrors, black cloth, filters and Photoshop.

Art's stand-ins invade my psyche. When I look at the deep-field and planetary nebula, I remember that even these 'objective' machine-made images are constructed. The rays of light, holes and gases are artistic experiments in photographic abstraction, examining what lies beyond vision. Imaging technology always transforms what is 'out there', and how we see it is determined by what is 'in here': our own subjectivity, what we bring of ourselves and our lives to the reading of the image.

The telescope is a photographer crawling through the cosmos, making more of the unseen seen – giving artists more references for appropriation, imagination and also critique. While scientists see structure and detail, artists see aesthetic and performative possibilities for asking pressing questions that concern the politics of space and place.

Art in space

Webb's images present a renewed opportunity to reflect on the work of American artist Trevor Paglen, who sent the world's first artwork into space. Paglen's work examines the political geography that is space and the ways in which governments aided by science use space for mass surveillance and data collection.

He created a 30-metre, diamond-shaped balloon called Orbital Reflector that was supposed to open up into an enormous reflective balloon and be seen from Earth as a bright star. It was rocketed into space on a satellite, but the engineers could not complete the sculpture's deployment due to an unexpected government shutdown.

Paglen's artwork was criticised by scientists. But unlike astronomers, he wasn't trying to unlock the mystery of the universe or our place in it. He was asking: is space a place for art? Who owns space, and who is space for?

Space is readily available to government, military, commercial and scientific interests. For the time being, Earth remains the place for art.

Don't say the Aboriginal flag was 'freed'. It belongs to us, not the Commonwealth

Bronwyn Carlson
Macquarie University

On 25 January, we woke to the news the Australian Government had negotiated with the designer of the Aboriginal flag, Harold Thomas, and copyright for the flag would be transferred to the Commonwealth. The government has now stated the flag is freely available for public use. Then prime minister Scott Morrison stated: 'We've freed the Aboriginal flag for Australians.'

While many Indigenous people are celebrating and rejoicing in the idea the flag has been 'freed', I am not so sure. I think we should all take a moment to pause and consider what this new 'ownership' might represent.

A brief history of the flag

The flag was first flown at Victoria Square on Kaurna Country, on National Aborigines Day in July 1971. The following year it became the official flag for the Aboriginal Tent Embassy, which was established on

Ngunnawal Country. In 1995, William Hayden, then governor-general of Australia, proclaimed both the Aboriginal flag and the Torres Strait Islander flag (designed by the late Bernard Manok) as 'Flags of Australia' under the *Flags Act 1953*.

But the truth is the Aboriginal flag has always been our flag. We didn't need an Act of Parliament to recognise its significance.

A national flag?

National flags are seen as sacred objects by many: in many countries, to desecrate the flag carries penalties. As citizens, we are expected to revere the national flag and to be proud of what it represents. But the Australian national flag represents white sovereignty and a belief in national unity.

The national flag symbolises both patriotism and nationalism. Nowhere was this more evident than when Morrison wore a mask sporting the design of the flag. The flag/mask draped his face with the most prominent national symbol for all to see. When wearing this mask, the prime minister literally embodied the symbolism of nation and all that stands for.

The national flag is flown at schools and all prominent government buildings. It is, for many Australians, a site of heightened emotion where the main response is a sense of belonging to what Benedict Anderson called an 'imagined community'.

Of course, the Union Jack is another nation's flag. It belongs to the United Kingdom. It represents our dispossession and is a constant reminder of our forced and continued colonisation. The Union Jack does not represent us, our history or our future aspirations.

A symbol of strength

The Aboriginal flag is a symbol of our strength as an ancient people who preceded the symbolic and real effects of national borders. The Aboriginal flag does not belong to all Australians. It belongs, like the land, to us as a symbol of our sovereignty. Morrison's statement about having 'freed' the flag for all is offensive.

It is ours; he has no authority to 'free' it. The Aboriginal flag cannot just be 'freed'. It is an emblem of our emotion, our loves and losses. It holds our faith, our hope and our future.

I grew up in the 1970s and 1980s. When I saw the Aboriginal flag, I felt a sense of pride and belonging. As a young person, I wasn't aware there were any copyright issues or that there were legalities that needed to be considered.

I always knew I belonged to what the flag stood for: our survival, our resilience as Indigenous people, and our steadfastness in the face of the ongoing and omnipresent colonial struggles that continue to affect us today.

Our sorrows and our unity

On Australia Day, we see the Australian national flag-waving take place. There is both banality and symbolism to this ritual. For some, the flag is waved without thought as to what it might mean to others: it is just part of the ritual of the national holiday. For many, it is emotionally charged and can generate fervour and national pride. I am not sure many people stop to think about the flag's design, its history, or what it might mean to some non-white Australians.

But the design of the Aboriginal flag is intimately connected to our struggle for land rights. The red represents the land, the yellow the life-giving Sun, and the black Aboriginal people. The flag is a symbol of the unceded sovereignty of our lands. It represents a powerful symbol of resistance in our ongoing battle with the Crown in terms of the unlawful claiming of our lands as terra nullius.

How is it possible that the Aboriginal flag can be so seamlessly hijacked in order to be incorporated – 'freed' – into another set of meanings, to be allowed onto the market for anyone to use? I see this act of 'freeing' our flag as an act of arrogance at the very least.

One could also say it is a violent appropriation of what Aboriginal people deem to be a symbol of reverence. Our flag contains our sorrows and our unity as a colonised people. It is not a 'free-for-all' symbol. Nor is it a symbol that can be neatly injected into the national psyche as a means of expressing some kind of racial unity that overshadows the injustice and inequality Aboriginal people experience on a daily basis.

It is the fabric of our souls. When it flies, we can see ourselves in flight as we once were – free nations.

At once an open book and a master of disguise, Shane Warne had an allure that extended far beyond the cricket pitch

Chris Wallace
University of Canberra

Pure box office, pure genius, was how former England cricket captain Nasser Hussain summed up the late, great Australian bowler Shane Warne, who died unexpectedly on 4 March at just fifty-two. But limelight is illumination of the most unreliable kind, as I noted at the beginning of *The Private Don*, my book on the inner life of Australia's peerless batting genius Don Bradman.

Though Bradman and Warne had strikingly different attitudes to public attention, there was more to both their lives than the limelight revealed. Warne used it like a nuclear reactor uses uranium: it fuelled him. We gave him our attention. In exchange, he shared an exhilarating intensity and appetite for life that riveted us for years.

The combination of Warne's libido and laser-like focus was compelling. The libido made him relatable. Only the unworldly could find no empathy for, and occasional vicarious pleasure in, Warne's hedonism, in which misogyny was notably absent. The laser-like focus gave us the most thrilling individual sporting performances we will see in our lifetimes. The excitement it generated was contagious among the cricket-indifferent and cricket lovers alike.

Millions of conversations around the world between people swapping stories about Warne since his death included this with a cricket-indifferent corporate lawyer. She recounted being at a Test match at the MCG one day as her cricket-buff husband's 'handbag'. Warne put on a star turn and, she said, 'Melbourne exploded'. She did too. It was ecstasy.

This was quintessentially to do with Warne, not just his bowling. Australia's current top spinner, Nathan Lyon, is an extraordinary third on the ladder of most wickets taken in Australian cricket, behind only Warne and Glenn McGrath. As good as Lyon is, the cricket-indifferent likely have never noticed him and never will.

And as much as people go on about Warne's larrikinism, his dominant characteristic was the mesmeric intensity with which he pursued his quarry. He had a superhuman stillness that demanded and commanded attention as he hauled the wickets in. This was both his big cricket brain at work and a visceral understanding, shared by top politicians, that combining effective theatre with the substance of one's performance maximises success.

This was central to Warne's later career as an elite poker player, too, where the 'poker face' and the well-timed and convincingly executed bluff are essential tools. Here is the paradox of Warne: that someone loved for his authenticity was so good at the mask, one he curated literally as well as figuratively. There was plenty of cosmetic 'work' and hair-loss treatment in his attempts to keep time at bay.

Warne's nonchalant waving-away of problems in public was put down to an ability to compartmentalise. But this is just another way of saying he could give himself over totally to, and deliver, the performance required in the moment.

On the eve of his death he shifted gear, letting the public into more of the complications of his large life, including in relation to his family and his body, via the documentary *Shane*. This was presaged by an *Australian Men's Health* magazine joint interview a few months earlier with Warne and his son, Jackson. 'Now, people can take the mickey out of me,' he said. 'They can do whatever they like. They can call me vain because it doesn't worry me in the slightest. Because in my mind it's always been look good, feel good.'

Superficially, the body preoccupation did not seem obsessive. 'Not everyone should worry about their weight – they should worry about feeling good,' Warne sensibly said. 'But, for me, mate, I look at a cheeseburger and put on three kilos, whereas I know other people can have five of them and nothing happens.'

But one didn't have to read between the lines to work out the issue was more significant than this. '[If] I'm quite strict with my diet and I combine that with my fitness routine, I'll be fine,' Warne said, vocalising the unbidden thought track in the heads of most Australian women as well as many men. The unspoken question was, of course, whether the public adoration (and Tinder success) would continue if Warne's weight blew out. For very sad reasons, this is a worry no more.

The most tender part of the interview concerned the impact of cricket as then played, with long months away from family, on him and them, along with the limelight's particular effect on son Jackson, now twenty-three. (Daughters Brooke, twenty-five, and Summer, twenty-one, are mentioned but presumed to have escaped the gendered impact of being a famous man's child.)

This was a worry for Don Bradman, too, who was close to daughter Shirley but struggled to help his depressed son John. Bradman was devastated when John changed his name to 'Bradsen' to escape the burden of others' expectations. Unlike Warne, who began to open up before his death, Bradman remained silent on this all his life, except in correspondence with Australian journalist Rohan Rivett, a close friend. John's depression was 'the supreme tragedy of my life for I seem so powerless to help', Bradman told Rivett.

Asked whether he felt his father's 'long shadow', Jackson Warne commented that the 'shadow is quite warm … [and] you can have a lot of fun in the shadow'. *Australian Men's Health* magazine's description of Jackson as 'sensitive, self-contained and likeable' hints, however, at the weight of masculinist expectations on the young man's shoulders, as does the list of sports he tried and failed to shine in before finally finding salvation in the gym.

Like Bradman, Warne's star will shine on. Unlike Bradman, Warne had begun using the limelight to work through his life's complications. We will understand him better over time than we ever really did the Don.

Is the #MeToo era a reckoning, a revolution, or something else?

Zora Simic
UNSW Sydney

Review: *Sexual Revolution: Modern Fascism and the Feminist Fightback* by Laurie Penny (Bloomsbury)

'The world', declares Laurie Penny on the first page of their new book, 'is in the middle of a sexual revolution.' And unlike earlier sexual revolutions, this one is for real – provided we eradicate capitalism, fascism and the patriarchy. With this call, it's business as usual for British writer and activist Penny, who has never sugar-coated their feminist and radical politics.

Penny, who is genderqueer and uses they/them pronouns, first came to public attention in the 2000s with the blog Penny Red and regular columns in left-leaning outlets such as the *Guardian* and *New Statesmen*. A steady stream of books followed, with arresting titles like *Unspeakable Things* (2014) and *Bitch Doctrine* (2017), in which Penny dared to call out the sexism of the radical-left circles in which they moved.

Anticipating the first-person feminism of Australia's Clementine Ford, among others – and updating the 1970s mantra 'The personal is political' for a new generation – Penny has often shared difficult and intimate personal experiences, from anorexia to masturbation to sexual assault. And while they have been what would now be described as 'extremely online', they have also gone in person to where the action is, whether taking part in the Occupy movement or travelling to Greece to observe the financial crisis up close.

Given all that Penny has been writing and protesting about for well over a decade, it was inevitable that they would write what could broadly be described as a #MeToo book – indeed, most of their six previous books have been #MeToo books of a kind. Penny deserves recognition for writing about sex and power in unapologetically feminist terms when mainstream feminism was widely considered to be in the doldrums, passé, and/or no longer necessary. Still, it's no longer 2007, which, as well as being the year Penny started blogging, was also the year that African American activist and survivor Tarana Burke launched the #MeToo movement, her hashtag raising awareness of the pervasiveness of sexual harassment and assault.

Since 2017, when #MeToo went viral and then global, countless words have been written about it by feminists, including Burke, whose memoir *Unbound: My Story of Liberation and the Birth of the Me Too Movement* (2021) is essential reading. Penny is entering a crowded field, inviting the question of what is new and distinctive about the grandiosely titled *Sexual Revolution: Modern Fascism and the Feminist Fightback*.

At their best, Penny offers a rousing and enticing prediction for what sits on the other side of the #MeToo era. For Penny, the present moment is one in which 'sex and gender are in crisis'. #MeToo is part of a 'Great Reckoning' that almost nobody saw coming, because 'when it came, it came from women'. We are now 'living through a profound and permanent alteration in what gender means, what sex means, and whose bodies matter'. Everywhere, 'women, men and LGBTQ people ... are walking quietly away from the expectations posed on them by thousands of years of patriarchy'. The changes underway promise 'ways of life that are not based on competition, coercion and dominance but on consent, community and pleasure'.

Yet rather than telling us more about the 'paradigm shift' that is remaking 'our civilisation', Penny's book mostly explains the present moment by covering similar terrain to their earlier titles, with some new piecemeal research and updated terminology. Frequently, Penny's declarative mode undercuts rather than generates analysis. The abrupt pivots throughout suggest a book written in some haste. Anecdotal evidence and personal experience drive the narrative and analysis, so much so that Penny's own journalism is alluded to rather than showcased.

For instance, Penny tells the reader that they have spent years 'researching and attempting to understand the mindset behind the incel and "men's rights" and "seduction" communities' and that the 'problem is getting worse'. But rather than properly extrapolate, Penny references a few random studies and concludes with an ode to the heroes of the global pandemic – 'not fighters or soldiers', but 'doctors, nurses, care workers and community leaders'.

The flashpoints of sexual and gender politics

There's no doubting Penny's ambition. Across fourteen chapters, most with an arresting if formulaic opening ('Pain is political, and so is pleasure'; 'Heterosexuality is in trouble'; 'Sooner or later, every revolution comes down to who does the dishes'), Penny covers the flashpoints of contemporary sexual and gender politics, including #MeToo and the backlash against it. Much of what is argued is easy to agree with: capitalism exploits some people and bodies more than others; women continue to carry the weight of domestic and caring labour; economic and sexual exploitation are not separate issues but are intimately linked.

In the chapter focused on work, Penny refreshingly moves #MeToo beyond the realm of celebrity to other industries, such as hospitality, agriculture and domestic work. They devote the most attention to sex work as paradigmatic of all labour under capitalism. Yet Penny cuts short rather than enhances another promising thread by focusing on arguments that have been made more powerfully by others. These include sex workers themselves, as showcased in the anthology *We Too: Essays on Sex Work and Survival* (2021).

The organising themes of sexual revolution, modern fascism and feminist fightback provide some cohesion, but not in an especially sustained or persuasive fashion. In Penny's telling, 'modern fascism' is a catch-all term that includes 'neo-masculinist' strongmen like Putin, Bolsonaro, Trump and Johnson, the 'overwhelmingly White men' who voted for them (a claim in need of some qualifications), incels, the far right, and any man experiencing a crisis or threat to his masculinity. It is a 'brutal political backlash' provoked by 'changes in the balance of power between men and women'.

Now, it is clear that authoritarian governments everywhere are much more likely to take away women's rights than extend them, as Penny covers in a chapter on reproduction that focuses mostly on the United States. But to make the case that 'modern fascism' is best understood as a backlash against feminism requires more work than Penny is willing to do.

Other feminist thinkers have offered far more probing and genuinely disturbing accounts of contemporary misogyny, including another British journalist, Laura Bates, in her book *Men Who Hate Women: From Incels to Pick-up Artists* (2020).

The genealogies of #MeToo

Like 'modern fascism', the 'feminist fightback' is taken as a given, rather than something to be accounted for or documented. Penny prefers sweeping statements about 'the greatest challenge to the social order in this century' coming from 'women, girls and queer people, particularly women, girls and queer people of colour, finally coming together to talk about sexual violence and structural abuse of power'.

Furthermore, the 'feminism' most often referenced is not the left, black or trans feminisms Penny seems most aligned with. It is the 'choice', neoliberal, mainstream feminism she criticises (as have many other feminists in far more encompassing fashion). For a self-proclaimed feminist book, *Sexual Revolution* is sparsely populated with actual feminists and largely bereft of feminist history. It is as though #MeToo came from nowhere.

Genealogies have been identified and scrutinised by Tania Serisier in her important book *Speaking Out: Feminism, Rape and Sexual Politics* (2018), among many others, including Tarana Burke's. Yet in place of proper details about 'feminist fightback', we get Penny's intervention: sexual revolution. Cognisant that the concept of 'sexual revolution' comes with hefty historical and cultural baggage (though not to the extent that they engage with relevant critiques), Penny attempts to rehabilitate it anyway. This sexual revolution, writes Penny, will deal 'not just with sexual licence but with sexual liberation' – as though they are the first rather than the umpteenth person to make this argument. This 'new sexual revolution is a feminist one'.

The idea of sexual revolution as unfinished business is decades old. So are expressions of what a 'feminist' sexual revolution might entail. Penny's update is to advocate for consent as the fundamental basis of the new sexual and economic order. Of course! But if we are at the midpoint of a sexual revolution, as Penny suggests, there is very little sense of positive developments in the sexual sphere. Instead, Penny's focus is overwhelmingly on how dire heterosexual relations are and how abhorrent the sexually desiring woman continues to be.

Sexual Revolution is a bulldozer of a book in which Penny opts for full-throttled polemic instead of nuanced analysis at almost every turn. There has always been a place for such books in the feminist canon, and Penny brings flair and spirit to the task. But beyond its potential value as a primer for contemporary feminism, it is difficult to discern who *Sexual Revolution* is written for. I suspect most readers are already familiar with 'patriarchy', 'rape culture', 'toxic masculinity', 'intersectionality' and other key terms.

From the rote to the muddled

Though Penny was once a welcome feminist voice at a time of 'post-feminism', *Sexual Revolution* reads as outdated, or not up to its proclaimed task, despite its contemporary focus. It suffers from comparison with other books that have tackled similar material with more depth and insight.

The major titles of the #MeToo era have involved forensic investigative reporting. *She Said: Breaking the Sexual Harassment Story that Started a Movement* by Jodi Kantor and Megan Twohey, and *Catch and Kill* by Ronan Farrow, both released in 2019, focused on the case of film producer Harvey Weinstein and the women he targeted. Penny promises a more wide-ranging and grassroots approach to sex and power, but only really skims the surface. In contrast to the polyphonic format of numerous anthologies, including the edited collection *#MeToo: Stories from the Australian Movement* (2019), Penny's voice eclipses the voices of people they know have often been marginalised, including Indigenous women, women of colour, and trans, queer and non-binary people.

Penny is attentive to the racial and racist dynamics of both the far right and mainstream (or White or carceral) feminism. But these discussions are too condensed to take root and sometimes read as rote. 'Quite apart from being ethically suspect,' Penny states, 'any movement to end exploitation that fails to centre race is intellectually useless.'

In terms of connecting the dots between White feminism and political Whiteness, a more illuminating book is Alison Phipps' *Me Not You: The Trouble with Mainstream Feminism* (2020). Phipps carefully and powerfully draws out the racist logic of what has come to be known as 'carceral feminism' – an approach that advocates for increased policing, prosecution and imprisonment as key strategies for combating violence against women – evident in some parts of the #MeToo movement.

Penny's book is muddled by comparison in the solutions it offers for dealing with perpetrators of sexual violence. As for the victims, Penny is sensitive to how and why they are often dismissed as 'mad' or unreliable, but Sara Ahmed's recent book *Complaint!* (2021) takes the subject much further and in new directions.

Proper comprehension of what consent entails is at the heart of Penny's sexual revolution. Given that it was only last year that NSW police commissioner Mick Fuller thought a consent phone app was a good idea, Penny's promotion of 'real, continuous, enthusiastic sexual consent' is welcome. Yet as Kathleen Angel persuasively argues in *Tomorrow Sex Will Be Good Again: Women and Desire in the Age of Consent* (2021), the contemporary fixation on consent as the solution to the pervasive problem of sexual violence can place additional burdens on women, including the need to know emphatically what they want sexually. In making this argument, Angel hardly disavows the 'bare minimum' of consent as central to contemporary sexual ethics. But she's also sceptical about the very notion of 'sexual revolution' that Penny so heartily advocates. Her book's title is a reference to philosopher Michel Foucault's highly influential critique of what he saw as one of the delusions of the earlier so-called sexual revolution of the 1960s and 1970s – that tomorrow sex will be good again.

As Penny recognises, #MeToo is not a standalone event or movement but an expression of wider social patterns. It is a tipping point in understanding the ubiquity of sexual and gendered violence. It has galvanised feminism, and redirected and refocused contemporary discourses around gender and sex. But its effects are too varied, diffuse and contradictory for the sledgehammer treatment Penny favours. Other feminist thinkers, such as British academics Amia Srinivasan and Jacqueline Rose, have pursued far more generative approaches. Srinivasan has productively revisited the feminist 'sex wars' in *The Right to Sex* (2021), while Rose has consistently turned to psychoanalysis, most recently in *On Violence and Violence Against Women* (2021).

A reckoning

Penny is more successful in capturing the affective dimensions of the #MeToo era. On this front, *Sexual Revolution* is a worthy successor or companion to Soraya Chemaly's *Rage Becomes Her: The Power of Women's Anger* (2018) and Rebecca Traister's *Good and Mad: The Revolutionary Power of Women's Anger* (2018), two early responses to #MeToo and the Trump presidency. These books are clearly part of the same zeitgeist, as their almost identical subtitles indicate.

While Penny clearly shares their faith in the political potential of rage (not all feminists do), *Sexual Revolution* is more useful in its reflections, right at the end of the book in an extended endnote, on 'trauma politics'. Penny writes that 'pain is not supposed to be part of the political conversation'. But it has become so, and the connections or continuities between intimate and structural forms of violence have become much more explicit.

Where Penny leaves us is where Australian journalist Amy Remeikis begins in *On Reckoning* (2022), her recently released and already best-selling monograph: the moment at which the complicity of modern politics in gendered violence is made starkly and painfully apparent. For Remeikis, this was the day after former parliamentary staffer Brittany Higgins went public on 15 February 2021 with the allegation that she had been raped by a male colleague in Parliament House in March 2019. Some twenty-four hours later, Prime Minister Scott Morrison addressed the nation. At the prompting of his wife Jenny, Morrison declared that 'he'd been reminded to think of the situation as a father'.

A parliamentary reporter, Remeikis was at work, typing out the prime minister's words. She was first traumatised, then enraged by them: 'Somebody else's daughter. We always have to be somebody else's daughter.'

Soon after, Remeikis shared her own experience of sexual violence in the *Guardian*, becoming a spokesperson for survivors in the process. *On Reckoning* powerfully reiterates and extends her key point that being 'thought of as someone else's daughter is not empathy'. It obliterates the experiences of real, rather than imagined, victims. It sets limits on whose pain can even be conceived. Is it any wonder then, writes Remeikis, that 'First Nations women, women of colour, trans and culturally and religiously diverse women have found it so hard to be heard?'

In the #MeToo era, the word 'reckoning' has been used so often it can slip into meaninglessness. But Remeikis – like another Australian journalist, Jess Hill, in another recently released essay with an almost identical title, *The Reckoning: How #MeToo Is Changing Australia* (2021) – imbues it with fresh force.

As records of Australia at a moment of profound cultural change, these works offer vital local and personal perspectives of a global phenomenon that has, among its many effects, reinvigorated feminist writing for the mainstream, mostly for the better.

From Charlene the mechanic to Australian TV's first gay marriage: Was *Neighbours* feminist?

Sarah Casey
University of the Sunshine Coast
Juliet Watson
RMIT University

From its early days, *Neighbours* reinforced stereotypes of white Australian heteronormative suburbia. But it also evolved to push boundaries around representations of gender, sexuality and feminism. As we farewell the residents of Ramsay Street, we are also saying goodbye to thirty-seven years of a popular-culture juggernaut and how it mirrored – or didn't – social change since the mid-1980s.

Soap operas like *Neighbours* can be an important route for feminist ideas. Popular culture is a critical vector for challenging dominant understandings around gender and sexuality. Was *Neighbours* a feminist triumph or a lucky-dip grab bag of progressive concepts and representation? To assess its feminist success is to reckon with how gender and sexuality have been depicted over the past four decades, and how this was received by audiences.

Early strands of feminism

Like feminism, *Neighbours* has many forebears to thank. Before Charlene, Madge and Izzy, there was Bea Smith on *Prisoner* (1979–86), Sister Scott on *The Young Doctors* (1976–83) and Pat the Rat on *Sons and Daughters* (1982–87). Characters like these were both archetypes and boundary pushers, with these inherent tensions contributing to their enduring popularity with fans.

When *Neighbours* started in 1985, Julie Robinson (Vikki Blanche) was a bank teller, Helen Daniels (Anne Haddy) was the wise matriarch, and Daphne Lawrence (Elaine Smith) was working unashamedly as a stripper before being 'tamed', experiencing ostensible upward social mobility navigating a career change to cafe owner.

During *Neighbours'* peak in the late 1980s, Mrs Mangel (Vivean Gray) was an older woman and busybody around Ramsay Street. Her status of ultimate disrupter is one shared with many feminists accused of being 'out of turn' – to the point Gray left the show in 1988 due to the abuse she copped in public.

Charlene Mitchell (Kylie Minogue) was the mechanic defying gendered career expectations with the 'Girls can do anything' attitude. Yet anxiety over portraying teenage sex on primetime television was resolved through marrying her off to Scott Robinson (Jason Donovan) at age seventeen.

Women like Daphne, Mrs Mangel and Charlene might have been challenging stereotypes, but they would eventually submit to palatable norms.

Feminism enters more spaces

By the turn of the century, more explicit references to feminism were made, and the women became increasingly complex.

Flick Scully (Holly Valance) was a dedicated teen feminist, passionate about social justice, yet her storylines focused more on her romantic entanglements. In 2004, single mother of six and unruly woman Janelle Timmins (Nell Feeney) parked her caravan on Ramsay Street, gambling, grifting and taking credit for writing *The Bogan's Tipped Hair*, a riff on feminist novel *The Bride Stripped Bare*, Australia's bestselling novel of 2003.

From the 2010s, the women of *Neighbours* began holding their own in the corporate world. Therese Willis (Rebekah Elmaloglou), the most prominent, juggled a tempestuous relationship with Paul Robinson alongside running Lassiters Hotel.

Gender and sexuality

In August 2018, *Neighbours* broadcast the first same-sex – and mixed-race – wedding on Australian television, when David Tanaka (Takaya Honda) and Aaron Brennan (Matt Wilson) were wed by Magda Szubanski. They were soon joined at the altar by Sky Mangel (Stephanie McIntosh) and Lana Crawford (Bridget Neval), who had shared the first lesbian kiss on *Neighbours* back in 2004.

While familiar soap opera tropes see most marriages ending in death and divorce, same-sex marriage on *Neighbours* proved to be more stable and ultimately more traditional. Since their wedding, David and Aaron have been depicted as the conjugal ideal when compared with the marriages between *Neighbours* stalwarts: the serial philanderer Karl Kennedy (Alan Fletcher) and his wife, Susan (Jackie Woodburne), and three-times-married Jarrod 'Toadfish' Rebecchi (Ryan Moloney).

In 2019, Georgie Stone joined *Neighbours* as the show's first trans character, Mackenzie Hargreaves. In 2022, *Neighbours* had its first non-binary character, Asher Nesmith, played by non-binary actor Kathleen Ebbs.

Work to be done

The word 'feminism' was unlikely to be heard in *Neighbours*' early days, but explicit references have been made in more recent times. By 2017, the series was even making casual references to a popular Australian feminist. When teenager Xanthe Canning (Lilly Van der Meer) was working through a romantic problem, she said: 'The only thing I can think of is getting in touch with Clementine Ford.'

Right until the end, the series was critiqued for lack of representation on screen, and in 2021 there were accusations of racism behind the scenes.

Neighbours was not a feminist triumph on or off screen. But it provided some entry points to feminist thinking and diverse ways of being that may not otherwise be accessible or sought out. And popularity procures broader audiences and hopefully understanding.

Was it enough? No. As the till rings for the last time at Harold's and the streetlights fade over Ramsay Street, there remains significant work to be done.

Everyone loves Bandit from *Bluey*, but is he a lovable larrikin or just a bad dad?

David Burton
University of Southern Queensland
Kate Cantrell
University of Southern Queensland

Bandit Heeler is a hero. The cartoon father of Bluey and her younger sister, Bingo, Bandit is the much-loved dad dog at the heart of Australia's favourite four-legged family. He balances the drudgery of housework with the creative escapades of his daughters, repurposing everyday objects and actions for imaginative play and engagement.

Awarded a Father of the Year award in 2019 and widely cited as the model of modern fatherhood, Bandit's engaged presence in his daughters' lives has been hailed as a watershed moment in children's television. In a break from TV's 'bad dad' trope, Bandit has been worshipped as a 'dad-idol', even inspiring a Facebook group of 14,000 dedicated dads who identify as *Bluey* superfans.

Child psychologists have explained how Bandit inspired their approach to pretend play and improvisation. An article published in *The Journal of Paediatrics and Child Health* lays out 'what *Bluey* can teach us about parenting and grandparenting'.

But there is a darker side to this lovable character. Bandit never strays far from the reductive stereotype of the Australian larrikin: the likeable roguish male stuck between childhood and adulthood, and whose disrespect of authority and rough-and-ready masculinity reflects Australia's emotional attachment to the working-class underdog.

A familiar breed of larrikin

It is difficult to overstate the cultural power of larrikin ideology in Australia. Generally regarded as a sign of authentic, rugged masculinity and anti-authoritarianism, the figure of the larrikin has been coopted for car and beer adverts, international tourism, and even conservative politics. Today, the image of the larrikin has been sanitised for public consumption; however, the history of larrikinism is firmly rooted in Australia's colonial literature.

The original larrikins of the late 19th century were young urban mischief-makers who sometimes ventured into serious violence and crime. At the turn of the century, these transgressive characters were endowed with hearts of gold in outback drama and literature. In some cases, they were domesticated, as was the case for Dad and Dave from Steele Rudd's *On Our Selection* (1899). Rudd established the family dynamic that would be replicated in a multitude of Australian comedies, from *Kingswood Country* (1980–84) to *The Castle* (1997) to *Bluey*: energetic and inexhaustible children, a long-suffering sensible wife, and a larrikin father who knows how to play to an audience.

From this mythos, we see the birth of Bandit: the underdog who knocks authority, mocks pomposity, and regularly breaks the rules to get what he wants – even resorting to cheating when he can't outsmart or outpace his children. In one episode, Bandit holds Bluey back from the finish line so he can win an obstacle course. In another, he lauds victory over his younger brother, Stripe, taunting that 'big brothers always beat little brothers' – a jibe Bluey imitates when she teases Bingo: 'Big sisters always beat little sisters. That's just the way it goes.'

Even Bandit's name conjures up the small-time crimes of bushrangers, Australia's revered outlaws who also achieved a type of perverse folk hero status.

Bandit the bully

Undoubtedly, Bandit's larrikinism contributes to his likeability: he is an entertaining and engaged father who is heavily involved in his children's lives. Occasionally, however, we catch a glimpse of Bandit's darker side, with his playful teasing of his young daughters sometimes devolving into bullying. In one episode, Bandit agrees to open Bingo's ice block before repeatedly licking her frozen sweet in front of her. Afterwards, Bandit apologises to his daughter for being 'a bit mean'.

While the show itself restrains judgement, often it is Bandit's wife, Chilli who pulls him into line. When Bandit forgets to pack sunscreen and snacks for a swim at the pool, it is Chilli (the 'boring' parent, in Bandit's words) who saves the day. Yet it is Bandit who is praised for his parenting prowess, while Chilli is figuratively and literally in the background. In fact, the creators of *Bluey* were recently accused of mother-shaming when they described Chilli as 'falling a bit short' due to her status as a working mum.

The universal veneration of Bandit is perplexing since, in situations like at the pool, he comes across as a mildly incompetent caricature, lampooned as an overgrown child in need of regular supervision and training.

Bandit is also surprisingly conservative when it comes to gender values. Bandit is a 'traditional' man who wishes to be viewed as the head of the Heeler household. When he reluctantly submits to wearing make-up, he is subsequently mocked by his mates for doing so. He censors himself from engaging in full imaginative play when under the gaze of other men. He teases his wife on the pains of pregnancy and labour.

Taken individually, most of these moments are punchlines. But over the course of three series, *Bluey* creates a complex portrait of Australia's favourite dad. Bandit is present and playful, but he is still a larrikin at heart. His continued popularity, despite his personal shortcomings, only speaks to the stereotype's strength in contemporary Australian life.

PART V

The power of nature

This is Australia's most important report on the environment's deteriorating health. We present its grim findings

Emma Johnston
University of Sydney
Ian Cresswell
UNSW Sydney
Terri Janke
UNSW Sydney

Climate change is exacerbating pressures on every Australian ecosystem, and Australia now has more foreign plant species than native, according to the highly anticipated *State of the Environment Report* released on 19 July. The report also found the number of listed threatened species has risen 8 per cent since 2016 and more extinctions are expected in the next decades.

The document represents thousands of hours of work over two years by more than thirty experts. It's a sobering read, but there are some bright spots.

Australia has produced a national state of the environment report every five years since 1995. They assess every aspect of Australia's environment and heritage, covering rivers, oceans, air, ice, land and urban areas. The last report was released in 2017. This report goes further than its predecessors, by describing how our environment is affecting the health and wellbeing of Australians. It is also the first to include Indigenous co-authors.

As chief authors of the report, we present its key findings here. They include new chapters dedicated to extreme events and Indigenous voices.

Australia's environment is generally deteriorating

There have been continued declines in the amount and condition of our natural capital: native vegetation, soil, wetlands, reefs, rivers and biodiversity. Such resources benefit Australians by providing food, clean water, cultural connections and more. The number of plant and animal species listed as threatened in June 2021 was 1918, up from 1774 in 2016. Gang-gang cockatoos and the Woorrentinta (northern hopping-mouse) are among those recently listed as endangered.

Australia's coasts are also under threat from, for instance, extreme weather events and land-based invasive species. Our nearshore reefs are in overall poor condition due to poor water quality, invasive species and marine heatwaves. Inland water systems, including in the Murray–Darling Basin, are under increasing pressure.

Nationally, land clearing remains high. Extensive areas were cleared in Queensland and New South Wales over the last five years. Clearing native vegetation is a major cause of habitat loss and fragmentation, and has been implicated in the national listing of most of Australia's threatened species.

Climate change threatens every ecosystem

Climate change is compounding ongoing and past damage from land clearing, invasive species, pollution and urban expansion. The intensity and frequency of extreme weather events are changing. Over the last five years, extreme events such as floods, droughts, wildfires, storms and heatwaves have affected every part of Australia.

Seasonal fire periods are becoming longer. In New South Wales, for example, the bushfire season now extends to almost eight months. Extreme events are also affecting ecosystems in ways never before documented. For example, the downstream effects of the 2019–20 bushfires introduced a range of contaminants to coastal estuaries, in the first global record of bushfires impacting estuarine habitat quality.

Indigenous knowledge and management are helping deliver on-ground change

This includes traditional fire management, which is being recognised as vital knowledge by land management organisations and government departments. For example, Indigenous rangers manage 44 per cent of the national protected area estate, and more than 2000 rangers are funded under the federal government's Indigenous rangers program.

Work must still be done to empower Indigenous communities and enable Indigenous knowledge systems to improve environmental and social outcomes.

Environmental management isn't well coordinated

Australia's investment is not proportional to the grave environmental challenge. The area of land and sea under some form of conservation protection has increased, but the overall level of protection is declining within reserves.

We're reducing the quantity and quality of native habitat outside protected areas through, for instance, urban expansion on land and over-harvesting in the sea. The five urban areas with the most significant forest and woodland habitat loss were Brisbane, Gold Coast to Tweed Heads, Townsville, Sunshine Coast and Sydney. Between 2000 and 2017, at least 20,212 hectares were destroyed in these five areas combined, with 12,923 hectares destroyed in Queensland alone.

Australia is also increasingly relying on costly ways to conserve biodiversity. This includes restoration of habitat, reintroducing threatened species, translocation (moving a species from a threatened habitat to a safer one), and ex-situ conservation (protecting species in a zoo, botanical garden or by preserving genetic material).

Environmental decline and destruction is harming our wellbeing

In this report we document the direct effects of environmental damage on human health, for example from bushfire smoke. The indirect benefits of a healthy environment to mental health and wellbeing are harder to quantify. But emerging evidence suggests people who manage their environment according to their values and culture have improved wellbeing, such as for Indigenous rangers and communities.

Environmental destruction also costs our economy billions of dollars, with climate change and biodiversity loss representing both national and global financial risks.

Climate change is hitting ecosystems hard

Previous reports mostly spoke of climate change impacts as happening in the future. In this report, we document significant climate harms already evident from the tropics to the poles.

As Australia's east coast emerges from another 'unusual' flood, this report introduces a new chapter dedicated to extreme events. Many have been made more intense and widespread, likely due to climate change. We document the national impacts of extreme floods, droughts, heatwaves, storms and wildfires over the past five years. And while we've reported on immediate impacts – millions of animals killed and habitats burnt, enormous areas of reef bleached, and people's livelihoods and homes lost – many longer-term effects are still to play out.

Extreme conditions put immense stress on species already threatened by habitat loss and invasive species. We expect more species extinctions over the next decades. An extreme heatwave in 2018, for example, killed some 23,000 spectacled flying foxes; in 2019, the species was uplisted from vulnerable to endangered.

Many Australian ecosystems have evolved to rebound from extreme 'natural' events such as bushfires. But the frequency, intensity and compounding nature of recent events are greater than they've experienced throughout their recent evolutionary history. For example, marine heatwaves caused mass coral bleaching on the Great Barrier Reef in 2016, 2017, 2020 and 2022. Such frequent disturbances leave little time for recovery.

Indeed, ecological theory suggests frequently disturbed ecosystems will shift to a 'weedy' state, where only the species that live fast and reproduce quickly will thrive. This trend will bring profound shifts in ecosystem structure and function. It also means we'll have to shift how we manage and rely on ecosystems, including how we harvest, hunt and otherwise benefit from them.

Including Indigenous voices

Indigenous people of Australia have cared for the lands and seas over countless generations and continue to do so today. In Australia, a complex web of government laws and agreements relate to Indigenous people and the environment. Overall, they are not adequate to deliver the rights Indigenous people seek: responsibility for and stewardship of their Country including lands and seas, plants and animals, and heritage.

For the first time, this report has a separate Indigenous chapter, informed by Indigenous consultation meetings, which highlights the importance of caring for Country. Including an Indigenous voice has required us to change the previous approach of reporting on the environment separately from people. Instead, we've emphasised how Country is connected to people's wellbeing, and the interconnectedness of environment and culture.

Failures of environmental management

Australia needs better and entirely new approaches to environmental management. For example, the inclusion of climate change in environmental management and resilience strategies is increasing, but it's not universal.

As well as climate stresses, habitat loss and degradation remain the main threats to land-based species in Australia, impacting nearly 70 per cent of threatened species. More than a third of Australia's eucalypt woodlands have been extensively cleared, and the situation is worse for some other major vegetation groups. Experts say within twenty years, another seven Australian mammals and ten Australian birds – such as the King Island brown thornbill and the orange-bellied parrot – will be extinct unless management is greatly improved.

Of the 7.7 million hectares of land habitat cleared between 2000 and 2017, 7.1 million hectares (93 per cent) was not referred to the federal government for assessment under the national environment law. Only 16 per cent (thirteen of eighty-four) of Australia's nationally listed, threatened ecological communities meet a 30 per cent minimum protection standard in the national reserve system.

Three critically endangered communities, all in New South Wales, have no habitat protection at all. These are the Hunter Valley weeping myall woodland, the Elderslie banksia scrub forest, and Warkworth sands woodland.

The bright spots

The report also highlights where investments and the hard work of many Australians made a difference. Individuals, non-government organisations and businesses are increasingly purchasing and managing significant tracts of land for conservation. The Australian Wildlife Conservancy, for example, jointly manages some 6.5 million hectares, actively conserving many threatened species. By building on achievements such as these, we can encourage new partnerships and innovations, supported with crucial funding and commitment from government and industry.

We also need more collaboration across governments and non-government sectors, underpinned by greater national leadership. This includes listening and co-developing solutions with Indigenous and local communities, building on and learning from Indigenous and Western scientific knowledge. And we need more effort and resources to measure progress. This includes consistent monitoring and reporting across all states and territories on the pressures on, and the health of, our natural and cultural assets.

Such efforts are crucial if we're to reverse declines and forge a stronger, more resilient country.

How not to solve the climate change problem

Kevin Trenberth
US National Center of Atmospheric Research & University of Auckland

When politicians talk about reaching 'net zero' emissions, they're often counting on trees or technology that can pull carbon dioxide out of the air. What they don't mention is just how much these proposals or geo-engineering would cost to allow the world to continue burning fossil fuels. There are many proposals for removing carbon dioxide, but most make differences only at the edges, and carbon dioxide concentrations in the atmosphere have continued to increase relentlessly, even through the pandemic.

I've been working on climate change for over four decades. Let's take a minute to come to grips with some of the rhetoric around climate change and clear the air, so to speak.

What's causing climate change?

As has been well established now for several decades, the global climate is changing, and that change is caused by human activities. When fossil fuels are burned for energy or used in transportation, they release carbon dioxide – a greenhouse gas that is the main cause of global heating. Carbon dioxide stays in the atmosphere for centuries. As more carbon dioxide is added, its increasing concentration acts like a blanket, trapping energy near Earth's surface that would otherwise escape into space.

When the amount of energy arriving from the Sun exceeds the amount of energy radiating back into space, the climate heats up. Some of that energy increases temperatures, and some increases evaporation and fuels storms and rains.

Because of these changes in atmospheric composition, the planet has warmed by an estimated 1.1 degrees Celsius since about 1880 and is well on the way to 1.5 degrees Celsius, which was highlighted as a goal not to be crossed if possible by the Paris Agreement. With the global heating and gradual increases in temperature have come increases in all kinds of weather and climate extremes, from flooding to drought and heatwaves, that cause huge damage, disruption and loss of life.

Studies shows that global carbon dioxide emissions will need to reach net-zero carbon emissions by mid-century to have a chance of limiting warming to even 2 degrees Celsius. Currently, the main source of carbon dioxide is China. But accumulated emissions matter most, and the United States leads on this measure, closely followed by Europe, China and others.

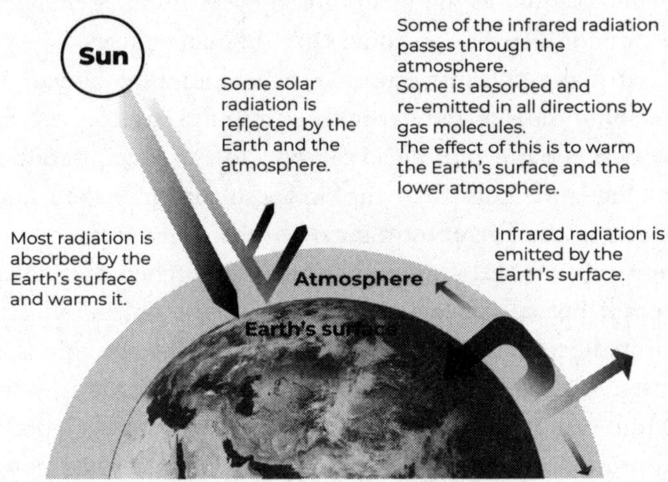

What works to slow climate change?

Modern society needs energy, but it does not have to be from fossil fuels. Studies show that the most effective way to address the climate change problem is to decarbonise the economies of the world's nations. This means sharply increasing the use of renewable energy – solar and wind cost less than new fossil fuel plants in much of the world today – and the use of electric vehicles.

Unfortunately, this changeover to renewables has been slow, due in large part to the huge and expensive infrastructure related to fossil fuels, along with the vast amount of dollars that can buy influence with politicians.

What doesn't work?

Instead of drastically cutting emissions, companies and politicians have grasped at alternatives. These include geoengineering; carbon capture and storage, including 'direct air capture'; and planting trees. Here's the issue.

Geoengineering often means 'solar radiation management', which aims to emulate a volcano and add particulates to the stratosphere to reflect incoming solar radiation back to space and produce a cooling effect. It might partially work, but it could have concerning side effects.

The global warming problem is not sunshine, but rather that infrared radiation emitted from Earth is being trapped by greenhouse gases. Between the incoming solar and outgoing radiation is the whole weather and climate system and the hydrological cycle. Sudden changes in these particles or poor distribution could have dramatic effects.

The last major volcanic eruption, of Mount Pinatubo in 1991, sent enough sulphur dioxide and particulates into the stratosphere that it produced modest cooling, but it also caused a loss of precipitation over land. It cooled the land more than the ocean so that monsoon rains moved offshore, and in the longer term it slowed the water cycle.

Carbon capture and storage has been researched and tried for well over a decade but has sizable costs. Only about a dozen industrial plants in the United States currently capture their carbon emissions, and most of it is used to enhance drilling for oil. Direct air capture – technology that can pull carbon dioxide out of the air – is being developed in several places. It uses a lot of energy, though, and while that could potentially be dealt with by using renewable energy, it's still energy-intensive.

Planting trees is often embraced as a solution for offsetting corporate greenhouse gas emissions. Trees and vegetation take up carbon dioxide though photosynthesis and produce wood and other plant material. It's relatively cheap. But trees aren't permanent. Leaves, twigs and dead trees decay. Forests burn. Recent studies show that the risks to trees from stress, wildfires, drought and insects as temperatures rise will also be larger than expected.

How much does all this cost?

Scientists have been measuring carbon dioxide at Mauna Loa, Hawaii since 1958, and elsewhere. The average annual increase in carbon dioxide concentration has accelerated, from about 1 part per million by volume per year in the 1960s to 1.5 in the 1990s, and to 2.5 in recent years since 2010. This relentless increase, through the pandemic and in spite of the efforts in many countries to cut emissions, shows how enormous the problem is.

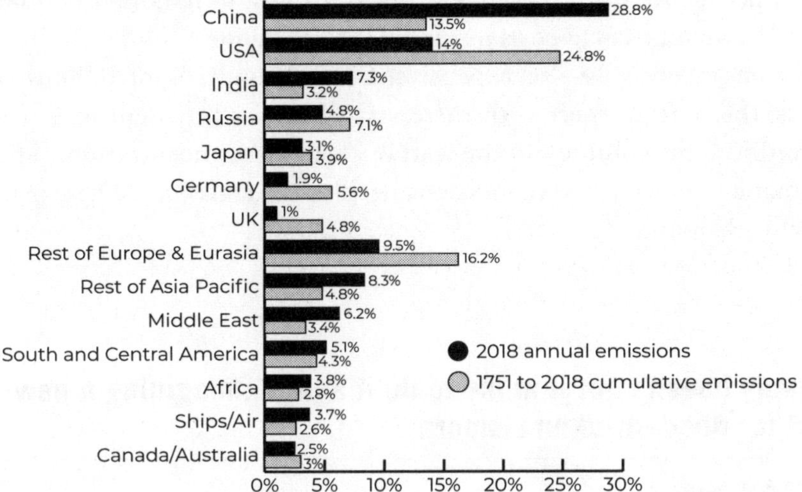

Usually carbon removal is discussed in terms of mass, measured in megatons – millions of metric tons – of carbon dioxide per year, not in parts per million of volume. The mass of the atmosphere is about 5.5×10^{15} metric tons, but as carbon dioxide (molecular weight 42) is heavier than air (molecular weight about 29), 1 part per million by volume of carbon dioxide is about 7.8 billion metric tons.

According to the World Resources Institute, the range of costs for direct air capture vary between US$250 and US$600 per metric ton of carbon dioxide removed today, depending on the technology, energy source and scale of deployment. Even if costs fell to US$100 per metric ton, the cost of reducing the atmospheric concentrations of carbon dioxide by 1 part per million is around US$780 billion.

Keep in mind that the carbon dioxide concentration in the atmosphere has risen from about 280 parts per million before the industrial era to around 420 today, and it is currently rising at more than 2 parts per million per year.

Tree restoration on one-third to two-thirds of suitable hectares is estimated to be able to remove about 7.4 gigatons of carbon dioxide by 2050 without displacing agricultural land, by WRI's calculations. That would be more than any other pathway. This might sound like a lot, but 7 gigatons of carbon dioxide is 7 billion metric tons, and so this is less than 1 part per million by volume. The cost is estimated to be up to US$50 per metric ton. So even with trees, the cost to remove 1 part per million by volume could be as much as US$390 billion.

Geoengineering is also expensive. So for hundreds of billions of dollars, the best prospect with these strategies is a tiny dent of 1 part per million by volume in the carbon dioxide concentration. This arithmetic highlights the tremendous need to cut emissions. There is no viable workaround.

'I simply haven't got it in me to do it again': Imagining a new heart for flood-stricken Lismore

Barbara Rugendyke
Southern Cross University
Jean S Renouf
Southern Cross University

The flood crisis in northern New South Wales, which unfolded during the early months of 2022, has left lives shattered. Those worst affected are dazed and struggling to comprehend the loss of life, homes, livelihoods and possessions.

We are both residents of the hard-hit Lismore region, as well as researchers with skills in geography, community development and resilience. One of us, Jean Renouf, also works for Fire and Rescue NSW. We are both helping people devastated by the recent floods and its aftermath.

We've seen the heartbreak in Lismore first-hand. Shock and pain are evident in people's eyes. The reality has hit that there's no longer a coffee shop in the town centre, no pub, restaurant, hairdresser, clothing store, pharmacy or newsagent. Horror at the annihilation of the town they love is palpable.

There is also a strange feeling of déjà vu. The town struggled back to life after the flood of 2017. Now, people talk of leaving Lismore. As one business owner said: 'I survived ten years here. I picked myself up and started again after the last flood. I simply haven't got it in me to do it again.'

So what will it take to rebuild Lismore? And how might the new town be more resilient?

A flood-weary town

Lismore sits on a vast flood plain beside the Wilsons River. In the town's early days, the river provided water and a transport route. Its fertile flood plains were ideal for food production and the river provided a major trade route for Lismore's timber and farming industries. Over the years, improvements in road transport and other services mean Lismore's riverside CBD location has become less necessary.

Lismore is a town accustomed to floods, but the most recent flood was at least 2 metres higher than those previously recorded. Aboriginal Elders, however, report that 'big floods' in the past topped Lismore's Cathedral Hill, as this one did. Climate change is expected to result in more frequent and intense rainfall, further increasing the flood risk.

A techno-fix won't work

Historically, engineered solutions have been introduced to reduce Lismore's flood risk. A one-in-ten-year flood levee was built in 2005 to protect the CBD. However, in 2017, water spilled over the levee and caused one of the most damaging floods this century. When levees are topped, floodwaters can rise rapidly and become trapped rather than draining away. Levees also give a false sense of safety to Lismore businesses.

Constructing buildings using specific materials and design can make them flood-resilient. But the contents cannot be flood-proofed or affordably insured. Other engineering solutions have been proposed, including excavating river bends to speed up the exit of floodwaters. But such measures can worsen flooding downstream and are unlikely to help during major floods.

Lismore residents are unlikely to support proposals for a new dam upstream, which would create environmental and social damage.

Lismore reimagined

Clearly, Lismore urgently needs radical change – and that requires bold and creative land-use planning.

Key to a reimagined Lismore would be a staged move of the CBD to higher ground. One strategy would be to encourage land swaps, with Lismore City Council exchanging commercial land in the CBD for land on high ground (either land it currently owns or land it purchases). A well-considered 'structure plan' – used to manage growth and change – with careful rezoning could encourage changed land use and attract new commercial development.

Financial incentives could encourage the owners of commercial premises to rebuild in safer locations. This could create new, smaller hubs for professional offices, a retail precinct or cultural activities.

Consideration should be given to locating multiple services on flood-free land owned by state or federal authorities. This might, for example, bring together emergency services, health services and government support offices.

Houses deemed unsafe should not be rebuilt in the same place. Housing blocks may need to be bought back by authorities. Where houses can be repaired, some may be relocated to higher ground. Before this year's floods, housing in Lismore was already in short supply. Creative planning could address this, perhaps allowing landholders to build tiny houses or granny flats on high ground.

During the recent floods, we saw police, SES and fire stations engulfed by floodwaters, rendering them inoperable. Emergency service bases located below maximum flood heights must urgently be relocated or adapted.

And what to do with the riverside land where the CBD sits now?

The riverine environment could be restored. Impervious surfaces such as asphalt and concrete could be replaced with regenerated bushland to slow water run-off. Expansive parklands could replace commercial premises beside the river. This 'green heart' could incorporate new facilities such as an amphitheatre and sports fields in areas less likely to flood, retaining some heritage buildings for public use.

If these sites did flood, they would be more easily restored afterwards than is the case for current commercial premises.

A new town heart

This new Lismore will not be easily achieved. Significant public and private funds will be needed. It will take political will and, above all, community support. This might all seem very hard, but towns have been fully or partially relocated for similar reasons in the past – most recently, at the Queensland town of Grantham. Many Lismore people would love to live in a safer and more prosperous town with a new CBD and verdant riverside community precinct.

Such changes will encounter justifiable resistance, however, including from business and property owners in the CBD. Lismore mayor Steve Krieg summed up the sentiment of some, telling the media: 'Forty years ago people tried to [move Lismore] but what you have to understand is that Lismore people love Lismore. They don't want it to move or be taken away from them.'

However, the economic, social and emotional cost of this flood is incomprehensible. Residents and businesses are considering leaving Lismore for good. This town with heart now needs a new heart.

Why the volcanic eruption in Tonga was so violent, and what to expect next

Shane Cronin
University of Auckland

The Kingdom of Tonga doesn't often attract global attention, but a violent eruption of an underwater volcano on 15 January spread shock waves, quite literally, around half the world.

The volcano is usually not much to look at. It consists of two small uninhabited islands, Hunga Ha'apai and Hunga Tonga, poking about 100 metres above sea level 65 kilometres north of Tonga's capital, Nuku'alofa. But hiding below the waves is a massive volcano, around 1800 metres high and 20 kilometres wide.

The Hunga Tonga–Hunga Ha'apai volcano has erupted regularly over the past few decades. During events in 2009 and 2014–15, hot jets of magma and steam exploded through the waves. But these eruptions were small, dwarfed in scale by the January 2022 events. Our research into these earlier eruptions suggests this is one of the massive explosions the volcano is capable of producing roughly every thousand years.

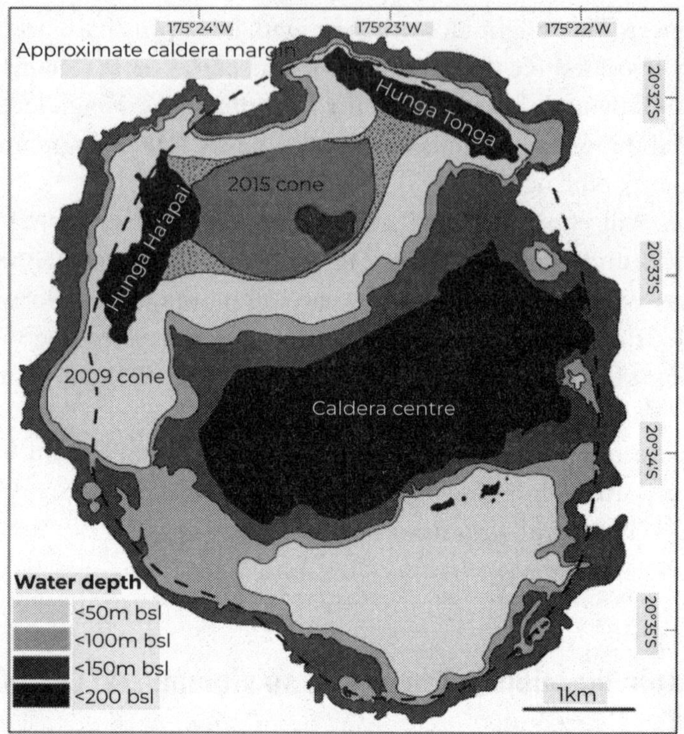

Map of Hunga Tonga–Hunga Ha'pai volcano

Why are the volcano's eruptions so highly explosive, given that sea water should cool the magma down? If magma rises into sea water slowly, even at temperatures of about 1200 degrees Celsius, a thin film of steam forms between the magma and water. This provides a layer of insulation to allow the outer surface of the magma to cool.

But this process doesn't work when magma is blasted out of the ground full of volcanic gas. When magma enters the water rapidly, any steam layers are quickly disrupted, bringing hot magma in direct contact with cold water. Volcano researchers call this 'fuel-coolant interaction' and it is akin to weapons-grade chemical explosions. Extremely violent blasts tear the magma apart. A chain reaction begins, with new magma fragments exposing fresh hot interior surfaces to water, and the explosions repeat, ultimately jetting out volcanic particles and causing blasts with supersonic speeds.

Two scales of Hunga eruptions

The 2014–15 eruption created a volcanic cone, joining the two old Hunga islands to create a combined island about 5 kilometres long. We visited in 2016 and discovered these historical eruptions were merely curtain-raisers to the main event.

Mapping the sea floor, we discovered a hidden 'caldera' 150 metres below the waves. The caldera is a crater-like depression around 5 kilometres across. Small eruptions (such as in 2009 and 2014–15) occur mainly at the edge of the caldera, but very big ones come from the caldera itself. These big eruptions are so large the top of the erupting magma collapses inward, deepening the caldera.

Looking at the chemistry of past eruptions, we now think the small eruptions represent the magma system slowly recharging itself to prepare for a big event. We found evidence of two huge past eruptions from the Hunga caldera in deposits on the old islands. We matched these chemically to volcanic ash deposits on the largest inhabited island of Tongatapu, 65 kilometres away, and then used radiocarbon dates to show that big caldera eruptions occur about every 1000 years, with the last one in the year 1100.

With this knowledge, the eruption on 15 January seems to be right on schedule for a 'big one'.

What we can expect to happen now

We're still in the middle of this major eruptive sequence and many aspects remain unclear, partly because the island is currently obscured by ash clouds.

The two earlier eruptions on 20 December 2021 and 13 January 2022 were of moderate size. They produced clouds of up to 17 kilometres elevation and added new land to the 2014–15 combined island. The latest eruption has stepped up the scale in terms of violence. The ash plume rose 20 kilometres into the air. Most remarkably, it spread out almost concentrically over a distance of about 130 kilometres from the volcano, creating a plume with a 260-kilometre diameter, before it was distorted by the wind.

This demonstrates a huge explosive power, one that cannot be explained by magma–water interaction alone. It shows instead that large amounts of fresh, gas-charged magma have erupted from the caldera.

The eruption also produced a tsunami throughout Tonga and neighbouring Fiji and Samoa. Shock waves traversed many thousands of kilometres, were seen from space, and were recorded in New Zealand some 2000 kilometres away. Soon after the eruption started, the sky was blocked out on Tongatapu, with ash beginning to fall.

All these signs suggest the large Hunga caldera has awoken. Tsunami are generated by coupled atmospheric and ocean shock waves during an explosion, but they are also readily caused by submarine landslides and caldera collapses.

It remains unclear if this was the climax of the eruption. It represents a major magma pressure release, which may settle the system. A warning, however, lies in geological deposits from the volcano's previous eruptions. These complex sequences show each of the 1000-year major caldera eruption episodes involved many separate explosion events.

Hence we could be in for several years of major volcanic unrest from the Hunga Tonga–Hunga Ha'apai volcano. For the sake of the people of Tonga, I hope not.

Meet the world's largest plant, a single seagrass clone stretching 180 kilometres in Western Australia's Shark Bay

Elizabeth Sinclair
University of Western Australia
Gary Kendrick
University of Western Australia
Jane Edgeloe
University of Western Australia
Martin Breed
Flinders University

Next time you go diving or snorkelling, have a close look at those wondrously long, bright-green ribbons, waving with the ebb and flow of water. They are seagrasses – marine plants that produce flowers, fruit and seedlings annually, like their land-based relatives.

These underwater seagrass meadows grow in two ways: by sexual reproduction, which helps them generate new gene combinations and genetic diversity, and by extending their rhizomes, the underground stems from which roots and shoots emerge. So when you see a meadow of seagrass, how many plants is it made of? This can be tricky question. To find out how many different individual plants are growing in a seagrass meadow, you have to test their DNA.

We did this for meadows of ribbon-weed seagrass called *Posidonia australis* in the shallow, sun-drenched waters of the Shark Bay World Heritage Area in Western Australia. The result blew us away: it was all one plant. One single plant has expanded over a stretch of 180 kilometres, making it the largest known plant on Earth.

We collected shoot samples from ten seagrass meadows from across Shark Bay, in waters where the salt levels range from normal ocean salinity to almost twice as salty. In all samples, we studied 18,000 genetic markers to show that 200 square kilometres of ribbon-weed meadows expanded from a single, colonising seedling.

How did it evolve?

What makes this seagrass plant unique from others, other than its enormous size, is that it has twice as many chromosomes as its relatives. This makes it what scientists call a 'polyploid'.

Most of the time, a seagrass seedling will inherit half the genome of each of its parents. Polyploids, however, carry the entire genome of each of their parents. There are many polyploid plant species, such as potatoes, canola and bananas. In nature they often reside in places with extreme environmental conditions.

Polyploids are often sterile but can continue to grow indefinitely if left undisturbed. This seagrass has done just that.

How old is this plant?

The sandy dunes of Shark Bay flooded some 8500 years ago, when the sea level rose after the last ice age. Over the following millennia, the expanding seagrass meadows made shallow coastal banks and sills through creating and capturing sediment, which made the water saltier.

There is also a lot of light in the waters of Shark Bay, as well as low levels of nutrients and large temperature fluctuations. Despite this hostile environment, the plant has been able to thrive and adapt.

It is challenging to determine the exact age of a seagrass meadow, but we estimate the Shark Bay plant is around 4500 years old, based on its size and growth rate. Other huge plants have been reported in both marine and land systems, such as a 6000-tonne quaking aspen in Utah, but this seagrass appears to be the largest to date.

Other huge seagrass plants have also been found, including a closely related Mediterranean seagrass called *Posidonia oceanica*, which covers more than 15 kilometres and may be around 100,000 years old.

Why does this matter?

In the summer of 2010–11, a severe heatwave hit land and sea ecosystems along the Western Australian coastline. Shark Bay's seagrass meadows suffered widespread damage in the heatwave. Yet the ribbon-weed meadows have started to recover. This is somewhat surprising, as this seagrass does not appear to reproduce sexually – which would normally be the best way to adapt to changing conditions.

We have observed seagrass flowers in the Shark Bay meadows, which indicates the seagrass is sexually active, but its fruits (the outcome of successful seagrass sex) are rarely seen. Our single plant may in fact be sterile. This makes its success in the variable waters of Shark Bay quite a conundrum: plants that don't have sex tend to also have low levels of genetic diversity, which should reduce their ability to deal with changing environments.

However, we suspect that our seagrass in Shark Bay has genes that are extremely well suited to its local but variable environment, and perhaps that is why it does not need to have sex to be successful. Even without successful flowering and seed production, the giant plant appears to be very resilient. It experiences a wide range of water temperatures (17–30 degrees Celsius in some years) and salt levels.

Despite these variable conditions and the high light levels (which are typically stressful for seagrass), the plant can maintain its physiological processes and thrive. So how does it cope?

We hypothesise that this plant has a small number of somatic mutations (minor genetic changes that are not passed on to offspring) across its 180-kilometre range that help it persist under local conditions. However, this is just a hunch and we are tackling this hypothesis experimentally. We have set up a series of experiments in Shark Bay to really understand how the plant survives and thrives under such variable conditions.

The future of seagrass

Seagrasses protect our coasts from storm damage, store large amounts of carbon, and provide habitat for a great diversity of wildlife. Conserving and restoring seagrass meadows play a vital role in climate change mitigation and adaptation.

Seagrasses are not immune from climate change impacts: warming temperatures, ocean acidification and extreme weather events are a significant challenge for them. However, the detailed picture we now have of the great resilience of the giant seagrass of Shark Bay provides us hope it will be around for many years to come, especially if serious action is taken on climate change.

PART VI

The power of money

How well off you are depends on who you are: Comparing the lives of Australia's millennials, generation Xers and baby boomers

Peter Abelson
Australian National University

Most Australian voters are either baby boomers (born 1946 to 1964), generation Xers (1965 to 1980) or millennials (1981 to 1996). Boomers are currently aged fifty-eight to seventy-six; they were aged 25–35 between 1971 and 1996. Gen Xers are currently 42–57, and they were 25–35 between 1990 and 2015. Millennials are in their twenties and thirties right now. And at one time or another, most have been told that their generation is better off (or worse off) than the ones that came before it.

It's tempting to think the most recent generation is always the worst off, with all the talk about the cost of living and other things in election campaigns. But without data, or living the lives of other generations, it is hard to be sure. For most of the dimensions of wellbeing in which we are interested, the questions turn out to be surprisingly easy to answer, so long as we remember that the data tells us a lot about lives on average, and little about the lives of individuals.

In a study prepared for the Australian National University's Tax and Transfer Policy Institute, I've attempted to provide answers for nine dimensions of wellbeing used by the OECD, ranging from income to housing, to personal safety and inequality.

Income and wealth

Net national disposable income per capita has been climbing over time, meaning that millennials aged 25–35 are 51 per cent better off than generation Xers were at that age, and 91 per cent better off than boomers at that age. And those figures are likely to understate how much better off their standard of living is.

The quality and range of goods and services, from food to cars to health care to computers to mobile phones with cameras, has improved in ways figures can't capture. Many didn't exist in the 1970s.

Although the Australian Bureau of Statistics attempts to adjust its measures for improvements in quality, it concedes its efforts are incomplete. The bureau's underestimation of quality improvements is likely to be significant.

Disposable income when each generation aged 25–35

Average real net national disposable income per capita when generation aged 25–35.

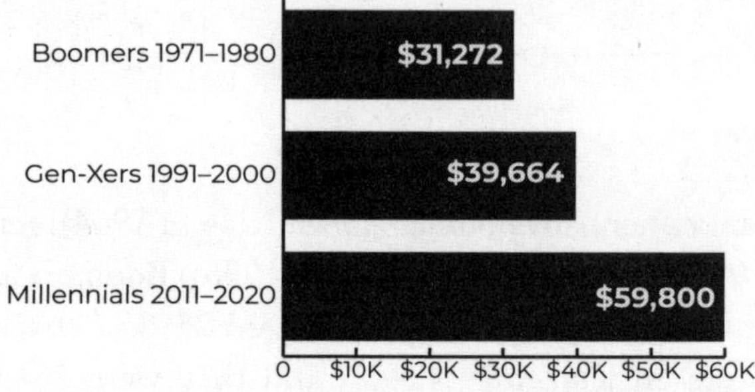

Millennials are also wealthier than gen Xers and boomers were at the same age, although recently the wealth of older Australians has been climbing more rapidly than the wealth of younger Australians, due in large measure to home prices. Offsetting this, in due course, should be big inheritances passed from boomers to gen Xers and millennials.

Housing

Millennials aged 25–34 are much less likely to own their homes than boomers were at the same age. Among those aged 25–34, home ownership has fallen from 60 per cent in 1976 to 37 per cent in 2017–18. While much of this is due to prohibitively high prices, some is due to millennials finishing education and entering the workforce and marrying later.

It should be noted that millennials who do own a home are no worse off in terms of payments relative to income than were boomers. But getting a deposit (unless there's an offer from the bank of Mum and Dad) has become much more difficult.

Home-ownership among those aged 25–34

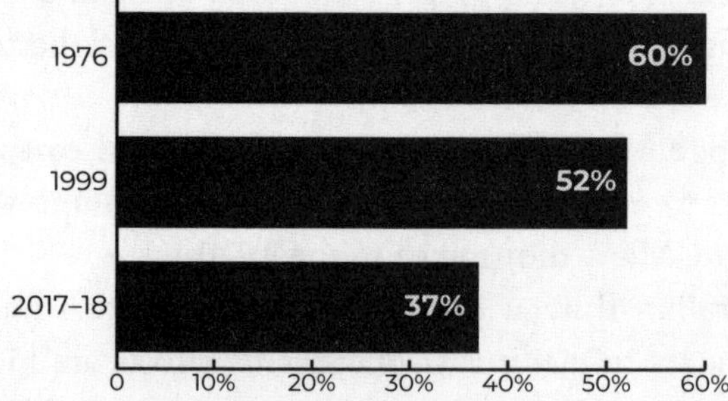

Private rents have been remarkably constant over the past twenty-five years, at about 18 per cent of average household income.

Rents for low earners (in the bottom fifth) remain extraordinarily high, in Sydney taking up about 30 per cent of household income. But this isn't a generational problem. Low earners' rents have been high and stable as a share of income for decades.

What is a problem for the most disadvantaged is that public housing has slid from 5.8 per cent of the housing stock in the late 1990s to about 3 per cent today.

Work

Women are much more likely to be in paid employment than forty years ago. Whereas in 1978, when boomers were aged 25–35, only 40 per cent of women were in paid work, by 2018, when millennials were that age, a record 57 per cent were paid workers, a proportion that climbed even higher during COVID to an unprecedented 60 per cent.

Men are less likely to be employed. Whereas in 1978, 75 per cent of men were paid workers, male employment fell to 67 per cent in 1998 when gen Xers were 25–35, and stayed there when millennials were that age in 2018.

Female employment as a share of working population

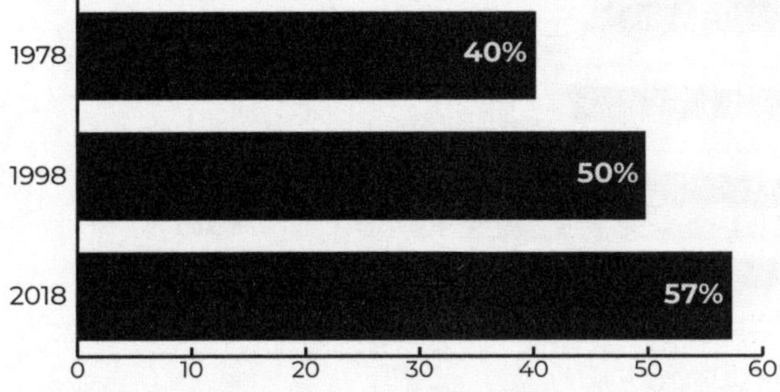

And there has been a major shift from blue-collar to white-collar work. As detailed in the *Intergenerational Report*, in 1966 machinery operators and drivers comprised 11 per cent of the workforce, and technicians and tradespeople 21 per cent. By 2016 these proportions had almost halved to 6 per cent and 14 per cent.

The share of the workforce employed in (generally less physically demanding) professional jobs has doubled, while the share employed in personal service jobs has nearly tripled. Arguably these changes mean more pleasant working conditions.

Work is also more part-time – the proportion of the workforce employed part-time has doubled, climbing from 15 per cent in 1978 to 30 per cent – and more casual. In 1988 only 19 per cent of the workforce was employed in jobs without leave entitlements. By 1998 the proportion had climbed to 27 per cent, and it has since declined to 22.5 per cent.

Health

Australians are taller and heavier than half a century ago, in part because of better nutrition. But we are more obese. Between 2007–08 and 2014–15, the proportion of children defined as overweight and obese women has climbed from 24.7 per cent to 26.4 per cent.

Despite this, the extra years of life expected by men who reach sixty-five have climbed dramatically, from 12.3 years for a boomer born in 1953–54, to 19.6 for a millennial born in 1994–96, to 22.3 for a man born more recently. The extra years of life for a woman at age sixty-five have climbed from 15 to 19.6 to 22.3.

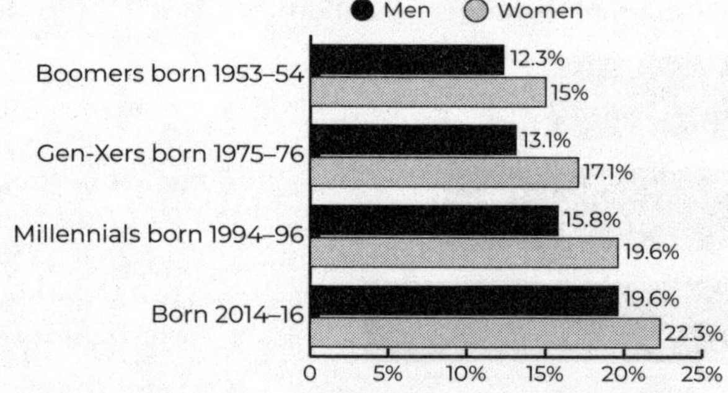

Importantly, the Institute of Health and Welfare finds most of the additional years are healthy years, with the proportion of lives spent in ill health little changed.

Suicide rates have fallen for women (from 7.8 per 100,000 females in the 1970s to 5.7 in the 2010s) but not for men (where they remained at about 18 per 100,000). On the other hand, both men and women experienced major increases in reported anxiety and mood disorders, with the proportion of women reporting anxiety climbing from 12 per cent to 16 per cent between 1997 and 2017, and the proportion of men climbing from 7 per cent to 11 per cent. But harmful alcohol use and illicit drug use fell.

Education

Millennials are much more educated (in terms of post-school qualifications) than baby boomers or generation Xers. Between 1975 and 2016, the proportion of men with a tertiary qualification climbed from less than 4 per cent to 20 per cent, and the proportion of women with a tertiary qualification from less than 2 per cent to 24 per cent.

The benefits for those with degrees go beyond the financial. The Household, Income and Labour Dynamics survey finds they extend to wellbeing, social interactivity and healthy behaviours, such as physical activity and abstaining from drinking and smoking.

Safety

Between 1996 and 2016, victims of homicide and related offences fell 50 per cent, victims of robbery fell 56 per cent, victims of motor vehicle theft fell 65 per cent and victims of other theft fell by 21 per cent. Reported sexual assaults moved in the opposite direction, climbing from eighty per 100,000 people in 1996 to ninety-five in 2016.

Driving on roads has become far safer. Between 1976 and 2016, road deaths per 100,000 people fell from 25.5 to 5.3.

Overseas, far more Australians (many of them conscripts) died in the Vietnam War than in Afghanistan, making the toll from overseas conflicts the greatest for boomers, much less for millennials and non-existent for generation Xers.

Loneliness and connections

The proportion of Australians actively engaged in community organisations fell from 33 per cent in 1967 to 18 per cent in 2004, with major declines in church attendance, membership of unions and political parties, and participation in organised sport.

Whereas in the boomer year of 1984, Australians had an average of nine trusted friends each; by the gen Xer year of 2018, that number had fallen to five. In 1984, people could drop in on ten neighbours. By 2018, it was only four. Seven per cent of people could not drop in on a single neighbour in 1984; by 2018 this had climbed to 17 per cent.

Offsetting this to some extent is evidence of substantial volunteer work in the recent floods and bushfires, social support services that did not exist twenty or thirty years ago, and the increasing use of online communication.

Environment

The US National Aeronautics and Space Administration finds the past seven years have been the hottest in recorded history. The CSIRO finds that Australia's climate has warmed on average by 1.44 degrees Celsius since national records began in 1910, and the Intergovernmental Panel on Climate Change expects Australia to suffer more from longer and hotter summers and more frequent bushfires than the rest of the world. More than 1700 Australian species and ecological communities face extinction.

Only partially offsetting this for millennials are less air and water pollution than in the 1970s, less water use, and better building standards.

Inequality

While the economy millennials entered in their twenties and thirties is richer than in earlier generations, its wealth and income are less equally distributed. The Productivity Commission finds income inequality has increased 'modestly' since the 1980s and wealth inequality has increased by more. Between 2003–04 and 2015–16, the wealth of the poorest tenth of households climbed not at all, while the wealth of middle-earners climbed 27 per cent, and the wealth of the top tenth by nearly 40 per cent, largely due to growing superannuation balances and home prices.

Assessing the overall position of millennial voters compared to gen Xers and baby boomer voters requires value judgements about the dimensions that matter the most, and also judgements about the future, including the ways in which Australia will buffeted by and respond to potential major threats including climate change, social media and the erosion of privacy, and conventional and cyber warfare.

Peter Abelson wishes to acknowledge the research assistance of Aliya Gul, a millennial.

'I just go to school with no food': Why Australia must tackle child poverty to improve educational outcomes

Gerry Redmond
Flinders University

About one in six children in Australia live in poverty. These children generally have poorer educational outcomes than more advantaged children. Our recently published research shows students who live in poverty also experience more social exclusion at school than their more advantaged peers.

These findings suggest disadvantage at home carries over into disadvantage at school. Interventions such as anti-bullying programs and increased funding for schools in disadvantaged communities can help. However, our analysis suggests there's a bigger structural problem. To reduce educational disadvantage, action is needed to reduce child poverty, which has remained stubbornly high since the early 2000s.

In 1987, then prime minister Bob Hawke famously pledged to end child poverty by 1990. As a result of his government's actions, child poverty initially declined before increasing again. Child poverty rates now are only slightly lower than in 1999. In that time, child poverty has been largely absent from policy agendas. Failure to act on poverty will cripple the life chances and productivity of future generations.

The high costs of social exclusion at school

Our research has looked at the schooling experiences of 3535 students aged 13–14 in every state and territory.

Children whose families lacked items most Australian households take for granted, such as cars, computers or holidays, were identified as experiencing family poverty. Children who reported lacking items that most children see as essential were identified as experiencing child deprivation. These items included clothes that allowed them to fit in with other children, and their family having money to send them on school camp.

The proportions living in family poverty or child deprivation were highest among children who experienced multiple forms of disadvantage. One in five children with a disability lived in poverty, as did one in three who had a caring responsibility for a family member. Over one in four

Indigenous children and children with a language background other than English also lived in poverty. By comparison, this was the case for only one in eight children who were not part of a marginalised group.

Teachers make great efforts to support the education of disadvantaged students. Despite these efforts, children living in poverty have lower school-completion rates and lower scores on national tests such as NAPLAN. And our study shows the effects of poverty still permeate school classrooms and playgrounds.

In our study, my collegues and I asked children how much they agreed with the statement: 'At my school, there is a teacher or another adult: who really cares about me; who believes that I will be a success; who listens to me when I have something to say.' The children experiencing deprivation reported less support from their teachers. They also reported higher rates of bullying than non-deprived children.

These experiences were in turn associated with students reporting lower levels of life satisfaction. That's an early indicator of mental health problems in youth and adulthood.

Children's potential is being stifled

The Programme for International Student Assessment conducts comparable academic tests of fifteen-year-old students in all OECD countries. Gaps in test performance between the most socioeconomically advantaged and the most disadvantaged students in Australia have hardly changed since the surveys were launched in 2000. The gaps for the most recent tests in 2018 represented around three years of education for reading, maths and science literacy. When students fall that far behind, it seriously blights their life chances.

Teachers recognise that children living in poverty face many challenges that impact their learning and relationships. Children also talk about the challenges of poverty. One boy explained:

> My mum would take me to the op shop because I keep on splitting my pants when I kneel down but she can't afford to buy me new pants. I don't get pocket money and have to make my own lunch and sometimes I don't even do that. I just go to school with no food.

That such experiences should be associated with poor educational outcomes is not surprising. What is surprising is how badly Australia's education system is failing to achieve a key objective: to support all children to reach their full educational potential.

It's time to focus again on child poverty

Child poverty and children's educational disadvantage require different solutions, but they are closely linked. The more poverty there is in Australia, the harder education systems and individual teachers have to work to compensate for its effect on student outcomes.

The Gonski 2.0 package of school funding reforms, launched in 2018, aims to at least partially address educational disadvantage. However, it is unlikely to break the poverty–educational outcomes nexus on its own.

The challenge that Hawke set thirty-five years ago, to end child poverty in Australia, needs to be taken up again. Both the Hawke government's actions in the years following his pledge and the current Australian Government's responses to the COVID-19 pandemic show how this can be done.

After 1987, family payments were significantly increased and targeted to lower-income families. This increased support helped reduce child poverty. In 2020, in response to the growing COVID-19 emergency, the Morrison government introduced the JobKeeper payment and added the Coronavirus Supplement to the JobSeeker Allowance. Poverty rates declined, at least temporarily, while these supports were in place.

Money does not solve all the problems of child disadvantage. But it does matter.

The next Australian Government could follow Hawke's example and set targets to reduce child poverty. History (in Australia and elsewhere) suggests that action will follow and child poverty will fall.

Reducing poverty will have positive flow-on effects for children's wellbeing, development and educational outcomes. It will also represent a major step towards Australia achieving the UN Sustainable Development Goal of halving poverty rates of all men, women and children by 2030.

Yes, $5 for a lettuce is too much. Government should act to stem the rising cost of healthy eating

Christina Zorbas
Deakin University
Kathryn Backholer
Deakin University

The cost of living is on the rise. The recent Consumer Price Index (a measure of inflation of a standard basket of goods) revealed Australians' grocery baskets are one of the biggest casualties. The latest data tell us the fruit and veg in our shopping baskets cost, on average, 6.7 per cent more than last year. Some items rose by far more. A cucumber, for example, went from $2.20 last year to $3.70 this year. The cost of lettuce became a touchstone during the election campaign.

The Australian Bureau of Statistics reports fruit and vegetable prices have gone up because supply chains were affected by the COVID pandemic (for example, border closures and loss of farm workers), floods and international conflict (increasing fuel and transport costs). But takeaway foods only went up by 0.7 per cent. The ABS suggests the cost of takeaway foods did not increase as much because of government-funded subsidies and voucher programs in New South Wales and Victoria.

The COVID pandemic has focused our attention on public health and government responses. But when it comes to building resilient food systems that support healthy and affordable diets for all – one of the most important actions for public health – governments struggle to act.

Do healthy foods cost more than unhealthy options?

There is some debate out there as to whether healthy foods cost more than unhealthy options. The verdict usually comes down to how you measure what constitutes healthy food and who you talk to.

Our assessments consistently tell us one thing: healthy diets are not affordable for everyone. For people who receive low incomes, healthy diets make up about a quarter of their disposable income (the money that comes into their household after taxes). One in four Australians say groceries are a big financial stress.

The price of 'brain food'

We've monitored diet prices for many years, and the implications of recent fresh food increases will continue to be heartbreaking for everyday people.

During our research, one single mother living in regional Victoria told us:

> People look at cost first and foremost … Bag of chips, $1.75, carrots, hummus and celery, $6 or $7. I know what I'm going to pick if I'm in a pinch, and it definitely ain't the healthy choice.

Another mother of two put the purchase of fresh fruit into context, saying:

> My little girl likes raspberries and blueberries. And I like her to have them, they're brain food. But they range from $4 to $7 for a punnet. And that's a huge portion of your weekly income.

All the nutrition knowledge in the world won't help guide healthy choices if people can't afford healthy food.

Supermarket specials can make unhealthy, ultra-processed foods and drinks look like good value for money. We've previously shown unhealthy options are on special twice as much as healthy alternatives. This pattern of discounting can be particularly persuasive for people on low incomes.

Finally, making food takes time. Buying takeaway foods may save time, even though regular consumption of them can cost us our health.

Making healthy diets affordable for everyone

Our food system does not prioritise the health of people or the planet. While lines for food banks are growing, discussions about removing the GST exemption on fresh fruit and vegetables have been brewing. As we face global food crises, our governments could be planning ways to keep healthy diets affordable for everyone – for example, by increasing subsidies to keep the prices of healthy foods down.

In the Northern Territory, the Aboriginal-led Bagala Community Store has shown governments what's possible by setting healthier supermarket pricing standards. When more specials were put on fruit and veg, consumption climbed by 100 per cent. In New Zealand, the government provides healthy lunches to kids at school to reduce food costs for families.

Price is only half of the food affordability issue. As the cost of living rises, our incomes are spread thinner. Even though the minimum wage has risen, we remain far from addressing the root causes of health inequalities as we head into this election. Healthy diets will only be affordable for all Australians if government income supports are lifted above the poverty line. Our government income support rates (provided through JobSeeker) are the second lowest of high-income countries.

Research from the beginning of the pandemic showed for the first time that JobSeeker made healthy diets affordable for people on low incomes. But the payments were later rescinded and people were put back into poverty. With rising housing costs, it's a wonder anyone who depends on JobSeeker ($345.50/week for a single parent) now can buy food, let alone seek out a healthy diet.

What's next?

Governments and food industries are not doing enough to make healthy diets affordable. The failure to respond to rising food prices, food insecurity and intergenerational poverty is a missed opportunity. Spikes in our food prices are a stark illustration of how vulnerable our food system is.

In the meantime, our team at Deakin University's Institute for Health Transformation will keep an eye on food prices and people's lived experiences of them. We will keep calling for appropriate policies that prioritise our right to affordable healthy diets.

Why did gas prices go from $10 a gigajoule to $800 a gigajoule? An energy crisis has engulfed Australia

Samantha Hepburn
Deakin University

Australia's east coast was plunged into an energy crisis just as winter took hold, which saw many people struggle to heat their homes due to soaring gas bills. On 1 June, Origin Energy confirmed it could not source enough black coal to power Australia's largest coal plant at full capacity, deepening shocks to the energy market. The electricity price surge was so dire, that small energy retailers such as ReAmped Energy advised customers to switch energy providers or be hit with much higher bills.

So what on earth is going on? It has a lot to do with Russia's war on Ukraine, which has disrupted the global energy market. Sanctions on Russian coal and gas exports mean there's simply not enough supply to meet demand. As a consequence, the global prices of gas and coal have soared.

Why are energy prices getting so high?

Australia is a net exporter of gas and coal. This means we export most of our fossil fuels overseas. As the global price of coal increases, the cost of generating domestic electricity from coal is increasing. What's more, many of Australia's coal generators are ageing, which means they fail more often. As of June, nearly 30 per cent of our coal generation was offline.

The price spike comes as coal plant owners look for the exit. Australia's largest coal plant, Eraring, has been operating for thirty-five years. In February, Origin announced it would shut Eraring seven years ahead of schedule, in 2025, because renewable energy was impacting profitability. Origin's new challenge is securing enough coal to run Eraring at its full 2.8-gigawatt capacity. The problem is set to persist into 2023. This is not only due to a difficult global environment, but also to domestic delivery difficulties due to supply chain disruptions.

In an attempt to meet rising electricity demand, some energy generators have increased gas-powered generation. However, given Australia exports so much of its domestic gas resources, any additional gas for domestic consumption must be acquired from the rising international market. To make matters worse, a June cold snap along the east coast led to a spike in demand for electricity as people heated their homes.

So what's the overall effect? To give you an idea, back in early 2022, gas was trading at approximately $10 a gigajoule. By June, wholesale prices in Victoria reached up to $800 a gigajoule – more than eighty times normal levels. This gargantuan spike caused the Australian Energy Market Operator to step in, temporarily capping prices at $40 a gigajoule until 10 June.

Will these prices continue?

These extraordinary prices will likely continue. The Australian Energy Regulator has warned that wholesale power prices are likely to remain high for at least two years. This will hit energy retailers and consumers hard. However, those likely to experience the most pain are small energy retailers on the east coast because of the so-called 'default market offer'.

Established in 2019, the default market offer serves as a price safety net for residential and small business customers by setting a cap on how much energy retailers can charge households and businesses. When advertising or promoting offer pricing, retailers must show the price of their offer in comparison to the default market offer price.

The default market offer for 2022 was released in late May. Alarmingly, it showed that from 1 July, default offers would rise by 14 per cent in New South Wales, 11 per cent in Queensland and 7 per cent in South Australia. In Victoria, the Essential Services Commission determines the default offer, and set the cap at 5 per cent.

So, while consumers will pay a bit more under the increased price cap, energy retailers will pay *a lot* more in a dramatically rising wholesale electricity market. Large retailers such as AGL may cope, but smaller players will be hit hard and may not be able to survive given these price hikes are on top of rises in 2021.

This is what led ReAmped Energy, a small energy retailer with 70,000 customers, to advise customers to look elsewhere.

Should we be surprised?

The state of the energy market reflects a deepening global resource crisis. However, in Australia, the writing has been on the wall for a long time.

Australia exports 85 per cent of its gas. Between 2000 and 2015, Australia's gas exports tripled. Between 2015 and 2019 they tripled again. As more Australian gas was exported overseas, the domestic electricity price rose. Exporting most of our gas means we often do not have enough for domestic consumption, and purchasing it on the international spot market is costly. The price of electricity rose a whopping 130 per cent between 2015 – when liquefied natural gas exports began at Gladstone in Queensland – and 2019.

Despite these increases, robust export controls have not been implemented. Unlike Western Australia, where liquefied natural gas producers must reserve 15 per cent for the domestic market, the east coast has no reservation policy. Adding to this is the failure to support a swift integration of renewables into the national grid through stronger, focused regulatory mechanisms, and improved policy has not occurred either.

All this has created, as new federal Climate Change and Energy Minister Chris Bowen put it, a 'perfect storm'. In a press conference on 2 June, Bowen blamed the previous government's stalling on renewables and changing energy policies, saying:

> Their ad-hoc-ery, their changes-of-policy approaches, have left Australia ill-prepared and our energy markets ill-prepared for the challenges we are facing today in relation to gas and energy supply.

Is the government doing anything about it?

One response could be for the government to trigger an emergency domestic gas pricing mechanism and declare this to be a shortfall year, a 2017 mechanism that hasn't yet been used. If 2022 is deemed to be a shortfall year, export restrictions would be imposed upon liquefied natural gas producers to protect domestic supply. This could help pricing, because gas reservations can change the supply balance and allow domestic prices to adjust. It may also assist with supply, given the recent cold snap resulting in the AEMO issuing a separate warning of gas supply shortfalls in Victoria, South Australia and Tasmania.

However, Bowen has ruled out using the emergency mechanism to deal with the energy price hikes. He said it wasn't designed to limit prices, and wouldn't have any impact until January next year.

At the time of writing, we are only in the early days of June, and more colder-than-normal weather is forecast for the coming winter months. Whether it uses the domestic gas pricing mechanism or not, the federal government must take steps to address rising energy prices and make the coming winter easier for Australians to bear.

Frydenberg's March budget was an extraordinary turnaround, but it left a $40 billion problem

Richard Holden
UNSW Sydney

It's often said in business circles that good companies manage their balance sheet and bad companies manage their P&L (profit and loss account). That same aphorism applies to governments.

And by that standard, treasurer Josh Frydenberg's fourth budget, handed down on 29 March, was a triumph. Net debt is forecast to peak at 33.1 per cent of GDP in 2024–25, compared to 40.9 per cent in last year's budget. Net interest payments stay below 1 per cent of GDP – a better result than every year from 1984 to 2000.

Net debt vs net interest payments
% of GDP, historical data and Budget 2022–23 forecasts, 1970–71 to 2032–33.

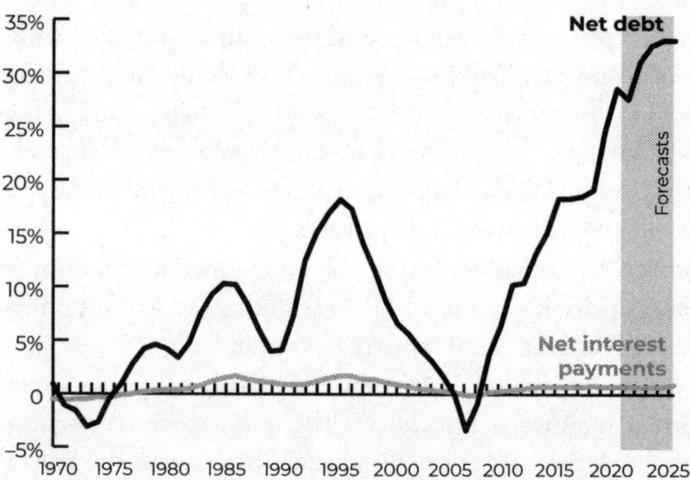

This is an extraordinary turnaround, and much of it comes in the twelve months to the end of June this year. Rather than net debt of $729 billion by June 2022 (as forecast in last year's budget), it is expected to be $632 billion. This reflects the stronger economy.

Unemployment is lower so welfare payments are too. High commodity prices have helped the budget bottom line, but so too have the tax receipts from increased employment and consumer spending.

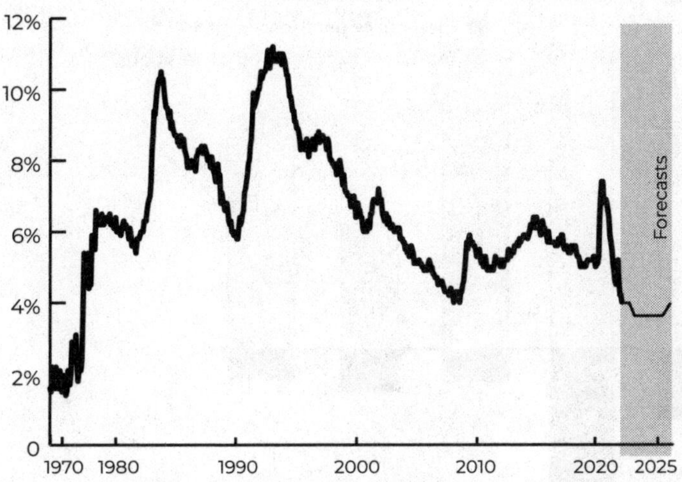

At the start of the coronavirus pandemic in 2020, the government outlined a clear fiscal strategy: spend big to support the economy, and shrink away the debt involved through higher economic growth. It worked. Australian GDP is 3.4 per cent higher than it was pre-pandemic. Only the United States, at 3.2 per cent, is close to that performance among the world's seven largest economies. France is up just 0.9 per cent, Canada 0.1 per cent, while Germany, Japan, the United Kingdom and Italy have all shrunk.

Amid this good news is a lingering concern. By 2025–26, the budget deficit is still estimated to be 1.6 per cent of GDP. That's a $43.1 billion gap between government revenues and expenses.

It is a reminder that while two governments – one Liberal and one Labor – have steered the nation through the global financial crisis and the coronavirus pandemic, they have not repaired our structural deficit.

Effect of government decisions versus effect of things the government can't control

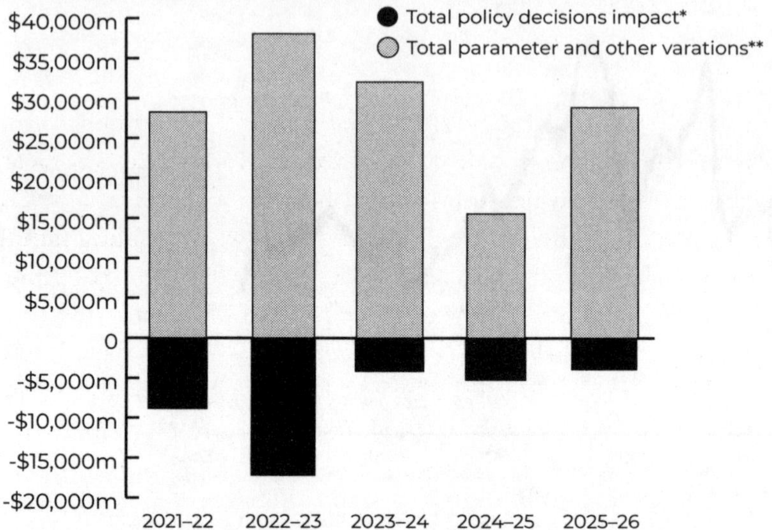

*Policy decisions are government policies announced since MYEFO 2020.
** 'Parameter and other variations' are external factors like the pandemic or global economic factors, etc.

The Albanese government now faces a difficult task. It needs to close that $40 billion structural gap without a turn to austerity that would damage the economic growth engine that's put us in this enviable position.

It's something of a high-wire act. And it is the litmus test of good economic management.

Some big spending

It's not hard to see why. Defence spending will grow from $35.8 billion this year to $44.5 billion by 2025–26. Given the global security outlook, it could easily go higher.

And spending on the National Disability Insurance Scheme will grow from $30.8 billion this year to $46.1 billion over the same time frame. That's growth of 10.6 per cent per annum. In fact, by 2033 the NDIS is forecast to represent more than $70 billion in government spending. That spending is life-changing for half a million Australians. But those figures tell us such spending is only sustainable with a strong economy.

If unemployment doesn't stay low and economic growth comparatively high, then spending growth in areas like the NDIS and defence will become unsustainable.

The fuel excise holiday

One hotly anticipated measure in the budget was a 50 per cent cut in the fuel excise from 44.2 cents to 22.1 per litre, for six months. Let's be clear: this is great politics. The treasurer said in his speech: 'Whether you're dropping the kids at school, driving to and from work or visiting family and friends, it will cost less.' This is a beautiful rendition of the time-honoured political tradition of feeling the voters' pain.

In one way this makes perfect economic sense, too. Why should households bear the risk of petrol prices bouncing around based on global conflict and decisions by the OPEC cartel? As the Australian Competition & Consumer Commission has demonstrated, prices at the pump basically move one-for-one with the Singapore price of the Mogas 95 unleaded petrol sold to Australia. By setting the fuel excise lower when oil prices are high, and higher when oil prices are low, the government acted like a big social insurance company. That's part of their job (see Medicare, NDIS, unemployment benefits).

But there's a wrinkle to this. According to figures from the Australian Bureau of Statistics' Household Expenditure Survey, the bottom fifth of households by income spend $27 a week or 3.5 per cent of their income on petrol. By contrast, the top fifth of households spend $42 a week or 1.8 per cent of their income on petrol. So, a per-litre cut in petrol benefits higher-income households more in dollar terms. It also doesn't discourage people from driving less.

It would be more progressive (and better for the environment) to just give all households a flat rebate.

A good plan, well executed

The tone at the budget press conference was in striking contrast to that at the announcement of the pandemic fiscal strategy in early 2020. Back then there were sharp questions about fiscal irresponsibility, leading then finance minister Mathias Cormann to exclaim: 'What would you have us do?'

This time, there were a series of relatively minor questions about whether Victoria was getting enough GST revenue or if medical students who studied in regional Australia would stay there. That is the consequence of a government that jettisoned decades of political branding in March 2022, laid out a compelling plan to get Australia through the pandemic, and delivered on it.

'Wellbeing': It's why Labor's first budget will have more rigour than any before it

Peter Martin
Business and Economics Editor, The Conversation

What if the most important thing in Jim Chalmers' first budget is the thing his critics are writing off as a gimmick?

Australia's new treasurer has a lot on his plate. He has commissioned a complete review of the way the Reserve Bank works, he has drawn up a statement to parliament he says people will find 'confronting', and he has prepared the second of two budgets in one year – in October, updating the Coalition's budget in March. In what some see as a gimmick, it will be Australia's first budget to benchmark its measures against their impact on the wellbeing of the Australian people: Australia's first 'wellbeing budget'.

When Chalmers proposed the idea in opposition, the treasurer at the time, Josh Frydenberg, described it as 'laughable'. Wellbeing was 'doublespeak for higher taxes and more debt'. Frydenberg asked parliament to imagine Chalmers delivering his first budget 'fresh from his ashram deep in the Himalayas, barefoot, robes flowing, incense burning, beads in one hand, wellbeing budget in the other'.

But here's the thing. In an important way, Chalmers' first 'wellbeing budget' will have more rigour than any of the budgets prepared by Frydenberg or any of his predecessors. It's the first to have a stab at a cost–benefit analysis.

Budgets are usually three things: a statement of accounts, with measures that will have an impact on the accounts (and sometimes measures that won't), as well as the legislation needed to authorise another year's worth of expenditure. What they don't do, as a rule, is assess the impact of those measures, even the impact on the economy.

Measures without outcomes

Frydenberg's first budget, for example, in 2019, included a measure named 'lower taxes for hardworking Australians'. The budget papers described what the measure would do and its impact on the budget, but not its impact on the economy. The calculations may well have been carried out, but they weren't included in the budget, as was typical. The budget papers told us what was being done, but not what it would do.

Until 2014 the budget papers at least told us who the budget would make better off and worse off. The standard table identified the impact of the budget as a whole on seventeen different types of households at different types of incomes. Prime Minister Tony Abbott and Treasurer Joe Hockey removed it in their first budget, perhaps because they didn't want the winners and losers to become apparent, and it hasn't returned. The budget papers neither tell us what the budget will do to economic growth, nor what it will do to incomes, nor what it will do to the environment or anything else other than the budget's bottom line.

Which is a pity, because the budget is massive. The government takes in just short of one-quarter of all the dollars spent in Australia and pays out slightly more than one-quarter of the dollars earned. The balance between that income and spending is called the budget deficit or surplus. It matters, but so too does what that income and spending do.

Encompassing rather than replacing GDP

What Chalmers has proposed, and what New Zealand and Scotland are doing, and what Canada is working towards, is a scorecard of how budget measures affect the things that matter, including how much we produce: gross domestic product.

During the first Rudd government, Angela Jackson was deputy chief of staff to finance minister Lindsay Tanner. Reflecting on that time at last week's Australian Conference of Economists, she said it was astounding that the expected effects of budget measures weren't made explicit. It meant what happened couldn't be assessed against expectations.

Introducing measurables wouldn't be about supplanting GDP but about including it along with other measures of prosperity as outcomes against which the budget could be assessed, along with measures of health, the environment, gender, children's welfare, and the welfare of Aboriginal and Torres Strait Islander people. It would let us see whether we are making progress or going backwards on the environment (where we seem to be going backwards) and on living standards, inequality, health and other things, and what the budget is doing about it.

The Australian Bureau of Statistics was on to this back in 2008 when it introduced a short-lived publication called *Measures of Australia's Progress* that reported on whether what came to be twenty-six key indicators were going forwards or backwards.

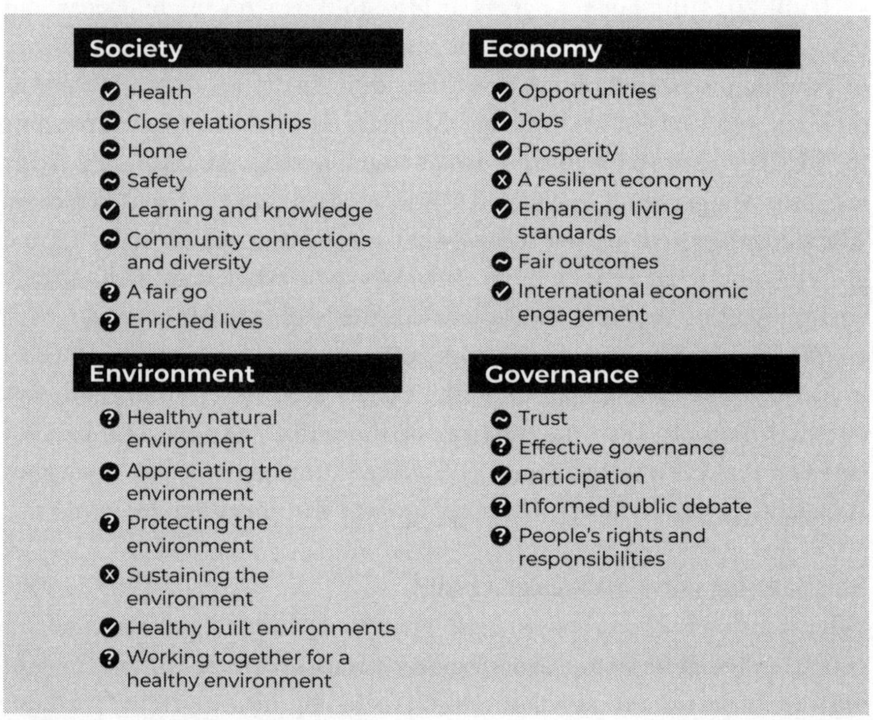

ABS *Measures of Australia's Progress*, 2013

Australia's Treasury was on to it earlier, in 2004, introducing its own wellbeing framework for internal use. It understands the concept.

Taking that concept public will improve or weed out budget measures before they are announced. They will need to demonstrate that they can improve wellbeing, or at least not make it worse. After it is established, it will require future treasurers to level with the public about the impact of what they are proposing, in the same way as Coalition treasurer Peter Costello's *Charter of Budget Honesty* required future treasurers to level with the public about the cost of what they were proposing.

It's already shaping up as Chalmers' most important legacy.

Going to private school won't make a difference to your kid's academic scores

Sally Larsen
University of New England
Alexander Forbes
University of New England

In Australia, around 30 per cent of primary and 40 per cent of secondary school children attend a private, or independent, school. School fees vary widely, depending on the type of private school and the different sectors that govern them. Catholic schools generally cost less than independent schools, where families can pay fees of more than $40,000 per year.

Despite the term 'independent school', all schools in Australia receive government funding. On average, Catholic schools receive around 75 per cent and independent schools around 45 per cent of their funding from state and federal governments.

Research shows parents believe private schools will provide a better education for their children, and better set them up for success in life. But the evidence on whether this perception is correct is not conclusive.

What does the research say about academic scores?

Our recent study showed that the NAPLAN scores of children who attended private schools were no different to those in public schools, after accounting for socioeconomic background. These findings are in line with other research, both in Australia and internationally, that shows family background is related both to the likelihood of attending a private school and to academic achievement.

While there may appear to be differences in the academic achievement of students in private schools, these tend to disappear once socioeconomic background is taken into account.

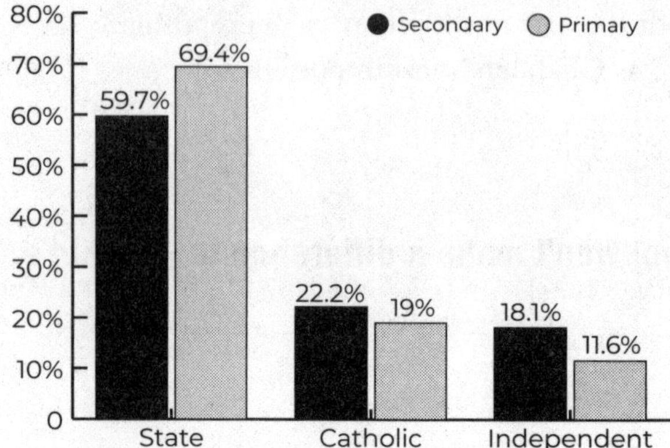

An analysis of sixty-eight education systems (mainly countries, but some countries only include regions, which are known as 'education systems') participating in the 2018 Programme for International Assessment tests showed attendance at private schools was not consistently related to higher test performance.

The OECD report says:

> On average across OECD countries and in 40 education systems, students in private schools … scored higher in reading than students in public schools (… before accounting for socio-economic profile) … However, after accounting for students' and schools' socio-economic profile, reading scores were higher in public schools than in private schools …

Do private schools improve student achievement over time?

Another argument used to support Australia's growing private school sector is the idea that private schools actually add value to a child's education. This means attending a private school should boost students' learning trajectories over and above what they might have achieved in a public school.

Our research is the first to examine whether students differ in learning trajectories across the four NAPLAN test years (3, 5, 7 and 9) depending on the school type they attended. We compared the NAPLAN scores of students who attended a public school, a private school, and those who attended a public school in years 3 and 5 and then a private school in years 7 and 9. The students in the latter group scored highest in reading and numeracy tests in each of the four NAPLAN test years.

This group outperformed students who attended private schools at all years, and students who attended public schools at all years. But there was no evidence that making the switch to a private school added to students' learning growth.

Average NAPLAN reading scores in years 3, 5, 7 and 9 for students attending public or private schools, and those who switched from public to private

NAPLAN scale score range from 0 to 1000 and are comparable across the four assessed years.

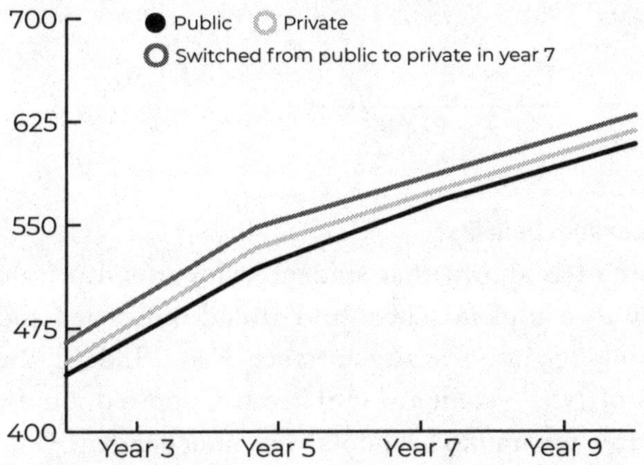

These high-performing students were already achieving the highest results in public school before they left for private school in Year 7. This suggests private schools may be enrolling the highest achievers from public primary schools.

Other analyses in our paper showed that once the socioeconomic background of these students was taken into account, apparent achievement differences between school sectors were no longer present.

The other interesting point is that there were no differences in achievement trajectories between the groups. So, making the switch to private schools in Year 7 did not affect the gains students were making in NAPLAN over time. Students in public schools made just as much progress as their peers who attended private schools. This undermines claims that private schools add value to students' academic growth.

Average NAPLAN numeracy scores in years 3, 5, 7 and 9 for students attending public or private schools, and those who switched from public to private

NAPLAN scale score range from 0 to 1000 and are comparable across the four assessed years.

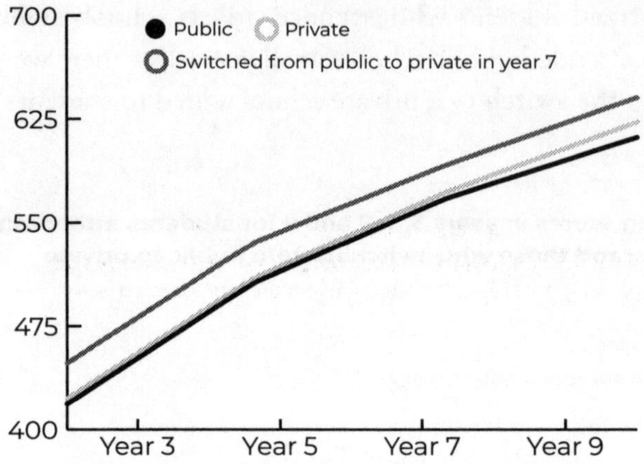

What about other private school benefits?

Some Australian research has shown that students who attend private schools are more likely to complete school and attend university, and tend to attain higher rankings in university entrance exams. Indeed, the recent announcements of NSW students' HSC results showed almost three-quarters of the 150 top-ranked schools were independent. The concentration of higher-achieving students in private schools could also magnify any peer effects on students' decisions about future career paths or attending university.

Nonetheless, the research on these questions is not definitive: it is very difficult to separate out the effects of background characteristics of students and the effects of the school sector given that more advantaged students tend to concentrate in private schools. Some Australian research has shown the characteristics of students before they enter private schools have a larger effect on their aspirations, behaviour and attitudes than the school.

Rethinking the system?

While the capacity for parents to choose a school that best suits their child is often seen as an advantage, many disadvantaged families are a lot more constrained in their ability to choose, and pay for, private schools.

Students attending private schools may have access to other non-academic benefits, such as more opportunities for sports, excursions and other extracurricular activities. But in terms of academic advantage, we know, from our research and other studies that explored similar questions, there is little evidence to show independent schools offer any. It is likely children will do equally well in any school sector.

Attending school every day counts, but kids in out-of-home care are missing out

Kitty Te Riele
University of Tasmania
Anna Sullivan
University of South Australia
Daryl Higgins
Australian Catholic University
Jesse King
Indigenous Knowledge Holder
Joseph McDowall
University of Queensland
Michael A Guerzoni
University of Tasmania
Rhonda Coopes
University of Southern Queensland
Sharon Bessell
Australian National University
Emily Rudling
University of Tasmania

Consistent school attendance is important in any child's education, but for many children in out-of-home care, going to school every day is no easy thing.

There are three main types of out-of-home care in Australia: relative (or kinship) care, foster care, and residential care (small-group homes). Children and young people who are unable to live safely at home, due to the risk of abuse or neglect, are removed and placed in care by their state and territory child protection services. In June 2020 there were 35,717 school-aged children (aged 5–17) in care in Australia; 40 per cent (14,444) of these were Indigenous children.

Research shows regular school attendance is crucial to educational achievement. Unfortunately, children in out-of-home care face myriad challenges when it comes to attending school every day.

What is education like for children in care?

Evidence shows that too often these students in care end up having negative experiences in school, and worse academic outcomes than their peers. For example:

- 82 per cent of students in care in Year 3 meet the national minimum standard in NAPLAN-Reading, compared to 95 per cent nationally. By Year 9, it drops to 69 per cent (versus 93 per cent).
- 81 per cent of students in care in Year 3 meet the national minimum standard in NAPLAN-Numeracy, compared to 96 per cent nationally. By Year 9, it drops to 61 per cent (versus 93 per cent).
- 57 per cent of young care leavers (aged 18–25) completed Year 12 or equivalent, compared to the national average of 85 per cent.

What are the issues and inequitable outcomes?

These young people are dealing with the impact of trauma and placement instability. But schools often lack expertise to support them.

Imagine what it's like to attend five or more primary schools. Imagine having to get used to new teachers again and again. Dealing with new approaches to learning, new rules, and new classmates. Constantly catching up on what has been missed. Being thought of as the kid who is 'behind'.

Aboriginal and Torres Strait Islander children in care also risk being disconnected from their culture and kin.

COVID-19 created and exacerbated problems. School closures have made school more difficult. COVID-19 uncertainty may have increased placement instability, schooling mobility, and economic and social stressors.

Quality education is essential for wellbeing and development. Improving education outcomes for students in care is of profound benefit to them. But it also benefits Australian society – now and for future generations.

Attendance is fundamental

Regular attendance is crucial to educational achievement. Absence from school flows on to negative effects like leaving school early, poor academic achievement and social isolation. Even short absences – including absences that are officially allowed, such as illness – can make it more difficult for children to keep up. The effects are cumulative. Each further absence makes things harder for the student.

The experiences that make school harder for children and young people in care (such as trauma and frequently moving to new care placements and schools) also lead to lower attendance. The statistics tell an alarming story.

The average number of days absent per term is double for students in care with a substantiated concern to the state child protection authority: seven days versus 3.4 days for students not in care. A substantiated concern means a report about the safety of a child or young person has been investigated by a caseworker, and they have been found to be at significant risk of harm.

Suspensions also mean students miss out on school. South Australian data suggest the proportion of students in care who were suspended is almost four times higher: 23 per cent versus 6 per cent across all students.

The best available data about absences and suspensions are from South Australia, but there is no reason to believe it is much different in other jurisdictions. They show attendance is fundamental to improving outcomes for children in care.

Aboriginal and Torres Strait Islander children and young people in care are doubly disadvantaged. For example, in a review of 1000 cases in Victoria, 30.5 per cent had been suspended in secondary school. In primary school, the proportion was 11.4 per cent.

What can be done?

Behind these figures sits a complex challenge. It's not the fault of these young people. They did not choose to go into care, or that their lives would be characterised by disruption and trauma. Nor should we blame schools and teachers. Frequent absences of children in care is a systems problem that goes beyond the responsibility of individual schools.

We've known about these problems for a long time. But several policy commitments now provide hope. The 2019 Alice Springs (Mparntwe)

Education Declaration names 'learners in out-of-home care' as a group needing targeted support. The 2020 National Agreement on Closing the Gap highlights school attendance as a key driver for ensuring Aboriginal and Torres Strait Islander students 'achieve their full learning potential'. The federal government's National Standards for Out-of-Home Care require state and territory governments to work to enhance life chances for children in care, including through appropriate education. And the relatively new Safe and Supported: the National Framework for Protecting Australia's Children 2021–2031 recognises access to education as a 'fundamental right'.

These commitments create a powerful opportunity to give children and young people in care a fair go at their education – to set them up for learning, and for life. But this will need collaboration across education and child-protection systems to ensure these children attend school. Every day counts.

PART VII

The power of technology

'This weird dinging sound that everyone dreads': What rapid deliveries mean for supermarket workers

Lauren Kate Kelly
RMIT University

Online grocery shopping has boomed since the pandemic began in 2020, with Woolworths and Coles steadily expanding their home-delivery offerings. Rapid delivery is the latest frontier.

Woolworths and Coles Express have been offering on-demand deliveries through Uber Eats and DoorDash since last year. Woolworths recently launched the Metro60 app, which promises home delivery within an hour to select suburbs. These arrangements have received little fanfare, yet they signal a significant shift for supermarket workers.

As part of ongoing research, I study how the gig economy is transforming conditions of work within traditional employment. To find out how interacting with delivery platforms affects supermarket employees, I interviewed sixteen experienced 'personal shoppers' at Woolworths and Coles who fill delivery orders from supermarket shelves.

The labour of on-demand grocery

In supermarkets that offer on-demand home delivery, the work of the personal shopper takes on a faster pace. For Woolworths employees, for instance, an Uber Eats order can drop in at any time, setting off an alarm until the order is accepted and picking begins. As one personal shopper explains:

> We get this weird dinging sound that everyone dreads. You have to pick that order within the half-hour or within the hour … it can drop in at any time. So if you're sitting there having lunch for an hour, you still have to go do it because you've got that KPI to hit. All the [scanner] guns in the store drop that sound. So it reverberates through the store. The customers can't hear it because they don't know what it is. But all of us know what it is.

The on-demand orders must be prioritised alongside existing orders, requiring the personal shopper to juggle competing time crunches simultaneously.

It's urgent, and they just pop out of nowhere. So you don't really know when they're coming until they're there. It's super-stressful. I dislike them immensely.

Enter the gig worker

Once the order is picked from the supermarket aisles, the employee hands it over to a gig worker for home delivery. Supermarket staff say their interactions are brief and often impersonal.

It's a complete mess. You have no idea who's coming to pick up these things. And it's just people showing up with their headphones in showing you that they've got this order on their phone. There's no real rhyme or reason to any of it.

For supermarket workers, gig workers are neither colleagues nor customers, yet they play an essential role in home delivery and customer service. When things go awry, however – such as a missing bag or broken eggs – it's the supermarket staff who field those complaints. Similarly, when personal shoppers run behind schedule, it has punitive flow-on effects for gig workers.

The on-demand model may, by design or otherwise, pit two groups of workers against each other, fostering frustrations at both ends.

Most of the time they're pretty good. They deal with it. It's just those bad times where we might be behind and then they don't deal with it very well.

A new labour regime

At first glance, the partnerships between supermarkets and gig-economy platforms look like the supermarket is outsourcing the work of delivery. But this is a simplification: in fact, the traditional companies are bringing the precarious and on-demand labour of the gig workers inside their own firm, and making it legitimate through formal partnerships.

How do supermarket employees view on-demand grocery?

Most personal shoppers I spoke with are ambivalent or wary of the expanding on-demand services.

> The people that I work with either love it or hate it. They like it because it's different, you never get bored, and you've always got something to do. But that's why other people hate it. Because you don't get a chance to just stand for a second, you always have to be doing something.

Some enjoy the fast pace and express satisfaction in meeting targets and making the customer happy.

> We've all gotten to the point now where we're attuned, we hear the chime, we know what actions we need to take. So it almost happens autonomously. And before you know it, here comes another one and you just keep going.

Others expressed concerns about burnout, unpredictable workloads and an increasing pace of work.

> It's obviously a very high-demand, high-speed job. That's probably the biggest frustration. We also have pick rates, essentially like Amazon, where we get told this is how many items we should average an hour … and a lot of the time people can't meet the average.

Staff who have been in the role more than a decade have seen the pace of work speed up significantly during their tenure, and are more critical.

> You're not a person when you walk in the door, you're a machine.

Some expressed broader concerns about the possibility of their role being taken over entirely by the gig economy. In the words of one shopper:

> I was a little dismayed when the whole DoorDashing started because it's like, oh no, the gig economy is getting closer and closer. Gig stuff always … makes me uncomfortable … It's all this whole long-term ploy to destroy some existing industry or place, or eliminate worker protections.

Another expressed a similar sentiment:

> My biggest worry is that they start outsourcing the actual shopping procedure. I think that would be the next logical step similar to what America has with Instacart.

Supermarket jobs of the future

All the personal shoppers I spoke with shared a pride in their work and their deep knowledge of the supermarket and its local community. How the role continues to evolve through partnerships with the gig economy is not inevitable but a matter of choice.

'Virtual influencers' are here, but should Meta really be setting the ground rules?

Tama Leaver
Curtin University
Rachel Berryman
Curtin University

In January, Meta announced it was working on a set of ethical guidelines for 'virtual influencers' – animated, typically computer-generated characters designed to attract attention on social media.

When Facebook renamed itself Meta in late 2021, it heralded a pivot towards the 'metaverse', where virtual influencers will presumably one day roam in their thousands. Even Meta admits the metaverse doesn't really exist yet. The building blocks of a persistent, immersive virtual reality for everything from business to play are yet to be fully assembled. But virtual influencers are already online, and are surprisingly convincing.

Given its recent history, is Meta (née Facebook) really the right company to be setting the ethical standards for virtual influencers and the metaverse more broadly?

Who (or what) are virtual influencers?

Meta's announcement notes the 'rising phenomenon' of synthetic media, an umbrella term for images, video, voice or text generated by computerised technology, typically using artificial intelligence or automation. Many virtual influencers incorporate elements of synthetic media in their design, ranging from completely digitally rendered bodies to human models that are digitally masked with characters' facial features.

At both ends of the scale, this process still relies heavily on human labour and input, from art direction for photo shoots to writing captions for social media. Like Meta's vision of the metaverse, influencers that are entirely generated and powered by AI are a largely futuristic fantasy. But even in their current form, virtual influencers are of serious value to Meta, both as attractions for their existing platforms and as avatars of the metaverse.

Interest in virtual influencers has rapidly expanded over the past five years, attracting huge audiences on social media, as well as partnerships with major brands, including Audi, Bose, Calvin Klein, Samsung, and Chinese e-commerce platform Tmall. A competitive industry specialising in the production, management and promotion of virtual influencers has already sprung up, although it remains largely unregulated.

So far, India is the only country to address virtual influencers in national advertising standards, requiring brands 'disclose to consumers that they are not interacting with a real human being' when posting sponsored content.

Ethical guidelines

There is an urgent need for ethical guidelines, both to help producers and their brand partners navigate this new terrain, and more importantly to help users understand the content they're engaging with.

Meta has warned that 'synthetic media has the potential for both good and harm', listing 'representation and cultural appropriation' as specific issues of concern. Indeed, despite their short lifespan, virtual influencers already have a history of overt racialisation and misrepresentation, raising ethical questions for producers who create digital characters with different demographic characteristics from their own. But it's far from clear whether Meta's proposed guidelines will adequately address these questions.

Becky Owen, head of creator innovation and solutions at Meta Creative Shop, said the planned ethical framework 'will help our brand partners and VI creators explore what's possible, likely and desirable, and what's not'. This seeming emphasis on technological possibilities and brand partners' desires leads to an inevitable impression that Meta is once again conflating commercial potential with ethical practice.

By its own count, Meta's platforms already host more than 200 virtual influencers. But virtual influencers exist elsewhere too: they do viral dance challenges on TikTok, upload vlogs to YouTube, and post life updates on

Sina Weibo. They appear 'offline' at malls in Beijing and Singapore, and on 3D billboards in Tokyo, and star in television commercials.

Gamekeeper or poacher?

This brings us back to the question of whether Meta is the right company to set the ground rules for this emerging space. The company's history is tarred by unethical behaviour, from Facebook's questionable beginnings in Mark Zuckerberg's Harvard dorm room (as depicted in *The Social Network*) to large-scale privacy failings demonstrated in the Cambridge Analytica scandal.

In February 2021, Facebook showed how far it was willing to go to defend its interests when it briefly banned all news content on Facebook in Australia to force the federal government to water down the Australian News Media Bargaining Code.

That year also saw former Facebook executive Frances Haugen very publicly turn whistleblower, sharing a trove of internal documents with journalists and politicians. These so-called 'Facebook Papers' raised numerous concerns about the company's conduct and ethics, including the revelation that Facebook's own internal research showed Instagram can harm young people's mental health, even leading to suicide.

Today, Meta is fighting US antitrust litigation that aims to restrain the company's monopoly by potentially compelling it to sell key acquisitions, including Instagram and WhatsApp. Meanwhile, Meta is scrambling to integrate its messaging service across all three apps, effectively making them different interfaces for a shared back end that Meta will doubtless argue cannot feasibly be separated, no matter the outcomes of the current litigation.

Given this backstory, Meta seems far from the ideal choice as ethical guardian of the metaverse. The already extensive distribution of virtual influencers across platforms and markets highlights the need for ethical guidelines that go beyond the interests of one company – especially a company that stands to gain so much from the impending spectacle.

What do TikTok, Bunnings, eBay and Netflix have in common? They're all hyper-collectors

Brendan Walker-Munro
University of Queensland

You walk into a shopping centre to buy some groceries. Without your knowledge, an electronic scan of your face is taken by in-store surveillance cameras and stored in an online database. Each time you return to that store, your 'faceprint' is compared with those of people wanted for shoplifting or violence.

This might sound like science fiction, but it's the reality for many of us. By failing to take our digital privacy seriously, as former human rights commissioner Ed Santow has warned, Australia is 'sleepwalking' its way into mass surveillance.

Privacy and the digital environment

Of course, companies have been collecting personal information for decades. If you've ever signed up to a loyalty program like Flybuys, then you've performed what marketing agencies call a 'value exchange'. In return for benefits from the company (like discounted prices or special offers), you've handed over details of who you are, what you buy and how often you buy it.

Consumer data is big business. In 2019 a report from digital marketers WebFX showed that data from around 1400 loyalty programs was routinely being traded across the globe as part of an industry worth around US$200 billion. That same year, the Australian Competition & Consumer Commission's review of loyalty schemes revealed how many of these loyalty schemes lacked data transparency and even discriminated against vulnerable customers.

But the digital environment is making data collection even easier. When you watch Netflix, for example, the company knows what you watch, when you watch it and how long you watch it for. But they go further, also capturing data on which scenes or episodes you watch repeatedly, the ratings of your content, the number of searches you perform and what you search for.

Hyper-collection: A new challenge to privacy

In late 2021, the controversial tech company Clearview AI was ordered by the Australian Information Commissioner to stop 'scraping' social media for the pictures it was collecting in its massive facial-recognition database. In July 2022, the commissioner was investigating several retailers for creating facial profiles of the customers in their stores.

This new phenomenon – 'hyper-collection' – represents a growing trend by large companies to collect, sort, analyse and use more information than they need, usually in covert or passive ways. In many cases, hyper-collection is not supported by a truly legitimate commercial or legal purpose.

Digital privacy laws and hyper-collection

Hyper-collection is a major problem in Australia for three reasons.

First, Australia's privacy law wasn't prepared for the likes of Netflix and TikTok. Despite numerous amendments, the *Privacy Act* dates back to the late 1980s. Although former attorney-general Christian Porter announced a review of the Act in late 2019, it has been held up by the recent change of government.

Second, Australian privacy laws are unlikely on their own to threaten the profit base of foreign companies, especially those located in China. The Information Commissioner has the power to order companies to take certain actions – like it did with Uber in 2021 – and can enforce these through court orders. But the penalties aren't really big enough to discourage companies with profits in the billions of dollars.

Third, hyper-collection is often enabled by the vague consents we give to get access to the services these companies provide. Bunnings, for example, argued that its collection of your faceprint was allowed because signs at the entry to their stores told customers facial recognition might be used. Online marketplaces like eBay, Amazon, Kogan and Catch, meanwhile, supply 'bundled consents' – basically, you have to consent to their privacy policies as a condition of using their services. No consent, no access.

TikTok and hyper-collection

TikTok (owned by Chinese company ByteDance) has largely replaced YouTube as a way of creating and sharing online videos. The app is powered by an algorithm that has already drawn criticism for routinely collecting data about users; similarly attracting disapproval is ByteDance's secretive approach to content moderation and censorship.

For years, TikTok executives have been telling governments that data isn't stored in servers on the Chinese mainland. But these promises might be hollow in the wake of recent allegations. Cybersecurity experts now claim that not only does the TikTok app routinely connect to Chinese servers, but that users' data is accessible by ByteDance employees, including the mysterious Beijing-based 'Master Admin', which has access to every user's personal information.

Then, it was alleged that TikTok can also access almost all the data contained on the phone it is installed on, including photos, calendars and emails. Under China's national security laws, the government can order tech companies to pass on that information to police or intelligence agencies.

What options do we have?

Unlike a physical store, we don't get a lot of choice about consenting to digital companies' privacy policies and how they collect our information.

One option, supported by encryption expert Vanessa Teague at ANU, is for consumers simply to delete offending apps until their creators are willing to submit to greater data transparency. Of course, this means locking ourselves out of those services, and it will only have a big impact on the company if enough Australians join in.

Another option is 'opting out' of intrusive data collection. We've done this before – when the My Health Record became mandatory in 2019, a record number of us opted out. Though these opt-outs reduced the usefulness of that digital health record program, they did demonstrate that Australians can take their data privacy seriously.

But how exactly can Australians opt out of a massive social app like TikTok? Right now, they can't – perhaps the government needs to explore a solution as part of its review.

A further option being explored by the *Privacy Act* review is whether to create new laws that would allow individuals to sue companies for damages for breaches of privacy. While lawsuits are expensive and time-consuming, they might just deliver the kind of financial damage to big companies that could change their behaviour.

No matter which option we take, Australians need to start getting more savvy with their data privacy. This might just mean we actually read those terms and conditions before agreeing, and being prepared to 'vote with our feet' if companies won't be honest about what they're doing with our personal information.

NFTs: An overblown speculative bubble inflated by pop culture and cryptomania

John Hawkins
University of Canberra

Comedian Robin Williams once called cocaine 'God's way of telling you you are making too much money'. This role may now have been overtaken by non-fungible tokens, the blockchain-based means to claim unique ownership of easily copied digital assets.

The latest NFT mania involves fantastic amounts of money being paid for 'Bored Apes', 10,000 avatars featuring variants of a bored-looking cartoon ape. In December 2021 rapper Eminem (real name Marshall Mathers) paid about US$450,000 in Ethereum cryptocurrency to acquire Bored Ape No. 9055 – nicknamed EminApe, because its khaki and gold chain resemble what Eminem wears. It purportedly joins more than 160 other NFTs in the rapper's collection.

The Bored Ape character seems derivative of the drawings of Jamie Hewlett, the artist who drew Tank Girl and virtual band Gorillaz. According to the creators, each variant is 'generated from over 170 possible traits, including expression, headwear, clothing, and more'. They say every ape is unique 'but some are rarer than others'.

So what does Eminem now own? He has an electronic version of an image, which he is using for his Twitter profile. But then so does anyone who copies it from the internet. The only difference is that he has a record in a blockchain that shows he bought it. He also gets to be a member of the 'Bored Ape Yacht Club', a members-only online space whose benefits and purpose beyond being a marketing gimmick are unclear.

That's about it. The intellectual property (such as it is) remains with the creators. He is not entitled to any share of merchandising revenue from the character. He can only profit from his purchase if he can find a 'greater fool' willing to pay even more for the NFT.

Which is unlikely. While publicity given to the rapper's purchase certainly seems to have boosted demand, the average price paid for Bored Ape NFTs so far in 2022 is about 83 Ether. Eminem may have been prepared to pay much more for the one that looked more like him, but would anyone else?

NFTs are a highly speculative purchase. The basis of the market is proof of unique ownership, which only really matters for bragging rights and the prospect of selling the NFT in the future. NFT mania arguably combines the most tawdry and avaricious aspects of collectibles and blockchain markets with celebrity culture.

The rise of the celebrity influencer

Eminem's monster payment in particular has lent credibility to the idea these NFTs have value. But he is not the only celebrity who has helped attract attention to the Bored Ape NFTs. Others to buy into the hype include basketball stars Shaquille O'Neal and Stephen Curry, billionaire Mark Cuban, electronic dance music DJ Steve Aoki, YouTuber Logan Paul and late-night television host Jimmy Fallon.

These well-publicised purchasers effectively act as a form of celebrity endorsement – a tried and true marketing tactic. It is a graphic example of the power of media culture to stoke 'irrational exuberance' in financial markets.

There has been a shift away from traditional investments and sources of investment advice. With prices disconnected from any future cash flows, there is less interest in forecasts from technical experts. Instead people turn to social media and 'doing their own research'.

One survey in mid-2021 (polling 1400 investors aged 18–40) suggested about a third of gen Z investors regard TikTok videos as a source of trustworthy investment advice. This has opened up the field for celebrity influencers.

A lot like Ponzi schemes

While not illegal, many NFT marketing ventures have some similarities with Ponzi schemes, such as that operated by Bernie Madoff, who sustained his fraud for decades by paying high 'dividends' from the deposits of new investors. Cryptocurrency markets work in essentially the same manner. For existing investors to profit, new buyers have to be drawn into the market. So too NFTs, with something illusory attached to the digital assets.

Some light on the worth of this attachment compared to the economics of NFTs themselves may come from the interesting (and also highly profitable) experiment by the (now not so) 'young British artist' Damien Hirst, himself a master self-promoter. Hirst's well-publicised 'The Currency' project has involved selling NFTs for 10,000 similar but unique dot paintings. The twist is that at the end of a twelve-month period, those who have bought the NFT must decide if they want the digital token or the physical artwork. If they keep the NFT the artwork will be destroyed.

No fundamental value

There's virtually nothing humans can't turn into a market. But increasingly there are speculative bubbles in things with absolutely no fundamental value. NFTs have joined bitcoin and celebrity meme-based cryptocurrencies such as Dogecoin and Shiba Inu as examples of tokens with no intrinsic worth, which speculators just buy in the hope the price will keep rising. Even Dogecoin, started as a satire on these excesses, is now valued at US$20 billion and promoted in Ponzi-like ways.

Some studies have suggested tweets or Facebook posts can now drive stock prices. Elon Musk's tweets certainly seem to have a large impact on cryptocurrency prices. We appear to be in the monster of all speculative bubbles. The creators of assets like NFTs will do well. It is not so clear about the holders.

Nor will the impact of NFT crashes be restricted just to the NFT market. Speculators, particularly if they have borrowed heavily, may need to liquidate other assets as well. This is likely to make all financial markets more volatile. The larger the bubble becomes, the wider the contagion when it bursts.

PART VIII

The power of hope

Albanese wants to 'change the way we do politics' in Australia. Here are four ways to do it

Ariadne Vromen
Australian National University

Prime Minister Anthony Albanese has pledged to 'change the way' we do politics in Australia by avoiding soundbites and 'actually answering questions'. This is part of his plan for 'rebuilding respect' for politics itself.

Even before the uninspiring, adversarial election campaign, we knew Australians had little affection for politicians and politics. Levels of distrust in government 'soared' in 2021, according to pollster Roy Morgan. But this does not mean Australians are disengaged. The record number of new independent MPs, coupled with the large numbers of volunteers who helped those campaigns, are serious indicators people will get involved if they feel like they can make a difference.

Now, with a new government, there is a rare opportunity to re-engage citizens in policymaking and politics. I research how people participate in politics. Here, I discuss four innovative democratic processes Albanese's government could adopt to actually change the way we do politics – not just talk about it.

But first, why do we need to change?

Albanese is right when he says we need a change. This is because the more citizens distrust politicians and switch off, the harder it is to hold a government to account.

At the same time, as the OECD points out in its public governance program, when citizens are more engaged in politics and involved in decision-making, it is more likely that good policies will result that can address critical, difficult issues. Citizens will be more invested in the outcome when they see their views are heard and acted upon.

This is not a call for governments to do better so citizens will just trust them to act in their best interests. It is a call for governments to trust citizens more – and use their expertise more. Other governments around the world, such as those of Germany, Denmark and Canada, trust their citizens to be actively involved in policymaking. It is about time Australia learnt to do this too.

There is also a long list of critical issues that are not being solved by 'politics as usual'. These issues affect all Australians and were largely ignored during the election campaign. Albanese committed to new policy directions for the first two issues in his election night speech, while the second set were raised as key issues by voters:

- the Uluru Statement from the Heart and First Nations Voice to Parliament
- effective, adequate climate change solutions
- intergenerational equity, including cost of living, affordable housing and secure work
- a caring economy that properly considers our health, aged care, child care and disability care needs.

What are the solutions?

Here are four innovative, citizen-centric ways to change politics in Australia that the new government can start working on today.

Online petitions

My research has found that for most of us, political participation starts online. Signing an online petition or making a donation to an online crowd-sourced campaign are the most popular acts of participation in Australia. Yet my research has also found the issues that matter to digitally active citizens rarely match the policy agenda of governments.

Petitions are one way to gather public opinion and make governments more responsive to citizen concerns. For example, the Scottish Parliament's petition process is easy to use, covers many issues, and ensures a government response. This is regarded by scholars as the international gold standard.

At the moment, Australia's use of online petitions is tokenistic. It is hard to create, sign and share petitions via the House of Representatives website. There are also no substantive government feedback mechanisms built into the process.

Town hall meetings

Governments are regularly criticised for not consulting, or consulting minimally, on decisions they have already made. There are much better ways to bring together decision-makers and citizens.

One way to do this is via 'town hall' meetings, where a topic or policy question is set and politicians and citizens engage in an open dialogue. It starts with a commitment from politicians to hear the diverse views and experiences of citizens, learn from them, and be clear about how these views will be used.

The 'Voices for' campaigns begun by Cathy McGowan in Indi in the lead-up to the 2013 federal election, and since taken up by the teals, are a good example of this. Many of these campaigns began with local 'kitchen table' discussions. This mobilised local voters to campaign for a local independent and become involved in the change they wanted for their electorate. In part, this was because they could see how that change could happen.

Beyond election campaigns, it is possible to set up new ways to connect the government with citizens. A large-scale project called Connecting to Congress has been run by Ohio State University academics since 2006. It has facilitated twenty-five live-streamed online town halls between US Congress members and a representative cross-section of their constituents. Borrowing from this experience, the University of Canberra ran two Connecting to Parliament experiments in Australia in 2020 and 2021. This saw two online town halls held with federal MPs on the issues of mitochondrial donation and youth participation.

Citizens' assemblies

Over the past decade, Ireland has held citizen assemblies on issues ranging from marriage equality to abortion, the ageing population, climate change, biodiversity loss, gender equality, referendums and fixed-term parliaments. They generally see 100 randomly selected people spend time together learning about and discussing issues, and then voting on options for policy change or constitutional reforms. As a result of these deliberations, there were successful referendums in Ireland on marriage equality in 2015 and legalising abortion access in 2017.

However, one of the main proponents of Irish citizen assemblies, political scientist David Farrell, suggests there is now a need for new innovations, learning from Belgium and France. In those countries, the agenda is less tightly controlled by governments and more driven by what citizens want to focus on.

In Australia, a similar process called a citizens' jury has been used by local and state governments to develop policy. For example, the City of Sydney used a citizens' jury comprising forty randomly selected citizens to help develop Sydney's plan for 2050. The jury discussed thousands of submissions from residents in order to recommend eight core concepts for change on issues such as First Nations leadership, accessible housing and a 24-hour city economy.

Advocacy and transparency

This fourth democratic 'innovation' is about making better use of the advocacy sector in Australia.

Over the past twenty years, we have seen increasing constraints on how registered charities or organisations that provide services can also engage in advocacy. This includes diverse groups ranging from the Australian Council of Social Service and the Australian Conservation Foundation to Vinnies and Amnesty International. Ensuring broad representation of diverse social groups is a fundamental part of good governance and integrity. We need to reform the Australian Charities and Not-for-profits Commission to make sure advocacy is no longer politicised but encouraged and seen as a useful public good.

At the same time, we need a more transparent lobbying system. This includes limits on political donations, and public diaries of meetings politicians have with lobbyists, as happens in Canada. The more information we have about who is lobbying whom, the less influence those with the most money are likely to have.

Then government needs to listen and respond

All these approaches need to include diverse voices and perspectives, not just the people we already hear from in new ways. Part of the problem with most existing forms of citizen participation is they entrench existing political inequalities. They are skewed towards the most vocal and most educated, and those with the most spare time. It is essential that new participatory initiatives for citizens systematically recruit diverse involvement.

They must also have what researchers call 'a theory of change'. This is a clear description of why this method will work and what will happen in the short, medium and longer terms. As David Farrell warns, we need to make sure these experiments do not just result in lengthy reports that nobody reads.

If Albanese is serious about changing the way politics happen here, he needs to lead a government committed to responding to what Australians say.

The Albanese government has committed to enshrining a First Nations Voice in the Constitution. What do Australians think of the idea?

Jacob Deem
CQUniversity Australia
Adrian Miller
CQUniversity Australia
AJ Brown
Griffith University
Susan Bird
Charles Darwin University

Prime Minister Anthony Albanese and his new government have committed to enshrining a First Nations Voice in the Australian Constitution. To do so, a majority of Australians in a majority of states will have to vote 'yes' at a referendum. But what are the other challenges along the way? Why might people support a Voice, or why might they be against it?

In 2021, CQUniversity and Griffith University conducted the Australian Constitutional Values Survey to answer these questions.

Survey questions and findings

The survey measured attitudes towards the Voice from more than 1500 respondents. Through quota sampling across participants' location, age, education and voting preference, we were able to obtain a nationally representative sample.

Our survey found substantial support for a constitutional Voice (51.3 per cent). Twice as many people supported the Voice as were against it (20.8 per cent, with 27.9 per cent undecided). But just as important are the reasons *why* participants said they were in favour, against or undecided.

Here are four key challenges that need to be addressed, our data suggest, on the journey towards a Voice.

Why have a First Nations Voice to Parliament?

As a first step, people must see a good reason to establish a Voice. The Uluru Statement from the Heart, which formalised calls for a constitutional Voice, is framed as a generous invitation towards reconciliation from First Nations peoples. The sentiments in the Uluru Statement are reflected in many survey respondents' support of the Voice. For example, one participant said: 'I believe that if Australia really wants to reconcile with the Indigenous community, that this is a very important step in that process.'

However, some people remain sceptical. While it seems most First Nations peoples support a Voice, this view is not unanimous. Some First Nations scholars and respondents to our survey questioned whether supporting the Voice further legitimates the Constitution, a colonial document.

At the other end of the spectrum, 10 per cent of respondents did not see the need for a Voice at all. Evidence of the disadvantages faced by First Nations peoples under all existing political institutions continues to suggest otherwise. For example, the inability to 'close the gap' is often attributed to the government's failure to genuinely engage with Indigenous Australians. Nevertheless, the view that reform is not needed is one the Voice campaign will need to confront.

Advocates for the Voice will be encouraged by the substantial number of survey respondents who are already convinced that institutionalising an Indigenous advisory body is a positive step. Many respondents cited the value in constitutionally recognising First Nations peoples, and viewed it as the 'right thing to do'. Further, when supporters of the Voice were asked how important this issue was, one in three thought it should be a priority for the government.

The general public's lack of knowledge

The Voice was proposed in the Uluru Statement in 2017, and calls for an Indigenous advisory body are even older. Despite this, public awareness remains a core issue.

More than half of respondents to the survey had never heard of the Voice before. Of the 27.9 per cent of respondents who were unsure whether they would be in favour of or against a constitutional Voice, most cited a lack of knowledge as the reason.

Encouragingly, the responses also suggest there is an appetite to learn more. Some 19 per cent of undecided participants said they wanted more information about the Voice, while 17.7 per cent had specific questions, such as how representatives would be chosen, and what powers the body would have.

The role of bipartisanship

While bipartisanship may not necessarily be essential to obtain a 'yes' vote in a referendum, a proposal with the support of the major parties is far less likely to fail. So far we know Labor is committed to pursuing a constitutional Voice, although the Coalition's position following its election loss is less clear.

One thing is clear from our survey: differences between the major parties' positions do not reflect voters' attitudes in a significant way. This is an important result, as it suggests the major parties should be able to find common ground in supporting the Voice. Senator Patrick Dodson's appointment as Special Envoy for Reconciliation and the Implementation of the Uluru Statement is an important step, as Senator Dodson is highly regarded on both sides of politics.

Delivering a Voice with substance

Support for Indigenous constitutional recognition is clearly strongest if believed to be likely to deliver practical benefits as well as symbolic value. Many survey respondents saw tangible outcomes such as improved health care and learning from Indigenous land management as reasons to support the Voice. When asked, 75 per cent thought the Voice would improve the lives of First Nations peoples. Therefore, the Voice many Australians want to enshrine is one that can make a practical difference in the lives of First Nations peoples.

The new government's commitment to the Uluru Statement is a hopeful sign for all those seeking constitutional change. While there is still a long journey ahead for the First Nations Voice, if these four challenges are met, then a majority of Australians are clearly ready to engage in this important step in the reconciliation process.

Since this essay was written in June, Prime Minister Anthony Albanese delivered a speech at the Garma festival setting out a proposed referendum question and constitutional amendment that addressed several of the challenges raised in our article. He explained the important need for a Voice, nothing that '121 years of Commonwealth governments arrogantly believing they know enough to impose their own solutions on Aboriginal people have brought us to this point – the torment of powerlessness.' He also rebutted concerns that the Voice would be purely symbolic, promising a Voice that could deliver practical benefits. The proposed amendment would set up a Voice that can 'make representations' to parliament and the government, ensuring First Nations' perspectives are heard. In making the Voice a national priority, Albanese has sparked discussion. and ensured more Australian's are aware of the proposal. At the time of writing, the Opposition is yet to reach a firm position on whether it will support the referendum, insisting it is waiting for more detail.

What the Queen's death means for an Australian republic

John Warhurst
Australian National University

The passing of Queen Elizabeth II has the potential to transform Australia's republic debate.

While the debate should not be about personalities, the monarch's identity clearly makes a difference. Former prime minister and republican Malcolm Turnbull once famously said many Australians were 'Elizabethans' rather than monarchists.

However, as we mark the transition from one monarch to another, republic supporters still need to be patient, for a number of reasons.

Speaking on talk radio on the day the news broke in Australia, Prime Minister Anthony Albanese declined to address the republic question, saying, 'Today is a day for one issue, and one issue only, which is to pay tribute to Queen Elizabeth II and to give our thanks for her service to our country.'

But what can we expect in the longer term?

The Charles factor

With the death of Queen Elizabeth II, Prince Charles has become King Charles III, not just of the United Kingdom, but of Australia and other dominions too. Camilla has become Queen Consort with Elizabeth's blessing.

Opinion surveys have regularly shown the idea of Charles becoming king raises support for a republic. I believe in 1999, at the time of the constitutional referendum, the figure was about 5 per cent. It was widely recognised that Charles was not as popular among Australians as his mother. That is still the case.

After the first, failed referendum, influential republicans, like Turnbull, believed Australia should not consider a second referendum until the Queen had passed away. The Australian Republic Movement disagreed – but that view became widespread. This has prevented any official preparatory initiatives prior to the end of her time on the throne.

Back to the start

Much has changed over the past twenty-three years since we last seriously considered a republic. This means the public discussion must begin again almost from scratch and under new circumstances. For one thing, any Australian currently under forty years of age did not vote in 1999.

Some lessons have also been learnt from 1999, including problems with divisions between republicans about what model to adopt, but many issues remain unresolved. The central arguments for a republic have not changed markedly, but the situation is different.

One important development has been the increased urgency for constitutional recognition of Indigenous rights. The republic movement and most republicans recognise the latter now has precedence over a second republic referendum.

Preferred models and public support

Experience and common sense dictate the move towards a republican Constitution should not be rushed anyway. There needs to be time put aside for considered community discussion. While the initial discussion can be led by civil society groups, like the republic movement, ultimately the discussion must be led by the federal parliament and government if we are going to make genuine progress.

The republic movement recently launched its preferred model for a republic, which is a starting point for public discussion. This follows years of stating the model should be decided by the community at a plebiscite prior to a referendum.

The new model proposes Australian parliaments nominate candidates for president before a popular vote to decide between them. It has been derided in some quarters for its complexity, but it is a creative attempt to resolve differences between direct election and parliamentary republicans. The model also reflects the realities of a federal system.

What are the mechanics?

The method of constitutional reform remains unchanged from 1999 (there has not been a referendum question put since then and the last successful referendum occurred in 1977). This recent history of our failure weighs heavily on any new referendum proposal.

Such proposals must effectively first win the support of both houses of federal parliament. Then the specific proposal must be put to a yes/no referendum.

There is no other legitimate constitutional way, even though some people would prefer an 'in principle' referendum to test the waters first. Realistically, the support of the federal government and Opposition is also a necessary condition for a successful referendum.

Another decade away?

At any rate, any radical transformation of the republic/monarchy debate will not happen straight away. There needs to be time for the public to mourn the loss of Elizabeth. Albanese has indicated that the referendum is not likely to happen during his first term.

That means a timetable for a second republican referendum, given King Charles has come to the throne in 2022, is at best five to ten years away (after the 2025 federal election at the earliest). By that stage Charles himself will be close to eighty years of age or even older.

Please excuse me, is there a place for politeness in Australian politics?

Kate Power
University of Queensland

Since former Australian of the Year Grace Tame declined to smile in a 25 January photo opportunity with then prime minister Scott Morrison, debate has raged about what counts as politeness and impoliteness in Australian political debate. Jenny Morrison subsequently told *60 Minutes* she wants her daughters to grow up 'fierce and strong' but also to 'be polite and have manners'.

Meanwhile, the gloves were well and truly off in Canberra. Labor claimed then aged care services minister Richard Colbeck had 'failed in his job' and should be sacked, Morrison accused Opposition Leader Anthony Albanese of 'clearly [being] on the side of criminals' during debate about deportation legislation, and he labelled deputy leader Richard Marles a 'Manchurian candidate' over past comments on China.

With every election cycle, the temperature of debate seems only to increase. Is politeness compatible with politics? And what standards should we expect from our leaders?

Defining 'politeness'

In 1978, American linguists Penelope Brown and Stephen C Levinson developed 'politeness theory'. This is the most influential scholarly work dealing with politeness. At its heart lies the notion of 'face' or the public image we want for ourselves.

There are two types of 'face':

1. 'positive face' – our desire to be 'appreciated and approved of'. It can be threatened by accusations, insults and expressions of criticism or contempt.
2. 'negative face' – our desire for autonomy, including both freedom to act and freedom from other people telling us what to do. It can be threatened by orders, requests, advice and threats.

Politeness might mean giving someone approval or praise, or minimising our imposition on them. But there are times when this is not possible or practical. In emergencies, for example, we might yell sharply at someone to get out of harm's way, or to protect ourselves. As linguistic anthropologists Horst Arndt and Richard W Janney observe,

> To not do this would require a radical suppression of one's own interests and feelings, and an almost slavish acceptance of those of others. The result would be a total loss of personal face.

In situations such as these, a lack of conventional politeness is not only understandable, it just might be essential.

Defining impoliteness

Politeness theory focuses on what we say, but impoliteness can also be communicated by non-verbal behaviour, such as facial expressions, eye contact, voice quality and body movements. So, not smiling in a photo opportunity may express positive impoliteness. Meanwhile, shaking someone's hand when they don't want you to arguably shows negative impoliteness.

Linguist Jonathan Culpeper says impoliteness involves 'the absence of politeness … where it would be expected'. And the more powerful and/or unfamiliar someone is to us, the more polite we are expected to be. He also explains that some behaviours can be perceived as impolite if they just clash with how someone expects or wants them to be.

So, who decides what counts as politeness? And what happens when we disagree?

Context matters

There is a longstanding consensus among linguists that nothing is inherently polite or impolite. Rather, the things we communicate take on these meanings from the cultures and contexts in which they happen.

For example, recent research suggests Australia's brand of politeness prioritises 'positive face', with a high value placed on 'being welcoming and showing solidarity and sympathy'. We also have an emphasis on what scholars call 'jocular mockery'. This includes various forms of teasing based on the view that people shouldn't take themselves too seriously, or what is more commonly known as 'taking the piss'.

But ideas about gender also play a significant role in our expectations here. For example, men who don't smile when they are expected to might be seen as 'tough' or 'serious', while women are labelled 'rude' or 'disrespectful'.

Politeness in politics

Politics is not a warm and fuzzy profession by any means. But in recent times, researchers have tracked a 'shameless normalisation' of verbal aggression, insults, racist and misogynistic attacks, and hostile forms of humour from leaders such as Donald Trump and Silvio Berlusconi.

Closer to home, the former Liberal MP Nicolle Flint decried the abuse she received during her time in politics:

> Men on the left, some of whom are public figures of influence, have done the following: they've stalked me, suggested I should be strangled, criticised the clothes I wear and the way I look, called me a whiny little bitch repeatedly, repeatedly called me weak, a slut …

More generally, politicians and scholars have both observed that rudeness is not only expected but rewarded in parliamentary debates. The risk here is that voters just tune out and turn off – as any regular viewer of parliamentary question time can attest.

Caution: Election ahead

Of course, there is a difference in how politicians or political opponents behave towards each other and how they behave towards the people whose votes they want. Politeness can play a potentially important role in image management. While he was Opposition leader, for example, Tony Abbott was quick to distance himself from placards belittling then prime minister Julia Gillard, after speaking in front of them at a public rally.

But here voters should take note of linguist Manfred Keinpointner's warning that 'some forms of politeness, such as manipulative or insincere politeness, should be seen as … impolite'.

And as we reflect on what behaviour we expect and want from our political leaders and those who shape the national debate, we also need to ask to whose benefit it is to be – or seem to be – polite. Perhaps what we want more than conventional etiquette is what political scientists call civility, or 'respect for the traditions of democracy'.

I am a climate scientist, and this is my plea to our newly elected politicians

Nerilie Abram
Australian National University

The 2022 federal election will go down in history as Australia's climate change election. Australians resoundingly voted for ambition on climate action, something that has been missing for a decade under a Coalition government, along with integrity and gender equality.

I am a climate scientist who has spent the last two decades studying how our climate is changing and sharing our increasingly urgent and frightening findings with the world. This is my plea to our newly elected politicians.

Dear Mr Albanese,

Congratulations on becoming the thirty-first Prime Minister of Australia.

If you wanted a clear mandate that the people are ready for ambitious and immediate climate action, then Australian voters certainly delivered that last Saturday. And how could they not?

Climate change is already impacting every inhabited part of our planet. Over the past few years Australians have suffered devastating bushfires and killer heat, catastrophic off-the-charts flooding, damage along our coasts from relentlessly rising seas, and the drawn-out hardship of droughts.

I spend every day looking at the data that tell us each of those climate extremes will keep getting worse. Every tonne of carbon dioxide that we emit adds to global warming. And every fraction of a degree of further warming will cause climate impacts to become more frequent and more intense.

So I implore you and the Labor Party to govern like every decision, and every year, matters. Because it really, really does.

You'll have a chance to prove on the world stage that the Australian Government is serious about climate action at the United Nations Climate Change Conference, COP27, in Egypt later this year. You've got some work to do, because COP26 last year was an embarrassment for our nation. We took little more than a three-word slogan to the conference in Glasgow and came away from those negotiations as a climate villain. The world is waiting for Australia to increase our 2030 commitment to reducing greenhouse gas emissions at COP27.

Labor's plan to reduce Australia's emissions by 43 per cent by 2030 is a good start, although it will still put us on track to contribute to more than 2 degrees Celsius of global warming – roughly twice the warming level we're currently at. Fortunately, the international climate negotiations framework is designed for ratcheting up ambition over time. This means Australia can still increase our 2030 ambition further and do our fair share to limit warming to 1.5 degrees Celsius, which would be a much safer pathway.

Climate change impacts worsen with every extra fraction of a degree of warming

This is what some of Australia is projected to experience:

Climate extreme	1.5°C warming	2°C warming	3°C warming
Extreme summer rainfall in eastern Australia (RX1day)	7% stronger	9% stronger	13% stronger
Drought in southern Australia in winter/spring (SPI-6)	20% more intense	23% more intense	33% more intense
Queensland heatwaves	3 times per year, lasting 7.5 days	4 times per year, lasting 10 days	7 times per year, lasting 16 days
Bushfire risk (FFDI)	15 to 65% increase in extreme fire danger days		100 to 300% increase in extreme fire danger days

To the Greens,

Well done on your record-high vote. Yours was a campaign with a climate policy aligned to the science of what's needed from Australia to keep the 1.5 degrees Celsius warming goal alive. I hope you're able to push from inside the House and the Senate to make that a reality.

The strength of the Greens vote in Queensland perhaps shouldn't have been a surprise to me. Nowhere else in Australia would the difference between 1.5 degrees Celsius and 2 degrees Celsius of warming be more apparent.

Earlier this year I wrote the saddest research proposal I have ever prepared. A decade ago I could not have imagined having to pen anything like it, but here we are.

I study climate change and its impacts using corals that have grown in the ocean for centuries. These ancient corals faithfully record natural and human-caused changes in the environment around them. But now those very coral records I use to study the climate are being destroyed by climate change. My proposal is to call for an urgent international effort to recover valuable scientific samples from coral reefs before they're lost forever.

Amid all of the bluster of the election campaign, the Great Barrier Reef quietly bleached for the fourth time in the last seven years. As scientists we knew to expect this – at 1.5 degrees Celsius of warming, 90 per cent of reefs will have been lost, and at 2 degrees Celsius, the wondrous Great Barrier Reef as we know it today will no longer exist.

This most recent bleaching event hits me hard. Maybe it hit Queensland voters hard this time too?

I wish the elected Greens well as they work inside parliament to do what's needed to give the reef a fighting chance.

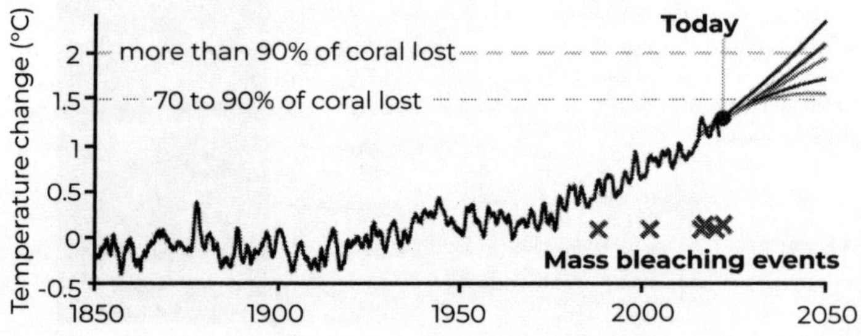

Graph of coral bleaching and temperature rise

To the teal independents,

Thank you for putting yourselves forward, for seeing the political status quo was not working for the people, and having the courage and conviction to provide Australians with an alternative.

It is well recognised that women need to be at the heart of climate action and solutions. Globally, female representation in politics has been shown to lead to stronger climate policies and better conservation outcomes. It makes me proud and hopeful to see the Australian people have elected so many strong, talented, independent women to our parliament.

To every member of our parliament,

It's time to get to work. The federal government has squandered the last decade and made the job harder. But fortunately, Australia's state governments have made a start while the federal government dallied. Australia's states and territories adopted net-zero targets before the federal government, and together those commitments are estimated to represent de facto national emission reductions of around 37–42 per cent by 2030.

Tackling the climate crisis is going to take a scale of ambition unlike anything we've seen before. But we have many solutions for decarbonising our energy and transport sectors ready to go. We will have to deploy these as quickly as possible to make the significant cuts to emissions needed this decade.

In future decades we will also need solutions that don't yet exist. This includes technologies and enhanced nature-based solutions that will help us to draw carbon dioxide back out of the atmosphere. These need to be underpinned by an investment in fundamental science today, so we can forge a pathway to those as-yet-unknown solutions.

People in Australia, and our neighbours in the Pacific, also need your help. Climate extremes are going to worsen and we need investment in the climate science and modelling capabilities to be able to improve adaptation decisions at the local scale.

To paraphrase our new prime minister, together you can end the climate wars and seize the abundant opportunities that Australia has to be a climate leader.

Good luck.